MARK CLARK
★ ★ ★ ★

Also by Martin Blumenson

Breakout and Pursuit
The Duel for France: 1944
Anzio: The Gamble That Failed
Kasserine Pass
Sicily: Whose Victory?
Salerno to Cassino
Bloody River: The Real Tragedy of the Rapido
Eisenhower
The Patton Papers: 1885–1940
The Patton Papers: 1940–1945
Masters of the Art of Command
(with James L. Stokesbury)
The Vildé Affair:
Beginnings of the French Resistance
Liberation
(with the editors of Time–Life Books)

MARK CLARK

MARTIN BLUMENSON

CONGDON *&* WEED, INC.

NEW YORK

To Blanche Gregory, with affection

Copyright © 1984 by Martin Blumenson

Library of Congress Cataloging in Publication Data

Blumenson, Martin.
Mark Clark.
Includes bibliographical references and index.
1. Clark, Mark W. (Mark Wayne), 1896–   .
2. World War, 1939–1945—Campaigns—Italy.   3. United
States—History, Military—20th century.   4. Generals—
United States—Biography.   5. United States. Army—
Biography.   I. Title.
E745.C45B58   1984   940.54'83'73   84-7614
ISBN 0-86553-123-4
ISBN 0-312-92517-4 (St. Martin's Press)

Published by Congdon & Weed, Inc.
298 Fifth Avenue, New York, N.Y. 10001
Distributed by St. Martin's Press
175 Fifth Avenue, New York, N.Y. 10010
Published simultaneously in Canada by Methuen Publications
2330 Midland Avenue, Agincourt, Ontario M1S 1P7

Photographs: The Archives-Museum, The Citadel, Charleston, South Carolina

Designed by Irving Perkins
Map by David Lindroth

All Rights Reserved
Printed in the United States of America
First Edition

"I shall keep of you the image of a great leader...the memory of a prompt and lucid intelligence, always perceiving clearly through the smoke of battle."
Letter, General Alphonse Juin to General Mark Clark, July 22, 1944

"A cold, distinguished, conceited, selfish, clever, intellectual, resourceful officer who secures excellent results quickly. Very ambitious. Superior performance."
General Jacob L. Devers, Chief of the Army Field Forces, rating the performance of General Mark W. Clark, Commander of the Sixth Army in San Francisco, July 1948

PREFACE

NO FULL-LENGTH study of Mark Clark has ever appeared in print, although he stands with Eisenhower, Patton, and Bradley in the quartet of American leaders who brought victory in Europe in World War II. This account, while tracing Clark's early and formative years, concentrates on his wartime career.

The narrative contains new material, with much from the Clark papers, never before opened in their entirety. His diary, devastating in its candor, reveals formerly unsuspected strains and frictions in the Anglo-American coalition and underlines the flawed Allied strategy of the Italian campaign. Recent disclosure of the Ultra Secret intercepts of German messages gives insight into battlefield strategy. The dramatic events of the war in Italy— Salerno, Naples, Anzio, the Rapido River, Monte Cassino, Rome, intriguing in their own right—emerge in startling perspective when regarded from Clark's point of view. Clark's closeness to Marshall and Eisenhower has generally been overlooked and unappreciated. His roles in the Darlan deal, the postwar Austrian occupation, and the negotiations leading to the Korean armistice are little known.

What the book offers are a reinterpretation of the campaign in Italy, a re-evaluation of Clark's central place in American military history from 1940 to 1953, and a portrait of the man himself.

CONTENTS

MARK CLARK
★ ★ ★ ★

CHAPTER 1

☆ ☆ ☆ ☆

WHAT MANNER OF MAN

"General Mark W"

GENERAL MARK WAYNE CLARK rose to eminence in World War II. Although he was well known throughout the Army before then, he entered popular consciousness as both a hero and international celebrity. Together with Dwight D. Eisenhower, George S. Patton, Jr., and Omar N. Bradley, Clark is a member of the essential quartet of American leaders who achieved victory in Europe.

They were all "Marshall men." They were in high positions of authority and responsibility because each had, somewhere in his career, attracted the favorable notice of George C. Marshall, the U. S. Army Chief of Staff. Marshall knew them well, and selected them for difficult tasks because he was sure of their professional efficiency and personal integrity.

Clark continued to serve his country after the war, yet the enduring accomplishment of his life was his participation in the Italian campaign. A forceful officer of undoubted competence, he was not merely a major

1

protagonist there but the central figure. As such, he placed his imprint indelibly on the drama of that time and place.

The fighting in Italy has generated more dispute than activities in any comparable area of the war. As a consequence of his significant status in the events, Clark is a controversial figure. Whether he was the cause or the victim of circumstances has been debated ever since, often acrimoniously.

The battles in Italy tested the Anglo-American coalition as nowhere else. Although the alliance was a strong and well-cemented partnership, tensions simmered beneath the surface. They resulted from and reflected not only personality clashes but, more important, divergent interests, as well as the growing strength of the Americans and the declining power of the British. What has been conveniently overlooked in public discussions and rarely mentioned in private conversations among experts were two sets of conditions pertaining in Italy: the Allied strategy and the command context, both of which shaped the exertions. Clark was responsible for neither. Struggling against confinements imposed by both the strategic intentions and the framework of command, he found himself opposed to many British aims, which he perceived as contrary to American expectations. By his driving will he prevailed, and many British historians and writers never forgave him. Their picture gained dubious credibility from unflattering portraits by Americans who resented Clark's success for one reason or another.

Like many strong and able figures in posts of authority, Clark attracted devotees as well as detractors. Those who worked closely with him and knew him well admired him intensely. He was, they said, a hard driver but fair, impatient yet considerate. He had an uncanny knack of getting at once to the heart of a matter, the intelligence to grasp immediately the nub of a problem, the ability to see at a glance what had to be done. Inspiring devotion among his staff, he had the facility, according to Eisenhower, to develop "a happy family in his command."

Some of his critics were jealous of his rapid rise in rank. As a lieutenant colonel in 1940, he passed over thousands of officers who were senior to him in age and length of service. By V-E Day he had moved up five grades and wore the four stars of a general. Too quick a climb, they said, to learn thoroughly the profession of arms. A contemporary recalled Clark as "a very ambitious, hardworking young major" and "an impressive officer in the peacetime Army"; but when "compared with people like Patton, Bradley, Joe Collins, and others, he lacked troop command as a junior officer, and I always had the impression that he really didn't have a feel for the tools of his trade."

Patton was eleven years older than Clark and had graduated from West Point seven years before him. Yet Patton became a lieutenant general and a general after Clark had reached these levels. They were good friends face to face—it was always Wayne and Georgie when they were together. In private, Patton referred scathingly to Clark. In numerous diary entries and letters to his wife, Patton castigated Clark as "very clever and indirect," "too damned slick," and simply "an s. o. b." So far as Patton could tell, Clark had neither interest in nor understanding of soldiers and warfare. To Patton, what concerned Clark above all was Clark.

Clark made enemies because he could be less than tactful, more than brusque, biting in his demands. Even his friends admitted that he had no aversion to being in the spotlight. He always had and nourished an ample ego. This too generated distrust and dislike. A retired general officer never closely associated with Clark said that while Clark no doubt "was a very able man," he was "famous for knocking off his friends." He did not specify who those friends were, or what those methods and what he wanted were.

Others charged him with being a publicity hound, ruthless in his quest for personal gain. Eric Sevareid, a war correspondent in Italy, wrote a devastating indictment of Clark, describing him as vainglorious, self-seeking, and driven by vanity and pride, "the victim of the natural pressures of his position and fame." Clark received publicity, Sevareid said, because of a well-managed effort, and Sevareid detailed the efforts of Clark's public relations officer, whom newsmen disliked and whose endeavors they resented. Sevareid reported the conference of senior commanders called by Clark in newly liberated Rome as a phony and embarrassing scene played for the benefit of newsreel cameras. He saw Clark's respectful treatment of journalists as merely a gambit to obtain "personal publicity."

A senior British officer explained Clark by paraphrasing Carl von Clausewitz's well-known statement that war is an extension of policy by other means. Clark, he said, believed war to be an extension of publicity by other means. Field Marshal Lord Harold Alexander of Tunis, Clark's direct and immediate superior throughout the Italian campaign, waited many years to take Clark to task. He disobeyed orders, Alexander implied, by driving to Rome. "I can only assume," Alexander wrote in his memoirs, "that the immediate lure of Rome for its publicity value persuaded

Mark Clark to switch the direction of his advance."

A good part of the trouble stemmed from the original news stories that made Clark prominent. There were too many sensational accounts in the press and in the radio broadcasts, and they had unfortunate repercussions. Clark had made a dangerous submarine voyage through hostile waters to a clandestine rendezvous on the North African shore. Filled with uncertainties, deadly serious in motive and execution, the adventure produced some details reminiscent of a Mack Sennett comedy. Inept policemen chased heroes who hid in a wine cellar and who, in trying to get back to their submarine, capsized boats in the surf and lost clothing and gold coins in the sea.

These elements came to light shortly afterward. Clark's superiors, Marshall and Eisenhower, encouraged him to meet with the newspaper correspondents and tell the tale. Unwilling to reveal and discuss the political and strategic problems involved, he bantered with the reporters and talked of the funny incidents that underlined the risk of the undertaking. The journalists loved every word. They spread far and wide in the news media how Clark took refuge in a wine cellar, how he overturned his boat, how he lost his pants. The story, splashed across front pages and poured with crackling intensity across radio air waves, captivated the public.

There was too much coverage, too much exposure, too much excitement for Clark's own good. Even Marshall, always Clark's staunch supporter, was exasperated by what he called the "cheap details" in the press. "There was more about the loss of pants and of his money," he said, "than there was of the serious phase of the matter."

Gradually, some of his peers began to wonder whether Clark had deliberately played up to the correspondents for self-aggrandizement. Others questioned whether he understood the basic Allied war aims, for he negotiated what to them was the odious Darlan deal. Many Texans never forgave Clark, "the butcher of Italy," for the casualties suffered by the 36th Division along the Rapido River. Quite a few Americans found his postwar activities distasteful, and they termed his political views as "just this side of Genghis Khan" and deplored his close association with conservative politicians who opposed the extension of civil rights and the integration of blacks into the military services.

And so a legend, largely unfair, was born. Absorbed by his need for personal glory, the thesis went, Clark mismanaged the Italian campaign because he failed to understand the terrain, the enemy, and the requirements of the battle and because he downgraded the value of the Ultra

Secret interceptions of German messages. Clark was to blame for the close call at Salerno, for the long duration of the Anzio beachhead, for destroying the Benedictine abbey at Monte Cassino, and for incurring needless losses among his troops.

None of the criticism of Mark Clark mattered to almost a thousand people who came to see him in October 1978, more than thirty years after the war. Veterans of the campaign in Italy and their wives and children, traveling from all parts of the United States, attended the Fifth Army reunion, held at The Citadel in Charleston, South Carolina. Their presence that weekend was a pilgrimage to honor their leader. They hoped to shake his hand, to talk and joke with him for a few minutes, to be close to him, to be recognized and remembered, to feel the warmth of his greeting and smile. Wherever they met, affection was visible. All of it converged on Clark, who accepted it easily and returned it with delight. They had talked earlier of revisiting their battlefields. But "this old Roman ruin," as he called himself, was, he said, hardly up to the trip.

The weather was perfect, the setting just right. They wandered about the well-ordered campus, where cadets marched and saluted. In the museum, they looked at mementos of their commander's life. They inspected the conning tower, now set in concrete, of the submarine that had taken him on his famous voyage. They congregated at Mark Clark Hall, where most of the festivities took place.

At the banquet, former Sergeant First Class Michael Zianna marched to and ascended the platform. He was dressed in his combat uniform, the clothing he had worn in 1944. As he stood there, a hush settled over the large room. It was a moment of nostalgia, and of respect for soldiers.

Several months later Zianna wrote to Clark. "General," he said, "you cannot imagine how extremely proud I felt just for that brief twenty short minutes I wore that uniform again for you, all the guests, and finally myself too. I felt like the 28 year old I was during our great war. I was so 'hyped-up' (as the kids say nowadays) that had you just suggested it, I would have gone off to any war at all that very moment, with you, right from Charleston on out. You were the greatest General of all Generals."

Gatherings of veterans were not the only places for sentimental remembrance. Four years earlier, in Carlisle, Pennsylvania, Carl Jumper's face lighted up with pleasure at the mention of Clark's name. "You mean General Mark W.," he said. "We all called him that." His eyes softened as he thought about what tied him forever to Mark Clark.

Jumper had been a corporal in Italy. In charge of eight men, he received what seemed to him to be a particularly hazardous mission. He was to guard a small bridge on a dirt road. At that lonely outpost, if Germans appeared on the other side of the stream, he was to prevent them from crossing.

He was less than reassured when he surveyed his situation. How could he and his squad keep the Germans from coming across? But he had an order to carry out, and he placed his soldiers in positions around the bridge and showed them where to dig their foxholes. He dug a hole for himself. Then he waited, worried about being overrun by the enemy.

A jeep came out of the woods behind Jumper. To his great surprise, he saw the Army commander on the front seat beside the driver. When the vehicle stopped, Jumper approached, saluted, and reported. The general returned the salute, uncoiled his lanky body, and got out. Together with Jumper, he inspected the foxholes, talked to the men. Satisfied and ready to depart, he said to Jumper, "Corporal, are you going to be able to hold this bridge?"

A few moments earlier, he would have said no.

"Yes, sir," Jumper said confidently. "If they come, sir, we'll hold it." He believed what he said. If the commanding general thought the bridge important enough to come personally to that place, he, Jumper, was going to do what was expected of him.

In good spirits, he waited all day long. The enemy failed to appear.

Jumper never saw the general again. But he often thought of Clark with affection. "Yes, sir," Jumper said with matter-of-fact understatement. "He was all right was General Mark W."

Eric Sevareid once watched Clark in Italy riding slowly in his jeep between two lines of infantry marching toward the front. From time to time Clark leaned out and called encouragement and praise to the men. They were at first startled, then, when they saw who it was, pleased to have him with them so far forward, so close to the fighting and the danger instead of back in a comfortable villa somewhere at the rear. His presence gave them heart and they walked more confidently. "It was good behavior for a general," wrote Sevareid.

During and after the war, Clark was instantly recognized wherever he went. There was no mistaking the tall figure, the beak of a nose. In restaurants as he was shown to his table, people stared at him, pointed him out to their children. On the street men stopped him to tell him of their service with him in Italy.

Once in New York in civilian clothes, he took a cab. The driver said, "You sure look like Mark Clark."

"Don't I, though?" he replied.

When the driver made an illegal turn and was stopped by a policeman, he said, pointing over his shoulder, "That's Mark Clark back there, and he's in a hurry." The policeman peered inside, saluted, then waved the taxi on.

"We sure fooled him, didn't we?" the driver chuckled.

His submarine trip to North Africa had given him the reputation of an officer who carried out dangerous missions. His subsequent invasion at Salerno, touch and go for several days, created anxiety among those at home who read their newspapers, then established him as a daring leader who took chances and won. His capture of Naples brought his name to headlines and radio broadcasts again as a successful commander. As he and his Fifth Army moved slowly up the boot of Italy against fierce opposition, he came to represent Allied determination.

For almost a year the Italian campaign was the only significant large-scale action on the European side of the conflict. The war on the seas and in the air competed for public attention, but the main focus rested on Italy. The dramatic events at Monte Cassino where the ancient abbey was destroyed and at Anzio where men fought with their backs to the beaches fixed the public view firmly on Clark. Then came Rome, the climax, but only for a brief moment before the Normandy landings on the very next day eclipsed what was happening in Italy.

In the public mind he was identified with his Fifth Army even though he stepped up to command the 15th Army Group and was at the head of all the Allied soldiers in Italy—half a million men of seventeen different nationalities—when the Germans surrendered. After the war he moved to Austria and took charge of the American zone of occupation. As Commander in Chief of the United Nations Forces several years later, he brought the armistice negotiations in Korea to a conclusion. Retiring from the Army, he became President of The Citadel, the Military College of South Carolina. Afterwards, as an elder statesman and historical figure, he received honors and tributes, spoke frequently to the press and on radio and television, campaigned for Republican Party candidates, and remained in touch with his comrades all over the world and with the cadets on campus.

He received at his home an average of thirty letters every day, requests from schoolchildren, students, and scholars for advice, information, or his autographed photo. Many veterans and admirers sent greetings and gifts. On his birthday truckloads, literally, of cards and correspondence wished him well.

Yet others continued to question his behavior and generalship.

Who was he and what did he do? Is the criticism of him justified? Was he truly a giant or the product of a shrewdly harnessed press? What confluence of personal traits and impersonal forces shaped his career? Can the controversies be resolved?

CHAPTER 2

☆ ☆ ☆ ☆

ORIGINS AND BOYHOOD

"don't you worry, little sweetheart, I will never give up"

MARK CLARK WAS the product of two distinct strains in his family heritage. His grandfathers were totally unlike save in their belief in the traditional virtues of hard work and personal integrity. One was American, Protestant, and rural, the other European, Jewish, and urban.

His father and mother were a study in contrasts. One was solid, the other imaginative. Each reflected dissimilar cultural legacies, but neither was religious in a formal sense, and their affection triumphed over what might have created tension.

Whatever subtle ambiguities these differences may have engendered in the child, Mark Clark appeared to be a remarkably stable youth, no doubt because of the love he received from his parents. From the one he inherited staying power and discipline, from the other drive and ambition. Yet he was enormously sensitive too. Above the heavy lips and long nose, the large eyes staring out of his boyhood photos are somber and bleak.

9

His paternal grandfather was Dr. Anson T. Clark. Of solid English stock, he was a surgeon in the Union Army during the Civil War and settled in western Pennsylvania and practiced medicine in the thriving coal mining communities around Sharon. In 1895, he traveled to Buffalo, New York, to read a paper on "Colles' Fracture" to a meeting of Erie Railway Surgeons, and the International Journal of Surgery published his report. Retiring to a small farm near Conneaut, Ohio, he died at the age of 80 in 1915, dimly aware of the horrors of the Western Front in Europe.

His son Charles Carr Clark, born in 1866, gained a congressional appointment to West Point at age 20. Upon graduation, he received his commission in the infantry. Solidly built, six feet tall, Charles Clark was, above all, decent. He believed fervently in duty, honor, country. Perhaps lacking originality, he was thoroughly reliable. Kindly yet strict, he was a man of few words. He enjoyed the solitary pastimes of hunting and fishing. His only quirk was a passion for cleaning his teeth.

At his first duty station in the Arizona Territory, he became acquainted with and eventually a good friend of a bachelor cavalryman, Major William A. Rafferty, who had graduated from the Military Academy in 1865, who was a veteran of Indian campaigns, and who was exactly twice Clark's age. Rafferty took a liking to young Clark and introduced him to a family he knew in nearby Tucson, a father and three daughters named Ezekiels.

Rafferty was interested in Rosetta Ezekiels, who was called Zettie. Lieutenant Clark quickly became enamored of Rebecca, who was known as Beckie. She was bright and articulate, a patrician in looks and temperament.

Their father, Mark Ezekiels, had come to the United States from eastern Europe, probably from Romania. As a Jewish immigrant escaping the old country and its restrictions, its ancient customs and outlook, he hoped to find a better life with broader horizons. The new land more than met his expectations. He was enthusiastically committed to the American promise, an open and democratic society that rewarded its members not on the grounds of origin and antecedent but on the basis of merit and achievement.

The ideas of the melting pot and of assimilation, to produce a superior race of Americans, were very much in the air. Mark Ezekiels subscribed completely to the concept. America, a place of boundless opportunity for all, was secular and vigorous, very much like himself.

Moving westward, roaming and exploring the vast expanses, he settled briefly in San Francisco where Beckie was born in 1869, resided in Tucson twenty years later, and eventually lived in Butte and Helena, Montana, where he operated a pawn shop and served in the state legislature before he died in 1919.

After a whirlwind courtship, Charles Clark and Beckie Ezekiels were married in August 1891. About the same time, perhaps at the same ceremony, Rafferty and Zettie became man and wife. Mark Ezekiels could not have been happier. The American dream had come true. Two of his daughters had entered and merged into the mainstream of American life. Henceforth they would carry the names Clark and Rafferty, and so would their children.

No one wondered or worried whether Jewish wives would hamper or ruin the military careers of their husbands. If intermarriage was hardly common, it was quite acceptable, especially if the woman was the "outsider." There were, of course, snobs and the bigoted. But what counted was conformance with the accepted conventions of Army life.

At Madison Barracks, later known as Pine Camp, then Camp Drum, at Watertown, New York, in the old stone officers' quarters on the eastern end of Lake Ontario, Beckie gave birth to a daughter named Janet. Four years later, on May 1, 1896, she and Charles had a son whom they named Mark Wayne Clark. His mother called him "Boy." He was a well-behaved baby who cried little and walked at twelve months.

During the Spanish-American War, Charles Clark saw action in Puerto Rico, took part in the occupation of Cuba, and served in the Philippines. Beckie and the children lived at Fort McPherson, Georgia, then with the Clarks in Pennsylvania, later in a rented house in Washington, D. C., near Zettie. When Charles returned from overseas, he found Beckie, as he noted in his diary, "looking quite young."

Two children blessed the Rafferty union. William A., Jr., whom everyone called Pat, was born about the same time as Janet, and Valencia was about Mark's age.

Colonel Rafferty was commanding the 5th Cavalry in the Philippines when he fell from his horse and died at the age of 60. Charles Clark filed the necessary papers for his sister-in-law and made sure that the insurance and pension claims were in order.

After a tour of Plattsburg Barracks on Lake Champlain, Captain Clark was transferred to Chicago, where Zettie was living. She had remarried, and her husband was John Marshall, a prominent businessman. The Clark and Marshall families saw much of each other. All four children attended the Elm Street Grammar School in suburban Highland Park.

The Clark household was a loving one. Mark respected his father, admired him for his firm attention to duty, and tried to emulate him in the soldierly qualities of discipline, manliness, and honor. He adored his beautiful and lively mother, who made a fuss over him and was generous with her affection.

They lived well, if modestly. An Army officer's salary was adequate and, like most of their military friends who depended on their monthly pay, the Clarks were careful with their money.

A frail boy, tall and skinny, Mark was anything but robust. He was often in bed for a few days with a cold, sore throat, or ear infection. He had most of the childhood diseases and the more serious scarlet fever. Somewhat of a loner, he tried to imitate his father by being closely controlled and stoic. Yet an occasional burst of fun and high spirits showed his debt to his mother. He made friends easily and was well liked.

When he was 12, he was away from home for a year at the Lower School of Racine College, an Episcopal institution with a picture-book campus near Lake Michigan. A fire one night destroyed the laundry building where the handyman and maids lived, and Mark described the exciting event in a letter to his father. At first he had lots of fun. But he learned that a janitor had "lost everything and I almost cried when he told me about it. Three of us boys to-day are going to try to buy him something with our spending-money." He admired the firemen—"My but they are brave." He heard the dean say, "I don't care if it burns. I have got it insured for about twice as much as it's worth."

He had opened rather formally, "My Dear Father," but he ended with, "Well, dear daddy, I will close." He added a postscript: "Love to mother and also for you. I wish you were here to scratch my back."

As Pat Rafferty entered West Point in 1909, the Clarks moved to Fort Leavenworth, Kansas. Captain Clark attended the Army's School of the Line, became a major, was a Distinguished Graduate, then completed the Army Staff College course.

There were frequent parties on post. Although his father never learned to dance, his mother danced, Mark Clark later said, "all the time." They came to know Douglas MacArthur, who courted his sister Janet.

Mark's sister married a young lieutenant and joined him at his camp along the Mexican border.

Mark swam, fished, and canoed in the Missouri River, shot ducks in the adjacent marshlands, played tennis and baseball, went hunting and fishing with his father. Next to his father, Theodore Roosevelt was his ideal, and for the rest of his life Clark admired the man who had been a weakling, who had built up his body by the strenuous outdoor life, and who personified forcefulness, righteousness, and a strong United States.

With Charles Clark transferred to Fort Sheridan and the family living again at Highland Park, a dashing figure seized Mark's imagination. He regarded from afar but with delight a recent West Point graduate, slim and handsome George Patton who was serving at his first duty station. Clark's sight of Patton was the beginning of a lifelong admiration, almost hero worship, of the colorful officer.

West Point was frequently in the family conversations. Charles Clark expected Mark to follow him into the Army and wanted the Military Academy to give his son strength of character and physical hardihood.

The decision came in the fall of 1912, when Major Clark received orders to China to command a battalion of the 15th Infantry. It was a choice assignment. Clark would be at the head of one of the few battalions in the Army, and that one in an elite regiment; in addition, overseas service meant a ten percent increase in pay and allowances. He would earn more than nine thousand dollars in 1913; his income tax in January 1914 would amount to twenty-one dollars and fifty-five cents.

"But what will we do with Boy?" Beckie asked.

Mark was 16 years old and a sophomore in high school. He could abandon his studies and accompany his parents overseas. Or he could stay with Aunt Zettie and finish his secondary education. Or perhaps it was time, even though he was rather young, to see about getting him into West Point.

The son of an officer on active duty could compete for a presidential appointment. About one hundred boys applied every year for a dozen vacancies. The young men who qualified were those who made the highest scores on the West Point admission tests. In order to give Mark a better chance of entering, Charles Clark decided to send him to Lieutenant Braden's School at Highland Falls, New York.

Charles Clark expected to depart for San Francisco and the Far East in November. Mark would then go to Highland Falls in January. Beckie would leave for China with Valencia Rafferty, Zettie's daughter. After Mark took the tests, he was to stay with Aunt Zettie and await the results. If he failed, he would join his parents and Valencia in China.

Frantic news then came from Janet. Her husband had disappeared into Mexico. She returned to Chicago to await the birth of her child.

As Major Clark arrived in China, his son was starting Branden's preparatory school. Mark was torn by conflicting desires. He wanted to enter West Point in order to please his parents. His father had inculcated in him a strong sense of duty to do his best and to persist. Yet he could not help hoping to fail, for in that case he would rejoin his family.

Several letters he wrote to his mother in February and March showed his dilemma, his struggle with himself to be grown-up and manly. He spoke often of his studies and how hard he was working—"I have not been to bed before midnight for almost all this week." He discussed his finances, his monthly check from the bank, paying his bills—"It sure does seem good to be even with every one." He told of his resolve to "try and save about ten dollars each month." He reported his bouts with colds and sore throat.

Yet inevitably, despite himself, despite his good intentions, he could not extinguish his lonesomeness, his regret over his separation from his mother and father, and, although he knew better, his feeling of being abandoned. His friend Whitcomb, he wrote, went home for the weekend "and it seems kind of lonely. I will begin studying pretty soon and then I will forget about his having such a good time. He is going to the Theatre tonight and to dinner with his Mother and Father. I will not let it worry me, for sometime we will all have as good a time together."

"Daddy told me not to worry about the exams and if I failed not to feel badly," he said in another letter. "I am glad that you all understand it, but just the same I will keep on working as hard as ever... I was real blue but now I am feeling better and am going to brace up. I can't help feeling discouraged once in a while, but don't you worry, little sweetheart, I will never give up."

He fought his emotions. "I am going to cheer up and get over the blues because everything will be all right."

And he stifled his concerns. "I am going to work very hard, so don't worry about my giving up. I am going to be happy and try not to get blue. Of course once in a while I can't help it, but I will cheer up and look on the bright side of things."

The last line in his letter summed up his feelings: "I hate to think of your going so far, but let's all cheer up and we will be happy some day."

In Chicago, Janet had a baby boy. Replacing Valencia on the trip, Janet and her infant traveled with Beckie to Montana and visited Mark Ezekiels. Then they went to China and joined Charles Clark.

Now Mark was all alone. He never even saw Pat Rafferty, who was at West Point nearby.

Braden's had its good moments. His roommates, Whitcomb and William C. McMahon, became close friends. His father had given him a subscription to the *Chicago Tribune*, and when it arrived, he opened the paper at once to his favorite comic strip, the adventures of Opie Dildock.

After passing the physical examination at West Point, Mark, together with Braden's pupils, traveled to Fort Slocum shortly after his seventeenth birthday for the written tests. Then there was nothing to do except to say goodbye and catch the train to Chicago and Aunt Zettie's. Would he obtain a vacancy?

The first notice said that he had won a place. A day or so later came word that he had missed by one. He could not tell which prospect pleased him more, West Point or China.

Mrs. John Marshall, his Aunt Zettie, resolved the issue. Taking advantage of her husband's numerous contacts in the worlds of business and politics, she went to Washington and called on Dudley Field Malone, Assistant Secretary of State. She explained the situation. Could Mr. Malone help?

Dining at the White House with President Woodrow Wilson, Malone mentioned Mrs. Marshall's request. Shortly thereafter, a congressman from New York was found who could make an appointment but had no candidate. He was persuaded to give the place to Mark Clark.

Thirty years later Clark sent Malone a letter of thanks. "I have always been mindful," he wrote, "of the start you gave me. Had it not been for your kindness, I would have been denied the privilege of going to West Point."

Had he been turned away then, he probably would have entered a later class. But that would have changed everything, all the circumstances that shaped his military career.

Had he failed in this, his first real undertaking in manhood, and traveled to China, his transformation from boy to young man would have been delayed and no doubt diluted.

Aunt Zettie helped at the critical moment, but the triumph was his. Through his study and hard work, through his tenacity in the face of his childish fears, he had not lost his nerve. His sense of duty and his need to do his best had worked. He may have appeared insecure and vulnerable, but he was ready for West Point.

CHAPTER 3

☆ ☆ ☆ ☆

WEST POINT AND THE GREAT WAR

"energetic, conscientious, and hardworking"

STANDING SIX FEET, three inches, and weighing a mere 140 pounds, Mark Wayne Clark was one of 185 young men who became cadets at the Military Academy in June 1913. His cousin Pat Rafferty had graduated a few days earlier.

Clark and Joseph Lawton Collins, "a smart, capable, good looking boy with drive," Clark recalled, "kind of cocky," were the youngest entrants. Both had been born on the same day and were the class babies. During the initial horseplay, they were diapered and powdered and put early to bed. In the years ahead both would gain the four stars of general. So would Matthew B. Ridgway, another classmate and close friend. Nine others would win stars in World War II, among them William C. McMahon, who had roomed with Clark at Braden's and was his roommate at the Academy.

The cadets were formed into units according to size, and Clark was

16

with the tallest men. Eisenhower, two years ahead of him, was the company's cadet sergeant and lived in the same barracks division. Although close relationships between members of different classes were discourged, Clark and Eisenhower struck it off. They formed the basis of what would be a deep and enduring friendship.

Clark had always been above average in his studies, but at West Point, solid geometry and trigonometry, which he had never had in school, were major problems. His roommate's coaching, as well as his hard work— he was usually up at 4 A.M. to study—got him through.

He distinguished himself by his outstanding neatness, soldierly bearing, military appearance, and attention to duty. He had few demerits. The Commandant of Cadets evaluated his habits and discipline as "excellent," his horsemanship as "very good." Clark qualified as a marksman with rifle and pistol, was "fair" as a swordsman. He participated in sports, played tennis, golf, and ping-pong, but was no athlete. His general qualities as an officer—judgment, originality, energy, efficiency, and character—were "very good."

Receiving a promotion every year in the cadet command structure, he served in turn as corporal, sergeant, and lieutenant. Collins made the same progression. Ridgway outstripped them and, as a senior or first classman, like Patton eight years earlier, was the corps adjutant.

Clark, who got on well with his fellow cadets and was well liked, was known as "Opie," after the comic-strip character. He was deemed versatile. The yearbook twitted him for being "an excellent purveyor...of more or less interesting rumors. No rumor ever suffered the diminution of its pristine splendor from having passed through Opie's hands or mouth. Always careful to give out said rumor at least as good as it was when he got it."

He came to a significant decision early in his cadet life. Although his parents had bothered little with formal religious observances beyond attending occasional nondenominational services at post chapels, Mark had himself baptized in the West Point chapel as an Episcopalian. This dispelled trifling or troublesome ambiguities, for military men were far more comfortable when they could firmly categorize people and things. He perceived, whether vaguely or clearly, the structure of American society and the advantage of being a Protestant with an Anglo-Saxon name. He had no Jewish identity, although he never denied his mother's heritage. As a boy he had spent several summers at his grandfather Clark's farm, and he felt more Clark than Ezekiels. Like his father and mother, he was never a fervent believer or strict churchgoer. Nor did he parade his faith. He was religious in the traditional American sense, that is, easygoing, tolerant, and fundamentally nonsectarian.

MacArthur's mother had lived at the nearby Thayer Hotel while he was a cadet, and Patton's mother or his devoted Aunt Nannie stayed there during his cadet years, but Clark was alone. If he missed his parents, he gave no sign of loneliness. His classmates characterized him as cheerful. He had, they said, an optimistic view of life.

He spent his few vacations with his Uncle John and Aunt Zettie Marshall until his parents, sister, and her son returned to Chicago from China at the end of 1915. In the following year his father became a lieutenant colonel. If he and Beckie ever visited Mark at West Point, Clark had no recollection of it.

Perhaps their absence prompted psychosomatic symptoms of illness, for Mark began to have nagging health problems. He had the usual colds that the Army called and dismissed as pharyngitis, but at the end of his third year, he was in the hospital with acute gastroenteritis. He continued to suffer distress in his stomach, feeling as though he had a heavy weight lodged there. Reporting on sick call several times, he was purged and received temporary relief. But pain and discomfort after eating became part of his daily existence.

He tried to disregard the condition and performed his duty as usual, not only because that was his habit and conformed with his family training but also because the exciting prospect of war lay over the horizon. Ever since 1914, when the Great War had erupted in Europe, the cadets had followed the campaigns closely. They hoped to practice their profession on the battlefield; all wanted a chance to show bravery and attain glory.

The United States entered the conflict on April 6, 1917, and two weeks later, a month and a half before scheduled, ten days short of Clark's twenty-first birthday, his class had its graduation ceremony. The government was mobilizing its energies and conscripting men for the military services, and the Army badly needed officers to train recruits.

Only 139 members remained of the original 185, and after Secretary of War Newton D. Baker's address, they received their diplomas and commissions as second lieutenants. Clark was 110th on the class list, well toward the bottom. Expressing his preference for the infantry as his branch of service, he received his wish. He was glad to follow his father.

He asked for assignment to the 11th Infantry, a regiment rumored to be returning from the Mexican border to Fort Sheridan, Chicago. No doubt he was thinking of being near his family. To his friends he jokingly talked of being close to the swell swimming and the good looking girls in Highland Park.

Clark had put on weight and was 157 pounds. He was balanced and even tempered, confident of his capacities. West Point had reinforced his values, confirmed his admiration for Theodore Roosevelt's virtues, given him stability no less than purpose, liberated him from boyhood and dependence on his parents, shaped him into a military man. Above all, the Military Academy inculcated in him a strong and lifelong dedication to the patriotic ideal that included devotion to the flag and commitment to a strong America. He would never swerve from these beliefs.

He was eager to prove his abilities and his courage on the battlefield. Only one thing bothered him. He was not feeling well.

Reunited with his parents and sister in Chicago, he immediately took to bed with severe stomach pains. His orders arrived and assigned him to the 11th Infantry, which was at Camp Forrest in Chickamauga Park, Georgia, near the Tennessee border and Chattanooga. Although he was still ill, he reported early in June. Posted to Company E, he took command of a platoon of 40 men. Twelve days later he had to request a month's sick leave. His company commander had only a fleeting impression of Clark but remembered him as "very willing and energetic."

Back in Chicago, he grew anxious over being absent from duty, apprehensive because his classmates might forge ahead of him in their careers, miserable because he was letting down his family, the Academy, the Army, and his country. He had to ask for an extension of his sick leave.

He visited a dispensary and was referred to a civilian specialist, who discovered a duodenal ulcer and an enlarged and tender appendix, requiring surgery. While he awaited hospitalization, the War Department promoted his father to colonel and him and all his classmates to first lieutenant. Happiness over his elevation in rank was short-lived. What, he asked himself, had he done to earn it? Nothing but be sick.

Clark entered the hospital. The doctors put him on an ulcer cure and removed his appendix. Several weeks later they took out infected tonsils.

Although he still suffered digestive troubles, Clark reported to duty in Georgia on December 1. His sickness had cost him six months. Would the loss of time affect his career? Except for his twelve days as a platoon leader, his military experience was nil. Determined to render efficient service, Clark received command of Company K of the 11th Infantry, about 200 men. He was conspicuously conscientious. He drove his soldiers relentlessly, but he had a way of joking with them too. He made more than a favorable impression on his immediate superior, Major R. W. Kingman, who commanded the 3d Battalion. Clark had turned his company, Kingman reported, into a "most excellent" unit. He was very well liked by his troops. He had a knack of creating a fine spirit among them and his capacity for command was well above average.

In March 1918, less than a year after graduating from West Point, he was promoted to the temporary wartime grade of captain. It had taken his father eight years to reach that rank.

The 11th Infantry, now part of the 5th Division, received orders for France. After an incessant round of inspections, Clark supervised and joked with his men as they boarded a troop train. At Hoboken, New Jersey, they marched directly aboard the giant German ocean liner *Vaterland*, which the U. S. government had seized and renamed the *Leviathan*.

The vessel set sail immediately and was in the port of Brest on May 1, Clark's birthday. This, he felt, was a good omen. He was 22 years old and except for a persistent and nagging physical discomfort that he tried to ignore, he felt ready to meet the challenge of combat.

The troops rode in boxcars across France, trained under French and American officers, and were inspected by General John J. Pershing and members of his staff. Then the division moved to the Colmar region behind what was known as the Anould Sector of the front and drilled again.

On June 11 came instructions to relieve a French division in the line. The Americans were to enter trenches in the Vosges Mountains, the southernmost part of the Western Front. In extremely rugged terrain where active warfare was impossible, where the opposing positions had remained unchanged for three and a half years, where deep dugouts protected the men from occasional enemy shells, the Americans were to have their introduction to combat in a relatively quiet area. They would become accustomed gradually to the sights and sounds of warfare.

As the units of the 11th Infantry started marching toward the front on June 12, Major Kingman, the 3d Battalion commander, became ill. He summoned Mark Clark, his best company commander, and turned over the battalion to him. Clark put his best platoon leader, a young Reserve lieutenant named John W. O'Daniel, in command of Company K. Clark then went to the battalion headquarters and assumed control.

His hard work and attention to duty had paid off. A year after graduating from West Point he was in command of a battalion of three rifle companies and a machine gun company, about 1,000 men. Regarded by his regimental commander as a quiet and unassuming officer, Clark had a good chance of remaining at the head of the battalion and of receiving promotion to major. He had made an auspicious beginning.

The regiment marched for two days to get into position to relieve the French. After resting on June 14—five years to the day since Clark had entered West Point—the troops moved forward when night fell. Carrying out the exchange of units, Americans shuffled and stumbled in the darkness to replace French soldiers who walked to the rear. The Germans commenced a desultory shelling. As Company I of the 11th Infantry moved into the trenches, the 5th Division took its first casualties of the war. Private Joseph Kanieski was killed, Captain M. W. Clark seriously wounded.

Clark had conscientiously been supervising the entrance of his battalion into the front line, making sure that his companies occupied their correct positions. As he emerged from the Company I dugouts to visit and inspect the next company, a shell exploded nearby. Fragments struck his right shoulder and upper back and knocked him unconscious.

Taken to a French hospital, Clark was placed under ether while surgeons dug bits of metal from his body. During the operation a hot water bottle accidentally tipped over and scalded his left leg. After he was sufficiently well, he was moved to an American hospital.

His father was serving at three posts in Kentucky and Georgia, alternately commanding a regiment, a brigade, and a newly formed division, all training for overseas movement. When they went to France, Colonel Clark would, no doubt, become a brigadier general.

He and Beckie learned of their son's injuries when they read his name on a list of casualties in a newspaper. A War Department telegram confirmed the fact. He had been "severely wounded in action." Mark, they thought, was surely dead. Then Pat Rafferty, who was in France, cabled, "Wayne all right."

As he lay in his hospital bed, Mark Clark reflected on his bad luck. Gone, at least temporarily, were his dreams of glory in combat. But if he recovered quickly, he could rejoin his regiment before the war ended.

Instead, after six weeks in the hospital, he was judged physically unfit for duty with the infantry. His cousin Pat Rafferty engineered Clark's transfer to the First Army Supply Section. There he would be a staff officer. Clark joined Colonel John L. DeWitt, the Chief of Supply, Lieutenant Colonel E. G. McGleave, who would marry Valencia Rafferty after the war, and Major Rafferty. Later Clark recruited Captain McMahon, his roommate at Braden's and West Point.

While the 5th Division fought in Lorraine, at St. Mihiel, and in the final Meuse–Argonne offensive, Clark had a less glamorous job. He supervised the daily shipments of food for the First Army's combat forces, which numbered more than half a million men. It was no small responsibility to get thousands of tons of rations flowing smoothly to ten or twelve divisions on schedule and in the proper quantities.

He performed exceptionally well, and his tall figure, pleasant personality, and intense dedication were favorably remarked around the First Army headquarters. In the process he learned much from the handsome, dapper, and efficient DeWitt, a Spanish-American War veteran.

More than satisfied by Clark's work and comportment, DeWitt recommended his promotion to major, citing Clark as "very conscientious and energetic." Unfortunately, no vacancy existed for another major on the staff. Although the First Army Chief of Staff asked Pershing's headquarters to make an exception for Clark, a negative reply came less than two weeks before the armistice.

DeWitt tried again, but in vain, to have Clark promoted after the war. Immensely regretful, DeWitt judged Clark to be "an excellent officer in every respect."

When the Third Army was formed for the occupation of Germany, McGleave was named Chief of Supply. He asked Clark to join him and McMahon in Coblenz. Clark decided to return home. He had been a staff officer long enough. He wanted to get back to the infantry and to command troops. He sailed from Rotterdam in June.

As he looked back on his wartime experiences, he was disappointed to have received neither promotion nor decoration. His friend O'Daniel, to whom he had turned over his company, had been wounded too, had earned the Distinguished Service Cross for gallantry, and was now a captain. Others had gained swift advancement.

Those were the breaks. Clark had done his duty. He never complained. He had been a good company commander. He had briefly commanded a battalion. He had an honorable wound. He had handled staff duties with success. Probably most important, he had attracted the respect of senior officers, particularly DeWitt, who would be influential in the Army during the postwar years.

If Clark had lost an opportunity to make his mark in the conflict and to win glory on the battlefield, he had no regret. He had broadened his knowledge and learned his strengths. Hard work and devotion to duty were virtues that Mark and his father shared.

Perhaps they were not enough. Charles Carr Clark was still a colonel in Georgia, for the armistice had made shipping the division overseas unnecessary. Neither Clark had capitalized on the career advantages offered by the Great War.

For his father who was approaching thirty years of Army duty, there would be no further chance. For Mark, he might have better luck next time, if there was to be a next time. If so, he would be ready. He would work hard and prepare himself professionally for additional responsibility. He would render faithful service to the Army.

Did his failure in the Great War to fulfill his personal expectations shape, unconsciously or deliberately, his behavior and career in World War II, when many observers thought him unreasonably, even ruthlessly, ambitious for advancement?

CHAPTER 4

☆ ☆ ☆ ☆

THE POSTWAR WORLD

"I desire a change of duty"

IN GOOD HEALTH, weighing all of 175 pounds, Clark was living at the Army-Navy Club in Washington, D. C., with other bachelor officers awaiting reassignment when at breakfast one morning he saw his name listed in the Army orders published regularly in *The New York Times*. He was to be on the staff of the Disciplinary Barracks, the jail for military offenders and criminals, at Fort Leavenworth, Kansas.

He packed, paid his bills, took the train, then discovered that another Captain M. W. Clark was meant. But Melville W. Clark was resigning from the service, the prisoners were rioting, and Mark Clark helped restore order.

At Fort Snelling, Minnesota, he took command of an infantry company. The countryside was beautiful, the hunting good. He bought a snappy Chandler touring car and acquired a dog.

His father retired in the spring of 1920 with a monthly pay check of

$312.50, and he and Beckie bought ten acres of land and a house near Washington, in the Ballston area of Arlington County, Virginia. Janet remarried, and she and her son moved to Norfolk.

Transferred to Fort Crook, Nebraska, near Omaha, where the 7th Corps Area headquarters came into being as a showcase post, Clark, trim and precisely military, commanded an infantry company. General Omar Bundy, the corps commander, noted him as "a promising young officer, enterprising, industrious, and active."

Clark was hoping for a tour overseas when he was suddenly called to temporary duty at Fort Dix, New Jersey. Expecting to be there a few days at most, he was furious when he learned what was in store for him: show business.

During the war many immigrants who spoke no English had entered the service. The Army had taught them to read, write, speak, and understand the language, made them familiar with American traditions and ideals, and helped them absorb the fundamentals of citizenship. After the armistice a group of soldiers who had been born outside the United States went on tour under War Department auspices. In uniform they drilled, sang songs, played musical instruments, and performed tricks to enthusiastic audiences. At a time when "Red" scares were very much in the air, when communism, socialism, and anarchism were widely regarded as threatening ideologies, the presentations offered a comforting message. Americanism was the best defense against all other "isms."

When the Secretary of War spoke publicly of the "importance of the Regular Army as a bulwark of Americanism," the War Department decided to educate the public on the opportunities and advantages of military life through the then popular Chautauqua programs.

A Chautauqua consisted of three consecutive days of educational, religious, entertaining lectures, musical events, and performances of various kinds in a particular town. On the first day, after completing their shows, the performers traveled to the next location on the circuit while those scheduled for the second day arrived. If groups of attractive, neat, well-behaved men in uniform performed on the circuits, they would no doubt promote Americanism and stimulate recruiting.

The Radcliff Chautauqua System Company, a prominent firm, had circuits in 1,700 towns ranging in population from 300 to 3,000, and Mr. Radcliffe himself was, he said, "patriotically interested" in Americanization. Wanting "to place a practical example of it" before his audiences, he offered to pay the travel expenses of several soldier parties, plus a daily fee of four dollars per person for meals and incidentals, if each group performed on one day of the normal three-day program in each town on a circuit.

The War Department accepted Radcliffe's proposal, formed four "Americans All" detachments, chose four officers who had attractive personalities to head them, and selected eight soldiers who were former illiterates of foreign birth for each group. They made such fine impressions in the small towns of rural America in 1920 that the War Department decided to continue the tours with three new parties in 1921.

Thus, early in January, Mark Clark arrived at Fort Dix and learned that he was to be in charge of eight men on tour for about nine months. He and his soldiers were to leave from Washington, D. C. in a few weeks. Until then, they were to rehearse their show.

The War Department removed his name from an order transferring him to the Philippines.

Instead of going overseas, he went to Washington with First Lieutenants Robert G. Gard and Paul B. Kelly and the 24 men of their three detachments. They had final rehearsals at the Radcliffe headquarters on 16th Street, then received special War Department instructions to advertise Civilian Military Training Camps.

Late in January the three teams departed, Gard to San Francisco to tour the west coast, Kelly to Atlanta for a circuit in the central south, and Clark to Charleston on the way to his first performance in Apopka, Florida.

Clark began each program with a brief lecture emphasizing the educational and vocational features of Army training and especially Americanization. The enlisted men introduced themselves in turn, told how the Army had improved them, marched in close order drill, sang, recited, and performed individual stunts, and thus illustrated how the Army produced intelligent and patriotic soldiers.

Following the circuit was wearing. They traveled by train and bus, frequently at night. The same entertainment soon became routine and monotonous. Many towns were isolated, meals were often irregular and poor, and accommodations less than desirable. Their monthly pay checks failed to arrive at Fort Lauderdale as promised, and Clark wired Washington for them to be mailed ahead to Homestead.

In Claxton, Georgia, trying to liberate his detachment from public transportation, Clark requested the Army to ship his Chandler automobile east. Turned down, he eventually persuaded the Radcliffe System to pay the freight costs on the basis of reducing travel expenses.

After three months, Clark was fed up. Writing to the Adjutant General, he said flatly, "I desire a change in duty." The War Department was powerless. Advertising the civilian training camps was a failure, and the Recruiting Bureau had already requested the Radcliffe System to discontinue the soldier groups.

Mr. Radcliffe refused to break the contract. His schedules were set. The soldiers cost him little. The detachments had to perform until the end of the season.

Clark saw much more than he wished of Florida, Georgia, Alabama, and South Carolina. He traveled, interminably it seemed, across Tennessee, Kentucky, Virginia, and West Virginia. He toured Pennsylvania and Ohio in better style in his Chandler. When the detachments were disbanded, he entered the Walter Reed Hospital with stomach trouble.

His Chautauqua experience was valuable. It taught him to know better the average American, to speak extemporaneously to audiences, and to understand the nature of public relations.

Quickly regaining his health, hoping for an assignment with troops, Clark stayed in Washington. He worked in the Munitions Building on Constitution Avenue for the Assistant Secretary of War, specifically for the Director of Sales, who had the enormous task of disposing of surplus War Department property, buildings, houses, land, installations no longer needed in peacetime. Clark prepared advertising copy, schedules, layouts, and descriptions of the Army's excess cantonments and structures. Displaying his usual zeal, he quickly mastered his new occupation.

His immediate supervisor wrote of Clark, who was then 26 years old, "Within a few months time he has, by diligence and strict attention to duty, qualified to a marked degree in a position which in the commercial world would correspond to that of an Assistant Advertising Manager of one of the largest corporations in the country, a position usually filled by a high priced executive with from 10 to 15 years of experience. His performance has been particularly creditable in view of the fact that he had no previous training in this line of work."

During two and a half years when his duties were entirely of a business character, Clark traveled extensively. In Chicago he conducted the final publicity campaign to dispose of the Symington Ordnance plant. At Mitchel Field, New York, he publicized the sale of the Army Supply Base. In Norfolk, Virginia, he sold extensive Army holdings. In Erie, Pennsylvania, he found a customer to purchase an abandoned howitzer factory formerly employing 8,000 people.

Wherever he went, he attracted favorable notice and comment as "an exceptionally capable officer" and as "an able, conscientious, and efficient executive" with "sound judgment and care in the expenditure of public funds."

Suffering almost constantly from poor health, Clark tried to ignore his symptoms. He rarely felt comfortable in his stomach, had gastrointestinal disturbances and slight nausea after every meal, lost ten pounds in two months. The doctors could determine no pathology. Potentially more serious was a cardiac condition. During three consecutive annual physical examinations, the doctors discovered a heart murmur and sent him each time to Walter Reed Hospital. There medical boards, although puzzled by his heartbeat, certified him as fit for duty.

Overriding his concern with his health was his courtship of a lovely girl. He remembered vaguely meeting her in the Munitions Building where she was a hostess in the Quartermaster General's office. She recalled far more precisely the important event.

Soon after her arrival in Washington in the summer of 1923, she had a blind date one afternoon. He turned out to be Mark Clark, who had been with the guard of honor in President Warren G. Harding's funeral procession earlier that day.

They drank coffee and joshed together in the canteen. Soon they were going to parties and picnics together. Before long Mark took her to Arlington to meet his parents. She enchanted them.

Maurine Doran was from Muncie, Indiana, where her father was sales manager for Ball Brothers. A graduate of Northwestern University and an accomplished pianist, she had been married briefly to a West Point classmate of Clark's named Oliver Brown Cardwell, who had taken his life on Christmas Day 1921.

On May 17, 1924, Maurine and Mark were married in the Bethlehem Chapel of the National Cathedral. His sister Janet was matron of honor. Major Pat Rafferty was best man. A reception in the bride's apartment on 17th Street followed.

Many years later a reporter asked Clark, "What was the best advice you ever received?"

After reflecting a few minutes, he said, "The best advice I ever had was to marry the girl I did."

"Who, sir, gave you that advice?" the reporter asked.

"She did."

It was an exceptionally happy marriage. He doted on her, and she returned his affection. Sweet tempered, easygoing, and smiling, she joked with him and looked after him. She had a way of putting people at ease and was socially gracious. She very much resembled her mother-in-law Beckie.

Her parents gave them a new car as a wedding present, and they drove to Fort Benning, Georgia. Unlike her husband, who was reserved and absorbed in his work, Renie Clark was light-hearted and had a fund of small talk. She quickly came to know the families on post, lunched with the ladies, engaged in charity affairs. In the following year she gave birth to their son William.

Clark was attending the Infantry School's Advanced Officers Course. Ridgway was a student too. Although the teaching of small unit tactics was somewhat stilted, Clark found it stimulating to be part of a group of alert young officers. He began seriously to read military history and started his own collection of professional books.

After visiting their parents in Washington and Muncie, he and Renie drove to San Francisco, where Clark reported to the 30th Infantry at the Presidio. He settled Renie and the baby into a house on post and went into the field for two months as an instructor at a summer camp. His battalion commander called him "capable in every respect of commanding a battalion in operations."

When Clark came down with a serious inflammation of the nose and throat, the doctors found his gall bladder diseased and sent him to Letterman General Hospital, where he remained nearly three months. The physicians recommended surgery, but Clark refused.

Except for this scare, he and Renie had a pleasant time. They made many friends. They felt fulfilled when their daughter Ann was born. She and her brother Bill were the center of the family existence, and the household was serene, affectionate, and happy.

Everything was going well for them until Colonel Frank C. Bolles appeared on the scene.

CHAPTER 5

☆ ☆ ☆ ☆

BOWSER BOLLES

"phenomenally outstanding work"

WHEN BOLLES TOOK command of the 30th Infantry and of the Presidio early in 1926, he became Clark's regimental and post commander. Known as "Bowser" because he barked, he was a tyrant. He was tough and demanding and could be abusive. Uncouth in manner and speech, he was oblivious to embarrassment. He had acquired an outstanding combat record in the war and had two Distinguished Service Crosses that some thought should have been Medals of Honor.

Bolles had twin basic drives. He wanted promotion to general officer rank and perfection in duty. Younger officers, he believed, were careless and lazy. Clark was a conspicuous exception.

He fastened on Clark to help him gain his desires. If Bolles could turn his regiment into a model and the Presidio into a showplace, he would impress the senior general who commanded the 9th Corps Area from an office across the parade ground.

Relieving Clark from command of his company, Bolles made him his unofficial aide, his general factotum, and his slave. He appointed Clark the Post Exchange Officer, moved him into an office close to his, and instructed him to be Bolles' junior alter ego in supervising all the activities.

Though flattered by his regimental commander's attention, Clark disliked being away from troops. There were also other disadvantages. Bolles telephoned Clark at all hours of the day and night. He had a tendency to bully and to badger. On two occasions he lost his temper and had Clark placed in arrest and confined briefly to quarters.

Yet Bolles appreciated Clark's steadiness, patience, and efficient service. He came to admire and eventually to like him, finally regarding him as a son. His ratings of Clark were more than favorable.

Clark repeatedly requested return to troop duty, and Bolles just as consistently refused to release him. He knew a good man when he saw one. Clark continued as the Post Exchange Officer for two years, and Bolles rated him the "most efficient business executive I have ever had serve under me, an officer of the highest type in every respect."

Major General John L. Hines, former Army Chief of Staff who was commanding the 9th Corps Area, called Clark "efficient, dependable, and energetic" and "a very presentable officer."

Bowser Bolles became a brigadier general early in 1928, and the War Department transferred him to Fort D. A. Russell, near Cheyenne, Wyoming, to be commander of the 4th Brigade and of the post. He wanted to take Clark with him, for, he said, "I regard you as a man of great integrity of character." Clark wished for foreign service with troops and liberation from bondage. Bolles had his way, and the Clark family drove to Cheyenne and settled in.

Bolles was about to make Clark the Post Exchange Officer again, but Clark protested. Another assignment in the same job would type him as incapable of anything else. Bolles then appointed him Executive Officer of the brigade. Clark handled the Post Exchange as an additional duty.

In his annual rating, Bolles called him "an officer of the highest attainments," qualified to be a colonel.

Clark's health collapsed in August 1928. He entered Fitzsimmons General Hospital in Denver, and the doctors removed his gall bladder. Hardly had he recovered when his hemorrhoids required attention. Hospitalization, surgery, and convalescence consumed more than eight months and left him exhausted and weak. He often wondered whether he might be forced to leave the Army.

The War Department sent Clark in 1929 to the Indiana National Guard.

Clark would ensure Regular Army standard training for the citizen soldiers who drilled one evening every week and attended two weeks of summer camp every year. He was an instructor of infantry and an adviser to the 38th Infantry Division. In the brand new armory in Indianapolis, Clark's duties were fairly light, and he built himself up physically. He met with National Guard units, staffs, and individuals, taught by lecture and demonstration, supervised close order drill, coached the rifle and pistol teams, visited units training in other towns and cities in the state, refereed athletic competitions held to enhance physical fitness, and umpired statewide contests in all the major sports.

The Clarks participated in the town's social life and made many friends. He joined the Mystic Tie Lodge and became a Master Mason.

The Wall Street crash in October 1929 and the subsequent Depression imposed austerity on the Army. Declining budgets meant reductions in manpower and cuts in pay and allowances. If the Army had to decrease the number of officers on active duty, would Clark's poor health make him a candidate for discharge?

At his annual physical examination in January 1930, the doctors ominously noted his weight of 154 pounds, about 25 below normal, and his long-standing cardiac condition, which they defined as a valvular heart lesion. They took no further action, but they raised a question in Clark's mind. If he had to leave the Army, how would he at 34 years of age provide for his wife and two small children?

Saving several months of leave, he traveled with his family to Muncie and worked for the Ball Brothers. The salary was much better than his monthly $250 pay, plus $80 rental and $36 subsistence allowances. He turned out to be a first-rate executive, and the firm offered him a permanent job if he would resign from the Army.

Two other employment offers came during the Depression years, one from Sears, Roebuck, which sent him $100 for traveling expenses to an interview in Chicago, the other from Pat Rafferty, who had retired from the Army and was in the real estate business in Florida.

Although civilian work would remove concern over his separation from the Army for physical reasons, Clark declined all prospects. "If I had started out with the idea of becoming rich," he said, "I wouldn't have gone into the Army in the first place."

Had he accepted employment, he would no doubt have been successful. His gift of judgment and his ability to make decisions would have taken him to the top. But the military needed those talents too. And that was where he wanted to be. He wanted, above all, to be a good soldier like his father.

His father, Charles Carr Clark, died in March 1930 after a brief illness. Traveling to Washington for the funeral and interment in Arlington Cemetery, Mark comforted Beckie and composed an obituary, which was also a moving tribute to his father's soldierly qualities, for the West Point class notes. Beckie soon moved to Kalorama Road in Washington, D. C.

Early in 1931, the doctors again noted his heart murmur, called him unfit for active field service because of organic heart disease, and sent him to Walter Reed for tests. A board of medical officers determined his systolic cardiac murmur to be no obstacle to full military duty. He was in relatively good health and gaining weight.

His supervisors termed Clark "mentally and physically alert, most intelligent, neglects no opportunity to improve himself, broad vision and fine personality," and found him to be "of the type who gets results without friction." Major General George Van Horn Moseley, commanding the 5th Corps Area, called Clark "an especially efficient officer of good judgment. He is tall and thin and presents a smart appearance. Dignified and somewhat reserved. Has an unusual ability to impart his knowledge to others."

He became a major in January 1933, the year that marked the end of the post-World War I era and the beginning of the pre-World War II period. Franklin D. Roosevelt was inaugurated President of the United States, and Adolf Hitler assumed power in Germany. On the other side of the globe, Japan had conquered Manchuria. A whole new world was in the making, and events already in motion were moving toward a climax.

Insulated from these affairs, Clark was a student at the Command and General Staff College at Fort Leavenworth. With him was Ridgway. Walter Bedell Smith and Donald Brann were also members of the class whom Clark came to know.

The College prepared officers to command divisions and corps and to serve on the general staff of important headquarters. Young men like Clark, who was then 37 years old, were to advance swiftly in a rapidly expanding Army in the event of war. The course work stressed the organization, supply, and maneuver of units in a theater of operations. Using a great variety of problems derived from historical examples and theoretical situations, the students planned and executed battles and campaigns.

Working individually and in teams, they were rigorously tested, with their proficiency always measured against the "school solution," the only one admitted and approved. This practice stifled originality and imagination, for many courses of action would work in a given case, although some would be better. But the students adapted and strove to perform as expected.

The Leavenworth system, imposing conformity and standardization, shaped several generations of graduates into a homogeneous pattern. The result enabled the Army to use officers as interchangeable parts. Anyone educated at Leavenworth was at home in any headquarters.

Faculty and staff members constantly observed and evaluated the students. Could they get along with people, work together, be flexible and cooperative, display leadership? These subjective judgments were also important in determining whether an officer was fit for high command.

Clark flourished. At his annual physical examination in January 1934, he weighed 161 pounds. And at the end of his first year, he was rated "dependable, careful, intelligent."

Hardly had the second year begun when an officer on the College staff slipped into the auditorium where the class was listening to a lecture and whispered into Clark's ear. The Commandant, General Herbert Brees, wanted to see him.

Standing at attention in Brees' office, Clark was astonished to hear the Commandant burst out with, "Clark, I don't understand you."

"Well, sir," he replied easily, "sometimes I don't understand myself. What have I done?"

Why anyone who had performed so well in the first year would want to leave the College and forego the second year was beyond him, Brees said.

But he had no desire to leave, Clark said puzzled.

Brees waved a sheet of paper at him, a letter stating his wish to depart.

It was Bowser Bolles, now a major general. Back from the Philippines, commanding the 2d Division at San Antonio, he had volunteered Clark's desire to serve under him again.

Clark convinced Brees to let him stay and complete the course, and Bolles agreed to wait until Mark's graduation.

As Clark, Renie, and the children drove to San Antonio and moved into a house on post, Bolles was appointed commander of the 7th Corps Area. Over Clark's protest, Bolles sent a radiogram to the War Department and demanded Clark's transfer to him. The Clark family drove to Omaha, where Clark served again with Bolles.

Clark had three jobs. He was the Corps Area Assistant Chief of Staff G-2 for intelligence, the Assistant Chief of Staff G-3 for plans and training, and the Deputy Chief of Staff for the Civilian Conservation Corps, which had come into being in 1933 to provide housing, food, and work for unemployed young men. The Army administered the camps, and Clark was in charge of the installations in the corps area. He traveled extensively to check on the state of morale, the quality of food, the conditions of cleanliness, and the progress of the public works undertaken.

As Bolles' published order showed clearly, Clark had the authority to "make all decisions and to take all necessary action in Civilian Conservation Corps matters that would normally be submitted to the Commanding General." That made plain Bolles' confidence in Clark.

Bolles sometimes accompanied Clark on his inspections, and one Sunday morning Bolles decided to visit several installations without warning the camp commanders ahead of time. At the first camp, which was in reasonably good condition, two flaws permitted Bolles to ask his favorite questions.

In the mess hall the mops were lined up vertically with the handles down. Bolles disliked seeing water run down the handles and considered it unsanitary. Who invented the law of gravity? he asked the mess sergeant. When the sergeant confessed ignorance, Bolles said triumphantly, "Newton."

Then he saw a man who needed a haircut. "Who can wear their hair long?" Bolles asked him. He did not know, and Bolles recited, with great satisfaction, "Poets, lovers, and musicians."

As Bolles and Clark were departing, Bolles asked where the next camp was. Clark gave its number. It was about six miles away. The camp commander must have overheard the conversation, telephoned ahead to warn of the imminent visit, and related Bolles' pet questions and answers. The second camp, as Clark's practiced eye quickly saw, was a little too neat for an unannounced inspection.

The first sergeant who met Bolles and Clark needed a haircut. Bolles' eyes gleamed wickedly. "Who can wear their hair long?" he demanded.

The sergeant was ready. "Newton, sir," he replied.

Clark almost fainted.

Throughout Clark's tour, Bolles wrote letters in his behalf, urging prominent officers to have Clark selected to attend the Army War College, the final preparation, the ultimate step after Benning and Leavenworth toward high rank and responsibility. To Malin Craig, Army Chief of Staff, to Edward Croft, Chief of Infantry, to John H. Hughes, War

Department G-3, to Harry E. Knight, War Department G-2, Bolles sang Clark's praises, extolling him as "one of the ablest young officers" in the Army. Would they give him "a friendly push?"

Clark's name appeared on the list of officers detailed to be students at the Army War College in the 1936–37 course.

Bolles had earlier tried to get Clark a Distinguished Service Medal for his wartime performance. Unsuccessful, Bolles enlisted the aid of DeWitt, now a brigade commander in the Philippines. Together, by correspondence, they pressured the War Department "to correct an act of omission in order that justice may be done." Unfortunately, too much time had passed since the war. Bolles and DeWitt were too late.

A few days after Clark had left for the War College, Bolles had a brilliant idea. He recommended Clark for the medal on the basis of "his phenomenally outstanding work" with the Civilian Conservation Corps. Nothing came of it.

"You have probably been in Washington long enough," Bolles wrote to Clark, "to know that a little politicking around often does a great deal of good." The advice was meant in a kindly way.

Clark later had conflicting thoughts of his association with Bolles. He had wished for troop duty, preferably overseas, but he was indebted to Bolles, who had taught him to be an aggressive and persistent perfectionist. Clark also learned to be patient.

Forty years old, in excellent health, intelligent, balanced, and alert, Clark at the War College was among the best and most highly regarded young officers in the Army. Ridgway, Bedell Smith, and Geoffrey Keyes were among his classmates. Despite their easy congeniality, their affectation of high spirited indolence, they were all serious minded, hard working, and avid for knowledge, not only because of the mutual pressures they exerted on each other, but also because the prospect of war loomed across both oceans. In Europe, Hitler was rearming Germany and making threatening sounds. In Asia, Japan had turned from Manchuria and was invading China proper. If the United States was drawn into armed conflict, the relatively young men at the War College would be leaders on whom America would depend. Their course work centered on preparing for war, and the students drew plans for various contingencies, worked on mobilization, shipping, training, weapons, equipment, and unit organization.

Clark's student committee looked into the structure and makeup of the infantry division, a massive and somewhat unwieldy organization suited for trench warfare as in World War I. Since then, developments in automobiles and trucks indicated to thoughtful officers the increasing need for mobility. Clark and his group recommended a smaller division without the brigade level of command.

The proposal made its way to the War Department, which appointed a board of three general officers, Fox Conner, Lesley J. McNair, and George C. Marshall, to consider the suggestion. Conner became ill, and the board never met. Yet the idea foreshadowed the eventual triangularization of the infantry division carried out by McNair in 1940. He reduced the size of the division by a third, trimmed the basic shape to three regiments, and dissolved the brigade headquarters.

Clark's committee also looked into the promotion system, which many officers believed to be stagnant, rigid, and overly oriented toward seniority. In time of emergency, bright, young, energetic leaders needed to move quickly into positions of responsibility. Clark made the oral presentation to his classmates on the group's findings and recommendations. Subsequent detractors of Clark who remembered his talk pointed to it as early evidence of his concern for promotion.

The intellectual and social exchanges with the students, the most promising officers of their age, sharpened Clark's professional attainments. The school year was a constant test of the leadership, intelligence, and understanding required for high rank. Even when they played baseball on the parade ground, they were under observation.

The commandant characterized Clark as being "of even disposition, an exceptionally good team worker, works methodically and thoroughly, appreciates the view of others."

The annual field exercise came at the end of the course when the students toured the major Civil War battlefields in Pennsylvania and Virginia and scrutinized the strategy and maneuvers of the divisions, corps, and armies. Then came graduation, following which everyone packed his furniture and personal belongings—Clark had 2,300 pounds of professional books—called the movers, said goodbyes, and set forth to their next destination.

The War Department had detailed Clark into the General Staff Corps, which was an honor, and was sending him to the 3d Infantry Division at Fort Lewis, Washington, which was an opportunity. He reported for duty toward the end of July 1937.

The times were critical. As international relations deteriorated and war threatened, American military budgets began to increase, and the Army started seriously to prepare for modern warfare. In this process Clark would play a prominent role and earn an Army-wide reputation. His work at Fort Lewis would firmly establish the ground for his later meteoric rise to fame.

CHAPTER 6

☆ ☆ ☆ ☆

FORT LEWIS: MARSHALL AND EISENHOWER

"no superiors and few equals"

THE CLARKS LOVED the Northwest, the exhilarating scenery, the breathtaking view of Mount Rainier, the beauty of Puget Sound, their proximity to Tacoma, Seattle, and San Francisco. Because Clark, like his father, needed to withdraw periodically to a place of solitude for reflection and self-renewal, the Clarks used a house and a few wooded acres on Camano Island where they relaxed quietly and Mark fished.

He was busy with his work in a world marching, seemingly inexorably, toward war. The United States had begun to look to its own security, and in that contemplation the American military forces appeared weak. The services were undermanned, understaffed, and underequipped, had old-fashioned and outmoded concepts, methods, and procedures, and possessed insufficient and obsolete weapons. Congressional appropriations began to increase, and the Army moved slowly toward a war footing, still a distant prospect. As the tempo of training accelerated, Clark became a key figure.

Fortunate to be with one of the few Regular divisions in the United States, Clark was also lucky to be with the organization that could most easily conduct large-scale exercises. Although all the divisions were fragmented and split, the 1st spread along the east coast, the 2d divided between Texas and Wyoming, the 3d had its major units relatively close to Fort Lewis.

After working with National Guard soldiers during their two-week summer camp and receiving a commendation for his "energy and capacity," Clark became the 3d Division Assistant Chief of Staff, G-2 and G-3, in charge of intelligence and training, then a normal combination.

Since the intelligence function, collecting information on actual and potential enemies, was minimal in peacetime, Clark relied for the most part on a young assistant, Captain Edwin B. Howard. Conventionally tied to the G-2 position was public relations, ensuring understanding between the military and civilian communities. Clark retained that for himself, and he spoke frequently to fraternal, patriotic and civic clubs in the area.

As G-3, his main responsibility was to prepare individuals and units, including National Guard and Reserve organizations, for war. Ordinarily, the division commander informed the G-3 of what he wanted, and the G-3 carried out his wishes. He could go back for guidance or for answers to specific questions before finally submitting his proposals for approval.

In Clark's case, the division commander was elderly, in poor health, and interested in social activities. The chief of staff, Clark's immediate superior, was much the same. So Clark had virtually a free hand. When he showed his projects, these officers said, "Go ahead, do it, fine, wonderful."

This was agreeable, for Clark could try out his favorite tactical theories and concepts in the field. But he was concerned about his relative youth and inexperience. To be sure that his ideas were practical, he needed the counsel of a mature infantry officer. He found his mentor in Brigadier General George Marshall.

Marshall commanded the 5th Brigade of the 3d Division at Vancouver Barracks, Washington, a few miles from Portland, Oregon. Well known and highly respected in the Army, he had graduated from the Virginia Military Institute, had been a superb staff officer in World War I, and then served as Pershing's senior aide. He was in China with the 15th Infantry a decade after Charles Carr Clark, Mark's father.

Having been the First Army's Chief of Operations in France in 1918,

Marshall was a good friend of DeWitt, who had been the First Army's Chief of Supply and Clark's boss. No doubt, Marshall and Clark had met at least briefly in France during the war. In any event, their previous service at the same headquarters permitted swift rapport, and Marshall was happy to look over Clark's projects and to offer advice.

Now when Clark discussed his plans with his division commander and chief of staff, he said, "Do you mind if I fly down and show them to General Marshall?" They replied, "No, he would love it." So Clark frequently went by small airplane to consult with Marshall, who came to appreciate Clark's clear mind, refreshing outlook, and energetic application to duty.

When Marshall visited Fort Lewis, he generally saw Clark. Sometimes he stayed overnight with the family. He bantered with Renie but was always quite formal with her husband.

Clark's annual physical examination in January 1938 almost brought his military career to an end as his heart murmur once again attracted the doctors' attention. They suggested that he retire but finally relented, "because of the long duration of the defect." He was across that hurdle, as it turned out, for good.

When the 15th Infantry, his father's and Marshall's old regiment, returned from China to the United States to become part of the 3d Division, Clark, perhaps as a tribute to his father, perhaps to please Marshall, publicized its arrival and debarkation at Tacoma. Calling on the skills he had mastered while advertising surplus government property, he generated a smooth promotion. The media coverage was outstanding, and Clark received much praise.

Planning a war problem, a simulated combat situation involving Marshall's brigade, Clark laid out a turning movement and an attack. The operation was to begin under cover of darkness. With the participants in their proper starting positions and umpires ready to observe the unfolding maneuver, Clark placed himself at Marshall's headquarters. In compliance with the instructions, Marshall marched his men out after nightfall and made his envelopment. In position to launch his attack, a commander would normally have waited until dawn to control the operation in daylight. Instead, Marshall directed the assault to begin at 2 A.M.

Surprised, Clark asked Marshall his reason for the unorthodox decision, which Leavenworth would have graded unsatisfactory. Marshall explained. Because his men had to cross open ground in the mock battle, they would suffer fewer casualties from the "enemy" at night.

The maneuver proceeded. At daybreak Clark called the exercise to an end. He then met with his umpires, discussed their observations, and wrote up his notes.

Later that morning, with all the division officers present, Clark presented his comments. He found fault with some actions, praised others. Some senior officers, he knew, considered Marshall's order to assault before daylight to be a serious mistake. Clark accepted Marshall's decision as correct because it was imaginative and based on realistic wartime conditions.

Marshall never forgot Clark's evaluation, not because he may have been the recipient of Clark's kindness but rather because he approved of Clark's concern with realism.

Shortly thereafter, Marshall was called to Washington, D. C., to become the War Department Assistant Chief of Staff. A few months later, he was elevated to the post of Deputy Chief of Staff. Despite his distance from Fort Lewis, he encouraged Clark to send him his plans, and he continued to offer advice. In one letter he suggested maneuvering off the reservation—"in other words out of sight of the Post water tower," a prominent landmark that helped participants plot their locations on the ground. In war, troops would have to orient themselves without familiar signposts.

He asked Clark to keep his remarks confidential, for he had no business sending hints on how to train the division. But he was in favor of "getting off the home grounds and doing things on a more warlike basis."

Clark understood. He always endeavored to make his exercises realistic.

In another letter Marshall asked, "Confidentially, will you let me know, most informally," whether it was practical to move troops by freight car as they had in France during the war instead of by passenger coach as the railroads in the United States insisted. "I would like to have you tip me off as to what you discovered. Hastily yours."

Clark investigated. The railways, he learned, preferred to have soldiers travel in coaches not only because of safety but also because of the higher rates they could charge. Clark sensibly suggested a meeting of railroad officials and War Department authorities to ensure safety as well as lowered costs.

After a year at Fort Lewis, Clark was judged "a hard working, conscientious, highly efficient officer with a pleasing personality." The field artillery brigade commander added unexpected praise. A "mere rating of superior," he wrote, "falls short of expressing my estimate of Major

Clark's abilities. He is one of the most brilliant all around officers I have met in 40 years of commissioned service."

Far from Fort Lewis, the meeting of Hitler, Mussolini, Chamberlain, and Daladier at Munich to assure "peace for our time" produced the opposite effect. As Germany moved to gobble up Czechoslovakia, European nations feverishly prepared for war. The United States stepped up its military activities.

A tough and decisive officer, Major General W. C. Sweeney, took command of the 3d Division, and his support of Clark's training program was directed and uncompromising. He relieved Clark of his peripheral responsibilities and permitted him to concentrate on war preparations.

"I know you are getting along fine," Bolles wrote to Clark, "and I look to see you go places, which I know you will. Personally, I think the opportunities for all officers in the next few years will be very great. I believe without doubt that the army will be increased."

He was right. New buildings were going up at Fort Lewis, McChord Field was being developed, and the G-2 map room had much of the world on its walls.

In the summer of 1938, Lieutenant Colonel Dwight D. Eisenhower, Douglas MacArthur's subordinate in the Philippines, came to the United States for a four-month visit. Early in October, on his way back to Manila, he stopped in Tacoma and spent a day with his brother Edgar. He called on General Sweeney, an old acquaintance, and saw Clark.

Clark's interesting tactical experiments impressed Eisenhower. To him, Fort Lewis seemed to be the center of intriguing activities. He decided to seek assignment there. With that thought in mind, he sent Clark a Christmas card.

Clark replied, "It was certainly a pleasure to see you recently after so many years. I have kept track of the fine jobs you have had throughout your service and expect to see you reach the top."

When the Inspector General of the Army offered to send Clark to the Harvard Business School in return for four years of service in his department, Clark declined with thanks. His present assignment, he said, was "proving most instructive."

Staging a series of maneuvers in May 1939, Clark suggested and Sweeney requested moving a battalion of infantry from Missoula, Montana, by air, quite a new and exciting idea. The corps headquarters disapproved because funds were lacking.

Marshall, now designated to be the Army Chief of Staff on Malin Craig's retirement in the fall, flew to Fort Lewis to observe the exercise.

The Chief of the Army Air Corps, Henry H. Arnold, accompanied him. Clark's work impressed them both.

The division chief of staff rated Clark "an alert, energetic, affable officer markedly efficient in all his work. The results of his efforts are outstanding. Intensely interested in his profession and a fine tactician. Of exceptional high all around professional attainments. This officer will go far in the Army." Sweeney concurred.

When the War Department published an order directing Eisenhower to report to Fort Lewis later that year, Eisenhower and Clark wrote each other on the following day. From Manila, Eisenhower informed Clark of the good news and asked about a school for his son John and about available living quarters on the post.

Clark had seen the order, was happy about Eisenhower's transfer, and Sweeney was "mighty glad" too. Anticipating some of Eisenhower's questions, he sent pictures of the post and information about housing. "When you arrive, please know that Mrs. Clark and I want to take care of you and the family until you get settled."

For the rest of the year they corresponded. Clark promised to keep an eye on John. He advised on the best way to ship a car from San Francisco to Tacoma. He reported the dimensions and the number of windows in the houses on the post so that Mamie could buy material for curtains more cheaply in the Philippines.

Eisenhower felt about going to Fort Lewis, he said, "like a boy who has been promised an electric train for Christmas."

Clark arranged for him to command a battalion of the 15th Infantry.

On September 1, 1939, Hitler invaded Poland and brought World War II to Europe. On the same day, Marshall officially became the U. S. Army Chief of Staff.

The outbreak of war gave added urgency to strengthening and modernizing the American military forces, and the German blitzkrieg in Poland showed clearly how far behind and out of date the American military establishment was. President Roosevelt increased the authorized size of the armed forces, and Congress voted additional funds.

At Fort Lewis the pace became hectic. Men signed up for service, and new soldiers crowded the barracks. Reserve officers recalled or volunteering for active duty arrived.

Throughout the fall of 1939, Clark worked hard on an unprecedented exercise to take place in January 1940, an amphibious operation involving both the Army and the Navy. The Fourth Army headquarters, now commanded by Lieutenant General John L. DeWitt, laid out the problem.

TOP: The Clark family in 1899. Clark, age two, is on the lap of his mother, Rebecca Ezekiels Clark, whom his father, Charles (left), met while on duty in the Arizona Territory; her forebears were among the first Jewish settlers in the Southwest. The girl in white is Clark's sister, Janet, and the other girl is a playmate.

ABOVE LEFT At West Point, six-foot-three and only 140 pounds, Clark was neither athlete nor scholar. He graduated 110th in a class of 139.

ABOVE RIGHT: Captain Clark, just after World War I—an infantry company commander at Fort Snelling, Minnesota.

September 1941: Brigadier General Clark with his old friend and fellow West Pointer, Colonel Dwight Eisenhower. In a few months would come the war that would send them both soaring to high command, with Clark forever the outranked.

A bit more than a year later, in Algiers, they are both lieutenant generals, and Clark is now Eisenhower's deputy.

The 3d Division was to come ashore on a narrow beach near Monterey, California, where the surf permitted landings without unduly risking soldiers' lives, then attack a mythical enemy force and capture San Francisco. The then astronomical number of 14,000 men would participate.

From Leavenworth, Clark obtained all available information on how to get a division on a hostile shore, then prepared field orders, charts, and checklists. He rehearsed the units that would take part. He traveled to talk with key commanders and staffs, to check on accommodations for troops, to reconnoiter terrain, and to deal with a multitude of details that were mostly new and untried.

By the turn of the year he was in a whirlwind. He had combat teams practice landing operations at American Lake and along the shores of Puget Sound. He sent groups of men to California to work with the Navy. He prepared the division to board ships in the follow-up landing.

Eisenhower arrived at Fort Lewis on New Year's Day. Clark appointed him chief umpire for the Army units in the joint exercise.

In accordance with plans, several hundred soldiers embarked at Tacoma in transports, which took them to Monterey Bay, where they clambered into lifeboats, paddled to the shore, and established a beachhead. A larger force at Tacoma marched aboard ships in a country fair atmosphere. Many from the post watched at dockside. A band played. Off Monterey, the men landed. Then all mounted an attack, a double envelopment, and surrounded the "enemy" in a matter of hours. Airplanes were featured throughout.

Compared to later operations, the maneuver was a primitive affair. Yet it attracted widespread military attention, for it demonstrated missions new to both services, as well as to the Army Air Corps. Marshall and many other prominent observers, among them McNair, were present. Instructors from the Army War College and from other service schools, as well as interested spectators from high headquarters, watched and learned, while the participants gained experience.

Sweeney was supposed to direct the show, but he took sick and retired to the Hotel Monterey. Clark took over. He called in the regimental commanders, gave the orders for the attack, and handed out operations maps. He unveiled a new technique—several small planes equipped with cameras had flown over the "enemy" positions and photographed the terrain; Clark then superimposed the developed and enlarged pictures on maps and distributed them to unit commanders. Afterwards, Clark presented the critique.

His performance was impressive. He handled the complicated details confidently. He introduced concepts hardly talked about. He issued instructions directly. His voice was firm and quiet. His decisions were quick and sure.

His West Point classmate Joe Collins sent his compliments. "You did a corking good job on the maneuver, and I enjoyed being with you."

"Ever since you have been out in the 3d Division," a friend wrote, "I have been hearing about the reputation you have made of yourself as the real Grand Cyclops of the outfit, and the real power behind the throne." Collins and others were lecturing on the landing and were building Clark's name. How he pitied Clark's successor, who would "have one hell of a time in even approaching the standards you have set as G-3 out there."

The greatest praise came from Marshall. After reading the official report of the exercise, including Clark's G-3 Summary, Marshall wrote to commend the Fourth Army commander, General DeWitt. Marshall's remarks, everyone understood, were meant for Clark.

"I think you and your assistants," Marshall said, "did an excellent job of handling that exercise. The careful planning and physical surveys preceding the exercises; the testing of plans; the care exercised in keeping the supply situation on a factual basis; the establishment and character of the aircraft warning service; and the tactical handling of the First Wing General Headquarters Air Force and of the 7th Cavalry Brigade during the exercise are considered to be outstanding."

Marshall was so taken by the manner in which Clark performed during the Army-Navy exercise that he suggested Clark's next assignment—to be an instructor at the Army War College. The Commandant of the College wrote Clark to inform him of this circumstance and explained why quarters on post would be unavailable to Clark. His was an additional appointment made after all the vacancies had been filled.

To be selected despite the lack of a vacancy meant that Marshall really wanted him in Washington, D. C. It did not occur to Clark that Marshall was gathering around him a team of officers on whom he could rely.

DeWitt, a former Commandant of the College, wrote to congratulate Clark. "You are going to have four delightful years of great benefit to yourself and to the College too." But normal tours would shortly become obsolete in a war-torn world.

The phony war in Europe came to a crashing end in May when German blitzkrieg forces overran western Europe, bringing Holland, Belgium, and France to defeat in six weeks. The lightning campaign produced consternation in the United States, along with concern for Britain, which stood alone and defiant against Hitler.

At Fort Lewis, as Clark prepared to depart, tributes poured in. Robert L. Eichelberger, a regimental commander who would later command the Eighth Army in the Pacific under MacArthur, wrote, "Among the many qualified general staff officers with whom I have served, I consider you to have no superiors and few equals."

Sweeney attested to Clark's invariable devotion and proficiency.

Before leaving for Washington, D. C., Clark and his family decided to spend a week at Camano Island fishing, then to go shopping in San Francisco. While driving to the island, Clark turned on the car radio. A news flash stunned him. All courses at the Army War College, as well as those at Leavenworth, were cancelled for the 1940–41 term; both schools were to close. Where then was Clark to go?

He stopped in downtown Seattle at the Olympic Hotel and phoned Sweeney. "First," he said, "please don't assign my house to anybody else." Second, would he try to find out what was happening?

The Clarks continued to Camano Island and stayed a few days. But Mark was impatient to learn about his next tour of duty. Abandoning their trip to San Francisco, they returned to Fort Lewis.

Sweeney had been unable to get any information on Clark's future, so Clark sent a telegram to Marshall. With the War College closing, he wired, he awaited instructions.

He received a typical Marshall reply. "Your message received. Comply with your orders."

On July 1, 1940, he was promoted to lieutenant colonel.

Then it was packing, 93 packages of household goods weighing 13,000 pounds, plus 10 boxes of professional books. He turned in his 1937 Buick at Tacoma and arranged to have a 1941 model delivered in Washington. With Renie carrying her canary in a cage, they took the train to San Francisco and embarked for the sea voyage to New York. They were in Washington in August. Quarters Number 11 on the main line of Fort Humphreys was available, for a senior faculty member had been promoted and transferred. The Clarks moved right in.

He was now at the center of the military establishment and, as Bowser Bolles had predicted, about to go places.

CHAPTER 7

☆ ☆ ☆ ☆

McNAIR

"He has everything."

CLARK ARRIVED IN Washington as the United States started to mobilize in earnest. Earlier efforts to expand the armed forces and to prepare them for war, although salutary, had been hesitant. Isolationists in the country still saw the conflict in Europe as of no concern to Americans and the violence in Asia as even less related to American interests.

Marshall, the U. S. Army Chief of Staff, warned repeatedly of the need for strength and modernization. The American Army, he said, stood seventeenth in size among the world's forces. Less than 25 percent of the units were ready to fight. The new techniques of warfare could not be improvised overnight.

After Germany invaded and overran Denmark and Norway and later when German forces rolled over Luxembourg, The Netherlands, Belgium, and France, then when Italy entered the war in June, most of western Europe lay under Axis domination. As Britain faced the prospect of

German invasion, Americans began to perceive the growing threat to their own security.

The fall of France in particular shocked Americans into a realization of how unprepared they were for war. The government reacted immediately to build up the military services. In June 1940, the authorized strength of the Regular Army enlisted men rose from 227,000 to 280,000, then swiftly to 375,000. In July the Armored Force came into being to develop a fighting team to match the power of the fast-moving German blitzkrieg combination.

Later that month, a few weeks before Clark reached Washington, General Headquarters, U. S. Army came into existence. GHQ, as it was called, was to organize and to prepare the field or combat forces for war. If the country entered the conflict, GHQ would presumably take command of an expeditionary force sent overseas to fight in an active theater of operations.

Marshall was the commander of GHQ even as he retained his post as Army Chief of Staff. Preoccupied with his duties in the latter position, he appointed Brigadier General McNair to be his Chief of Staff at GHQ. McNair was, according to Marshall's instructions, to "direct and supervise the training of troops," that is, to plan and to carry out a vast program designed to bring the Army to war readiness. Although Marshall retained nominal command of GHQ, McNair would have a relatively free hand to shape and drive the combat units into condition. He would do so from offices in the Army War College, which stood on the point between the Anacostia and Potomac Rivers at Fort Humphreys, sometimes called Washington Barracks, later named Fort Lesley J. McNair.

A relatively short and sandy-haired man of few words, intelligent and dynamic, McNair, like many artillerymen who had been close to the sound of guns, was hard of hearing. At meetings he was not always sure he understood correctly all that was being said. He therefore looked for a junior officer to represent him and to speak for him at conferences. He carefully scrutinized the seven young officers originally assigned to his GHQ staff. All were under 50 years of age, vigorous, alert, and smart. Marshall had handpicked them. Among them was Lieutenant Colonel Mark W. Clark.

On the day he reported to Washington, Clark was transferred from the Army War College faculty to GHQ. Asked routinely whether he had any aversion to flying, he replied that he was "perfectly willing in connection with this duty as required." He had no idea how much time he would spend in airplanes.

Having first met during Clark's impressive exercises on the west coast, McNair and Clark became closely associated, both officially and personally, as they started to give structure to a critical endeavor. To Clark, McNair was "brilliant, selfless, and devoted," had a penchant for observing events himself, "always wanted to see at first hand how things were working out." Clark had learned much from DeWitt, Bolles, and Sweeney, and McNair would bring him to maturity. Quickly establishing his usefulness to McNair, Clark was soon regarded as McNair's principal assistant. Clark traveled for his chief, conferred as McNair's representative with high-ranking officials, made decisions in McNair's name, and witnessed and reported on equipment being developed and on new combat techniques being tested and approved.

Although GHQ had additional missions—administering aviation matters until the air forces became largely autonomous, directing harbor defenses in all the major ports of the United States, and controlling the overseas departments, Hawaii, the Philippines, Panama, Puerto Rico, later Alaska—training was the paramount function, and GHQ provided a central focus to what earlier had been the fragmented responsibility of the four field armies. Hugh A. Drum, commanding the First Army, Ben Lear, the Second, Stanley D. Embick, later Herbert Brees, still later Walter Krueger, the Third, and John L. DeWitt the Fourth were jealous of their prerogatives and senior to McNair. Marshall at once promoted McNair to major general and, in 1941, to lieutenant general. By then, after the Selective Service Act had brought half a million men, all eighteen National Guard divisions totalling 225,000 men, and 100,000 officers of the Organized Reserve into federal service for a year, the combat forces consisted of more than 1,300,000 men in uniform. McNair's staff numbered twenty-one officers—among them Majors Lyman L. Lemnitzer and Alfred M. Gruenther—who prepared timetables for receiving, equipping, organizing, and training the manpower surging into military posts.

McNair delegated his responsibilities for the operating functions, the harbor defenses, the overseas departments, and the like, while he and Clark concentrated on training the field forces. To impose logic and order on a huge and complex enterprise, McNair instituted what he called progressive training, a cycle moving through a well-understood sequence, from basic soldiers to small units, to combinations of units, and finally to large organizations. He also made training standard. All men and units followed the same schedules and tests without exception or variation. No longer were Drum's emphasis on the care of soldiers' feet, Krueger's stress on feeding, and other commanders' quirks tolerated. An orderly program produced skilled soldiers and competent units.

GHQ reopened the college at Leavenworth to provide intensive education in special short sessions and thus qualify commanders and staff members rapidly for increased responsibilities in the new units. McNair and Clark chose senior officers, with McNair generally picking the artillerymen, Clark the infantrymen. They also had the delicate job of removing National Guard commanders and staff officers who were in important positions because of their state political connections but were unfit for military duty because they were too old or below par in health or deficient in military knowledge.

Traveling extensively, McNair and Clark spent about half their time away from Washington, visiting and inspecting units, consulting with commanders in the field, observing demonstrations and exercises, evaluating officers on their effectiveness. Clark now occasionally wore glasses to correct a slight astigmatism.

World War II spread eastward in Europe on June 22, 1941, when Hitler's military forces invaded the Soviet Union. The German blitzkrieg rolled across Russia, appearing again to be unstoppable.

At the end of June, as was customary, McNair rated Clark's performance. Clark was, McNair wrote, "A rare combination of a most attractive personality with a stout heart and fine tact and intelligence. He gets results smoothly and without friction, due partly to his consideration for the views of others and partly to his soundness. He is one of the very few ablest officers of his vintage whom I know." It would be desirable, McNair added, to promote Clark to the next higher grade.

About a month later, Clark and McNair returned to Washington from a trip. Their plane landed at Bolling Field, where McNair's driver waited to drive them to Fort Humphreys. He had, as always, brought McNair's official mail. While the two officers rode in the back seat of the sedan, McNair opened each letter, threw the envelope on the floor, read the communication, and handed it to Clark. If McNair had a comment, Clark made a notation on the paper.

This time, as they were going through the mail, McNair read a message, smiled slightly, folded the sheet, and put it into his pocket.

The car stopped in front of McNair's house to let him out. Then, normally, the driver would have continued down the street to Clark's.

But Betty McNair and Renie were waiting outside, and they came running up and calling out "Congratulations." They had heard the news over the radio.

Clark was puzzled until McNair pulled the letter out of his pocket and handed it over. He had wanted to give it to Renie first. It was a note from Marshall, and it said, "The President today has nominated Lieutenant Colonel Mark W. Clark to be brigadier general."

He was overwhelmed. He had surpassed his father. Hoping for promotion to colonel, he had jumped over that grade.

Renie wrote a note to thank Marshall. He replied, "You must address your thanks to your husband and not to me. He earned everything he has gotten."

A distressing disadvantage resulted. Clark had moved ahead of officers formerly senior to him, and some resented his sudden rise. Now when Clark visited units to inspect their training, it seemed to him, "everybody who came out to meet me was my senior by years." At a camp where Doc Ryder, West Point class of 1915, and Red O'Hare, class of 1916, both good friends who had graduated before him, were stationed, he no longer heard a glad cry of welcome, "Opie, how are you?" Instead, he received a sober stare, a correct salute, a formal yes, sir, and almost the cold shoulder. "Red, Doc, for God's sake," Clark pleaded, "listen, please, let's still be friends."

But, he remarked years later, "when you are catapulted over people" who were good, "who were senior to me, years senior," and who had every right to expect promotion, you had to anticipate envy and malice from some. He "always tried very carefully," he said, "to avoid making myself obnoxious, particularly with people who had been my senior and who had fine records." Yet he frequently encountered jealousy on the part of some whom he had exceeded in rank.

Throughout the remainder of his career he would often command older officers. Some of them would remember him as a youngster who, they believed, had received rapid advancement because of his ruthless ambition. Friends of National Guard officers removed by McNair and Clark added to the backbiting and bad talk. Because of McNair's deafness, Clark often sat for him in high level sessions dealing with important problems needing quick solutions. Without much time to consider alternatives graciously, the members of these boards acted swiftly. Clark's logic, thought processes, and decisions became more rapid as his self-confidence grew. This too exasperated some of his contemporaries.

If the United States went to war, Clark told McNair, he wished McNair to have a high command overseas and to take Clark with him. McNair's response surprised him. "You are apt to have high command yourself," McNair said. "Because you are the right age and rank, you have a good background and a good record, and you're in the right place."

In 1941, McNair and Clark were ready to see how effective their programs had been. They decided to put divisions, corps, and armies into competition in a series of maneuvers, first in Texas and Louisiana, then in the Carolinas. McNair instructed Clark to draw the plans and told him, "Keep the directives as simple as possible."

At Camp Polk, Louisiana, in September, they directed the largest exercise to date. A mock battle pitted Lear's Second Army against Krueger's Third, nearly half a million men in all. The war games showed much progress. A friend wrote to Clark, "As a detached onlooker I have been elated over the fact that such tremendous expansion could be made in the Army so hurriedly and with so little fuss and confusion." GHQ had "done a noble job in building up this new Army."

West Point classmate Colonel J. Lawton Collins wrote, "My congratulations to you for your part in engineering the very highly successful and instructive maneuvers which we have just completed. There is no question in my mind but they have been the best peacetime maneuvers ever conducted by the United States Army."

A personal report from the Inspector General to Marshall contained a flattering reference: "I was particularly impressed with the efficiency, balance, and judgment displayed by General Clark."

Sweeney, now retired, informed Clark of a letter he had received from Mark Watson, a distinguished military correspondent for the *Baltimore Sun* who had covered the Louisiana maneuvers. Clark's "efficiency and character" had impressed Watson. Clark "had made a very big name" and everyone recognized his "soundness and military judgment." Watson could be useful to Clark, Sweeney suggested, "in all sorts of ways, especially in public psychology which you will have to consider with growing attention. You have a marvelous opportunity under all the circumstances as I see them to go clear to the top in these coming years."

The thought was sobering.

During a critique conducted by Clark to a roomful of officers, a telegram containing a list of promotions to general officer rank was passed to him at the podium. At the end of his talk, Clark rapped the gavel and announced that he would read the names. He glanced at the paper and saw about ten men being advanced to major general, about twenty to brigadier general. Among the latter was Colonel Eisenhower, who had performed brilliantly as Krueger's Third Army Chief of Staff and who was in the audience.

Clark read the list. He skipped Eisenhower. At the end, he said, "That's it." Then immediately, "I'm sorry, I beg your pardon, I have omitted one name, Dwight D. Eisenhower."

As the gathering broke up, Eisenhower came toward Clark laughing. "You son of a bitch," he said, "I'll get you." Clark was laughing too as he extended his hand in congratulations.

The Carolina maneuvers involved more than 300,000 soldiers. "I always wanted to try air-borne troops," Clark wrote to Sweeney, reminding him of their request and the corps' refusal at Fort Lewis, "and now I have my chance. Am going to do it with both parachutes and air-borne units." The war games demonstrated the increasing competence of the Army's combat forces.

Secretary of War Henry L. Stimson called a meeting of the top Army leadership in his office on December 3. Attending were Stimson, Under Secretary Robert P. Patterson, Assistant Secretary John McCloy, Assistant Secretary for Air Robert A. Lovett, Marshall and his three deputies, Major Generals William B. Bryden, Richard C. Moore, and Henry H. Arnold, McNair, and Clark. They discussed why it took ten to twelve months to raise a new division to combat performance and whether acceleration was possible.

Four days later the Japanese attacked Pearl Harbor and brought the United States into the war. Clark's first thought when he heard the news was, "How lucky we are that we just finished our maneuvers."

As Clark was having a working lunch with Marshall, McNair, and several others, Marshall said, "I've got to relieve the fellow in war plans who is somewhat identified with Pearl Harbor." He asked Clark to give him the names of ten brigadier generals capable of becoming the new chief of the section.

"I'll give you one name and nine dittos," Clark said. "Dwight D. Eisenhower."

"I don't know him," Marshall said.

But he was mistaken. Marshall had met Eisenhower briefly in 1930 and again at the Louisiana maneuvers. Krueger had recommended him strongly for advancement. So had others. Perhaps Clark's statement clinched the case. Marshall called Eisenhower immediately to Washington, and he became Marshall's right-hand man.

Many years later Eisenhower told Clark, "You are more responsible than anybody in this country for giving me my opportunity." No doubt he was referring to Clark's kindness at Fort Lewis as well as bringing Eisenhower to Marshall's attention.

Eisenhower arrived in Washington on December 14, and a few days afterwards Clark phoned him. He suggested having lunch together once a week in order to coordinate Eisenhower's planning and Clark's training. This they did, usually at each other's homes, over soup and a sandwich.

Pearl Harbor brought mounting fear to the west coast. Numerous Japanese, most of them American citizens and relatively few aliens, lived near burgeoning airplane plants and other war factories, and many civilians and state officials grew frantic over the potential danger of the Japanese population. Were the Japanese a fifth column waiting to sabotage war industries and communications if Japan invaded the west coast?

DeWitt, the Fourth Army commander at the Presidio, asked the War Department for guidance on how to avert both violence against the Japanese and their possible hostile actions. He suggested barring Japanese from sensitive areas, but he could do so only by diverting troops from training schedules. Public sentiment in the west was clamoring to resettle all the Japanese inhabitants in the interior of the country. As hysteria mounted, DeWitt feared becoming a scapegoat. If Japan attacked and if the Japanese acted as accomplices, DeWitt would be held to blame.

Because of Clark's friendship with DeWitt and his familiarity with conditions on the west coast, Marshall asked Clark to go to San Francisco for a few days. When Clark returned, he reported to Marshall DeWitt's wish to create restricted areas from which to remove Japanese people. Stimson, McCloy, and Marshall asked Clark for his impressions. The Californians, he thought, were unduly alarmed. There was no possible chance for a Japanese invasion and no possible harm from the Japanese people.

When the President approved moving the Japanese, Stimson, McCloy, and Clark discussed the instructions to be sent to DeWitt. Clark disliked uprooting the Japanese. In addition, he hated to have the evacuation "absorb like a sponge, many divisions for this purpose" and "sabotage our expansion of the Army for offensive purposes."

Almost two years later, after young Japanese-Americans had been inducted and organized into segregated combat units and were ready to go overseas into action, the War Department debated where to send them. Reluctant to have them engage Japanese soldiers in the Pacific, Marshall offered the Nisei units to Eisenhower in Europe. Members of his staff, with or without his knowledge, declined to accept them. Marshall then asked Clark whether he could use them in Italy. "We will take anybody

that will fight," Clark said. A regiment of Hawaiian-Japanese in Italy
were magnificent warriors under Clark. As Marshall later said, they were
"superb! That word correctly describes it: superb! They took terrific
casualties. They showed rare courage and tremendous fighting spirit."
Their association with Clark made him a hero to Hawaiians and to
Japanese-Americans everywhere.

The War Department carried out a sweeping reorganization in March
1942. Marshall's Operations Division, headed by Eisenhower, was renamed the War Plans Division; continuing as Chief, Eisenhower became
a major general. GHQ went out of existence, replaced by three new
commands: Army Air Forces, Army Service Forces, and Army Ground
Forces, all with duties confined to the continental United States. As the
Commanding General of the Army Ground Forces, McNair was responsible for organizing and training the combat units. He named Clark to
be his acting chief of staff until Marshall could promote Clark to major
general. Marshall did so on April 17, 1942, two weeks before Clark's
forty-sixth birthday. With Eisenhower and Clark both wearing two stars,
they were about to be involved in a broader challenge.

The roots of the situation went back almost a year before the Japanese
attacked Pearl Harbor. British and American military representatives had
met informally and discussed courses of action if the United States entered
the war and faced Asian as well as European adversaries. Unofficially,
they decided on a "Europe First" strategy. The United States would defeat
its European enemies before turning in full force to the Pacific. The
agreement was merely an understanding and hardly binding.

Immediately after Pearl Harbor catapulted the United States into the
Asian conflict and after the German and Italian declarations of war brought
the country into the European struggle, British Prime Minister Winston
Churchill and his Chiefs of Staff came to Washington for conferences
with the President and his military advisers. The purpose was to find a
common method of fighting the war. Both political leaders restated and
made formal the earlier Europe First concept. The United States would
hold the Japanese in the Pacific while giving its main attention to Europe.

As a token of this pledge, Charles Ryder's 34th Division sailed to
northern Ireland in January 1942.

Two months later, Marshall presented to President Roosevelt his
thoughts on how to carry out the Europe First program. He proposed a
massive cross-Channel attack, a direct assault on the European continent
launched from England. The President approved the idea, and Marshall
instructed Eisenhower, his chief planner, to work out the major details.

Roosevelt then sent Marshall and Harry Hopkins, the President's assistant, to London in May to decide with British officials how and where combined Anglo-American forces could take action.

Hopkins and Marshall spent two weeks in London consulting with British authorities, who were reluctant to undertake landings on the European continent. Despite the arrival of the 34th Division in the United Kingdom and the projected sailing of two more American divisions that spring and summer, the American forces were too small and insufficiently trained to make an amphibious operation feasible in the coming months. The British were loath to furnish the bulk of the invasion forces, for the Germans defending the western European shoreline seemed altogether too strong to give an invasion across the Channel much chance of success. Agreeing in principle to an eventual cross-Channel endeavor, the British were more than pleased to welcome a flow of American troops and equipment as a necessary preliminary.

A month later Marshall became uneasy over the buildup of American military resources in Britain. American officers in London and in Washington seemed to be less than synchronized on intentions and procedures. In order to smooth processes, to survey conditions in Britain, and to learn where, for example, an increasing number of American soldiers could be housed and trained, Marshall dispatched a delegation of four officers to England: Lieutenant General Henry H. Arnold, commanding the Army Air Forces; Lieutenant General Brehon B. Somervell, commanding the Army Service Forces; and Eisenhower and Clark to represent, respectively, Marshall and McNair.

Touring Britain under the auspices of the War Office for a week, they talked with Churchill and his military advisers. Vice Admiral Lord Louis Mountbatten, head of Combined Operations, personally took Eisenhower and Clark in tow for much of the time. The Americans observed large field exercises and amphibious demonstrations. They discussed possible invasions of the European continent in 1943. If an emergency Channel crossing was necessary in 1942 to help the Soviet Union remain in the war, they agreed to have the U. S. forces in the United Kingdom serve under British command. They considered how to ensure standard training for the troops of both nations.

They visited the headquarters of Lieutenant General Sir Bernard L. Montgomery, who commanded the British forces in southeast England and who was abrupt and acerbic. He greeted them by saying, "I have been directed to take time from my busy life to brief you gentlemen."

As he took the pointer and was about to speak, Eisenhower lit up a

cigarette. Montgomery sniffed the tobacco and said, "Who is smoking?"
Eisenhower said, "I am, sir."

"Stop it," Montgomery said. "I don't permit it."

Eisenhower meekly put out his cigarette.

During their flight home, Eisenhower and Clark found their thinking
to be much the same. The War Department, they believed, should establish a high-powered headquarters in England with a well-known commander in charge of the American buildup for a European invasion in
the spring of 1943.

Soon after their return to Washington, Eisenhower suggested to Marshall appointing General Joseph T. McNarney, one of Marshall's principal
deputies, Commanding General, European Theater. In his diary he recorded, "Also I've recommended Wayne Clark to command the first
corps to be sent to England."

Marshall decided to create a new headquarters called the European
Theater of Operations, U. S. Army, known as ETOUSA, as an overall
administrative command dealing mainly with personnel and supplies.
Under ETOUSA would be the II Corps headquarters to handle the combat
training of the American divisions in the British Isles, in reality to command all the U. S. ground forces in Britain. The 34th and the two other
divisions scheduled to follow were to be under the V Corps headquarters
in northern Ireland, but the II Corps would supervise them and be a
miniature Army Ground Forces headquarters.

Summoning Clark, Marshall asked who he thought should command
ETOUSA. Clark had discussed the question with McNair, who favored
Joseph Stilwell, Patton, or Lloyd R. Fredendall, all senior major generals.
Clark passed along these suggestions.

"Suppose," Marshall said, "it was a younger man that we were looking
for. I want your opinion."

"I think General Eisenhower," Clark said, "would be the fellow."

Marshall had, unknown to Clark, already chosen Eisenhower. Because
Eisenhower had favored Clark for the II Corps, Marshall said, "It looks
to me as if you boys got together."

He then asked how soon Clark could be ready to go back to England
if he were selected.

Automatically, Clark glanced at his wristwatch.

Marshall smiled faintly.

"Any time," Clark said.

Marshall nodded, dismissing him.

So there it was, left hanging. Perhaps, Clark thought, he might receive command of a division in northern Ireland.

A few months earlier, a group of prominent Indiana citizens had invited Clark to command the 38th National Guard Division, which he had advised and instructed ten years before. He sought McNair's advice, and McNair brushed the idea aside. "You'll do better than that before this war ends," he said. Clark politely declined the offer.

Mountbatten came to the United States for a brief visit, and when he and Sir John Dill, the British Chiefs of Staff representative in Washington, expressed their wish to observe American soldiers in training, Marshall asked Clark to make the arrangements for a two-day trip to Forts Benning, Gordon, and Bragg. He and Clark would accompany the British officers. Clark planned an itinerary and made some phone calls.

At Fort Benning from a hilltop they watched a demonstration dubbed the "Mad Minute of Fire," an infantry assault with artillery support, together with tanks and fighter-bombers, all using live ammunition. At Fort Gordon, they saw the 4th Division at work. At Fort Bragg, they regarded a parachute drop by the single battalion in the Army so trained, 800 men jumping from planes to seize an airfield.

During dinner at the Pine Needle Lodge near Pinehurst, North Carolina, Mountbatten asked Marshall who was to command the II Corps.

The decision had yet to be made, Marshall replied.

Having learned privately from McNair that his name was among those under consideration, but figuring himself to be too junior for the post, Clark was surprised when Marshall leaned toward him and in a stage whisper said, "It might even be you."

On the following day, Clark was at his desk when Mountbatten telephoned his congratulations. Marshall had just told him of Clark's selection to command the II Corps. A few minutes later McNair came to Clark's office and confirmed the news.

One of the youngest major generals in the Army, Clark would prepare the American troops in Britain to take part in an invasion of the European continent, then, no doubt, command them in the landings.

Eisenhower at the head of ETOUSA and Clark at the head of the II Corps made an excellent team. Working directly with Marshall had developed Eisenhower's innately strong strategic outlook. Involvement with McNair's detailed training programs had strengthened Clark's organizational and executive capacities.

Both men were young, vigorous, and eager to make good. With several exceptions and for brief interludes, they had been staff officers, assistants and advisers throughout most of their careers. Eisenhower had during World War I commanded Camp Colt, near Gettysburg, Pennsylvania, where he had trained tankers; he had commanded an infantry battalion at Fort Lewis. Clark had commanded an infantry company, and a battalion in the 5th Division in France, then several infantry companies during the interwar years. Now they were to direct organizations at a high level. Their prospects, if they succeeded, were unlimited.

Clark's duties with McNair came to an end in June 1942, and McNair submitted his rating of Clark's performance. As the result of daily close association, McNair recommended Clark for high command. "He has everything, personality, poise, brilliant execution, sound thinker, splendid judgment."

He had been, as McNair had said, in the right place. Going to England would keep him at the center of activity, in the right place again for increased opportunities and heavier responsibilities.

CHAPTER 8
☆ ☆ ☆ ☆
WITH EISENHOWER IN LONDON

"an almost intolerable situation"

TRAVELING TO JACKSONVILLE, Florida, where the headquarters was located, Clark assumed command of the II Corps. He met and spoke with the staff members and did a certain amount of weeding out.

To Colonel Marius S. Chatignon, Clark said, "Chaplain, I think you are too old to go overseas."

Chatignon looked him squarely in the eye and said, "General, I think you are too young to command this corps."

Pleased by the forthright statement, Clark changed his mind and kept him.

To fill several key positions, Clark asked specifically for a few officers whose capabilities he knew and respected. Among them was Lyman Lemnitzer at Army Ground Forces, who was brilliant, durable, and popular—his laugh, resembling a schoolgirl's giggle, was infectious. Another was Edwin B. Howard, who had been Clark's assistant G-2 at Fort Lewis. In England he would secure John O'Daniel, to whom he had turned over his Company K in France in 1918, and who was a specialist in amphibious warfare; known as "Iron Mike" from the fact that a bullet had passed through his cheeks, later as "Soft Hearted John" after the Li'l Abner comic strip character, O'Daniel was tough and humorous, optimistic and inspiring.

In Washington, Clark moved his family out of government quarters and into an apartment at the Kennedy-Warren House on Connecticut Avenue. Because the Camano Island property was Clark's legal residence, he obtained the promise of Representative Henry Jackson to appoint son Bill to West Point.

Early on June 23, 1942, the Clark family drove to Bolling Field. Eisenhower and his wife Mamie arrived about the same time. McNair and several others were there to see them off. Together with a small party of officers and men, Eisenhower and Clark flew across the Atlantic. Staff and headquarters people were to follow by ship.

In London, Mountbatten and Major General John C. H. Lee, head of the U. S. Services of Supply in Britain, welcomed the two Americans and took them to Claridge's Hotel. Exhilarated and chipper on the following morning, they walked to their offices at 20 Grosvenor Square. They conferred with Admiral Harold L. Stark, chief of the U. S. Naval Forces in Europe, Major General Carl Spaatz, commander of the U. S. Army Air Forces in Europe, and others on how they could best be ready for a cross-Channel attack in the spring of 1943. Clark was to be both the principal trainer of the U. S. ground forces and the principal planner of the operation.

The 1st Armored Division had joined the 34th Division in northern Ireland, and the 1st Infantry Division was to come in August. Although all three were directly under the V Corps, Clark's headquarters exercised overall supervision.

"We've got to get some younger fellows over here to help us," Eisenhower said. "You know who they are." Clark drew up a list of names, and Eisenhower requested the War Department to send the officers to England. Among those whom they especially wanted and obtained was Gruenther, an intense, exacting, hard-driving executive who spared neither himself nor those who worked for him, yet who prompted admiration and loyalty from his subordinates. Known for the brilliance of his staff work, sometimes called the Brain of the Army, Gruenther had an international reputation as an expert bridge player who wrote on the subject and who frequently refereed matches.

Early in July, Eisenhower and Clark accepted the first of many invitations from Churchill to spend the night at his official country home, Chequers. They admired Churchill immensely. To Clark he was dynamic, charming, persuasive, "the greatest man I have ever met." Churchill liked them both, and he had a special affection for Clark, whom he dubbed "The American Eagle."

Driving to Chequers, they arrived in the evening. Churchill, wearing a baggy smock and carpet slippers, welcomed them. They walked in the woods and sat on a bench and talked about the war effort. They had a delightful time over cocktails. Mrs. Churchill and Lady Portal, wife of the head of the Air Forces, were at dinner. Much of the conversation was a frank discussion of the war, including secret plans. Everyone in the house, including the servants, then watched a movie, a hilarious comedy. Afterwards, Churchill, who had napped in the afternoon and was rested, said to the Americans, "Now let's get to work." Eisenhower and Clark were ready for bed, but they went with him to his study and talked well into the morning, interrupted by reports coming in to the Prime Minister from all over the world. They exchanged opinions on strategy, armament, forces, morale, and the most pressing problems of the moment. Where Churchill could help them, he did so. He had no hesitation to telephone his senior officials no matter what the hour to ask for advice or for clarification of a point.

Eisenhower and Clark arose at 7:45, and after a copious breakfast of ham and eggs, the two exhausted Americans drove back to London to resume work. Although they always enjoyed Churchill's company, they dreaded the late hours he kept.

On Wednesday evenings, Eisenhower and Clark frequently went to 10 Downing Street, Churchill's official residence in town, for dinner, conferences, and lengthy discussions.

When the convoy bringing the II Corps headquarters landed in Scotland, Clark was there to meet the men who boarded trains for Tidworth, near Salisbury, 8 miles southwest of London where Clark had opened his headquarters. On the following day he assembled his 180 officers, stood on a wooden bench to be visible to all, and told them to cooperate with the British and to be soldierly and courteous. They had a great opportunity. "You are on the ground floor," he said. Each officer filed past him, and he shook hands and chatted briefly. He similarly greeted and addressed his enlisted men.

Clark was well organized when he received a telephone call from Eisenhower asking him to come to London. Roosevelt had sent Marshall, Admiral Ernest J. King, who was the Chief of Naval Operations, Harry

Hopkins, and Presidential Secretary Stephen Early to confer with the British. The President had instructed them to decide on an Anglo-American offensive operation for the near future, if possible in 1942. He wished thereby to help the Russians, who seemed about to be overwhelmed in their second summer of fighting. The object was to launch the Europe First strategy.

Eisenhower wanted Clark in London for three reasons. Clark knew best the combat capabilities of the American troops in the United Kingdom. He was planning a relatively small emergency Channel crossing to the Cherbourg area if the Russians appeared at the point of collapse. He was looking into the conditions and requirements of a later and larger invasion of the Continent.

Roosevelt's four high-powered emissaries, Hopkins, Marshall, King, and Early, first consulted with the top American commanders in England—Eisenhower and Clark, Admiral Stark, Air Force General Spaatz, and supply chief Lee. After discussing their options and desires, all agreed that a major descent on the European continent in the immediate future was impossible. They simply lacked the resources for a significant and sustained operation. As Clark explained, the 34th Division had just started training for amphibious landings and had few antiaircraft guns and no tanks; the 1st Armored Division was awaiting the delivery of much equipment; the 1st Infantry Division had yet to arrive.

Was the Cherbourg invasion feasible? Only if the British committed the bulk of the forces needed. In that case, Clark's II Corps headquarters would direct the relatively few American troops.

When the Americans approached the British with this idea, they met objections. The British were reluctant to cross the Channel in 1942. They favored landing in French Northwest Africa.

As the Anglo-American talks continued, Clark returned to Salisbury. No invasion force, he was sure, could be ready before the spring of 1943, but even that date seemed very close at hand. To prepare troops for landing on whatever hostile shore might be chosen, he established an amphibious training center under O'Daniel.

Clark then went back to London, where the conferences had ended. At Roosevelt's insistence and over their own reservations, the Americans had accepted the British suggestion to land in North Africa. The operation was codenamed Torch.

The Americans disliked Torch because it would draw men and material away from the resources building up in the United Kingdom and defer a cross-Channel invasion until 1944. The delay, Clark thought, would postpone ultimate victory and be, he said, a "great calamity."

But the political leaders, Roosevelt and Churchill, had decided upon Torch, and the military men could only carry it out. Who was to command Torch and exactly how it was to go had yet to be determined. If it was to be executed before the end of 1942, precious little time remained to plan and prepare it.

These were no concerns of Clark's, and at Salisbury he concentrated on training his troops and planning for landings in Europe.

When the War Department revealed Clark's presence in England to the public, he held a press conference for the 39 newspapermen accredited to his headquarters. The Americans were not in England, Clark said, "to sit on their backends." They were there to go into action against the enemy, and the sooner the better. He wanted no personal publicity because, he said, "I haven't commanded troops in battle yet; until I have proved my fitness, the less said about me the better."

The reporters noted his youthfulness, vitality, and self-confidence.

When the 1st Infantry Division debarked from the *Queen Mary* in Scotland, Clark was there to greet them. Three divisions had arrived, and more were sure to come.

A telephone call from Eisenhower brought Clark to London again on August 10. He was surprised to find Patton, whom Marshall had sent to discuss the plans for Torch. Clark had first glimpsed Patton at Fort Sheridan when he, Clark, was 13 years old. He had met Patton at the Louisiana maneuvers when Patton was a major general and Clark a lieutenant colonel. Now they were both major generals, and Patton was dubious about Clark's rapid promotions. He was also envious of Clark's close friendship with Eisenhower, who was an old friend of Patton.

Roosevelt and Churchill had decided in favor of invading North Africa because the operation required fewer resources than landings on the European shore and could go more quickly. What was especially attractive, particularly to the inexperienced Americans, was the absence of German and Italian forces in French Morocco, Algeria, and Tunisia.

No Axis troops were there because of provisions of the armistice of 1940. In June of that year, after the Germans had overrun all of northern France, including Paris, and the Italians had entered into the region of Nice, 84 year-old Marshal Philippe Pétain, the hero of Verdun in World War I, had become the head of government. He immediately asked for terms of a cease-fire. The accords signed permitted Germany to occupy a large part of France in the north, Italy to hold a small area in the southeast, and Pétain to rule the nonoccupied zone in the south. With unlimited authority as the head of state, with his capital at Vichy, Pétain also administered the three French territories in North Africa. For the purpose of maintaining internal order there, Germany and Italy allowed Pétain to have an army of 100,000 men. In return, France promised to defend the North African possessions against invasion.

The only invaders then envisaged were the British. After the capitulation of France, French sentiment had turned sharply against their former ally. Many Frenchmen blamed their defeat on British reluctance to bring more airplanes to the continent during the campaign. They resented British withdrawal to their home islands and their refusal to surrender. The French were also embittered by the attacks of British warships against the French fleet to keep the vessels from falling into German hands. They were incensed by British support of General Charles de Gaulle who, from London, sought to continue the struggle against the Axis.

If the British invaded North Africa, the French were certain to oppose them. But if the French still harbored a desire to fight the Germans again, perhaps the traditional Franco-American friendship would lead them to welcome American soldiers ashore. To give Torch the appearance of an entirely American expedition, Eisenhower became Commander in Chief of the Allied forces making the landings.

Allied troops in French Northwest Africa would threaten the Axis in Libya and assist the British in Egypt. To meet the danger to Libya, Hitler would have to send more units to North Africa and thus decrease the strength he could bring to bear against the Russians. This was the immediate rationale of Torch.

The first plans projected two landings. An Anglo-American task force sailing from the United Kingdom was to land somewhere inside the Mediterranean. Another task force, this one wholly American and coming from the United States, was to land on the west coast of Africa near Casablanca. Patton was to command the second expedition.

To synchronize the two task forces, Patton flew to London and saw Eisenhower on August 7. They talked for four hours the following day on the discouraging prospect of assembling enough troops and ships to make the operation feasible. They spent all day on August 9 discussing the difficulties and risks, the uncertainties and problems. The naval authorities recommended cancelling Patton's crossing, but a single task force coming from the United Kingdom provided hardly enough margin for success.

At this point Eisenhower called Clark, who had demonstrated his ability to move fast and get things done. If anyone could pull together diverse elements and turn deficiencies into adequacies, if anyone could knock heads together and resolve problems, it was surely Mark Clark.

Eisenhower, Patton, and Clark had lunch together with Lieutenant General Sir Kenneth Anderson, who was to command the British troops in Torch. Eisenhower spoke of being overwhelmed by many demands. The British had offered him a deputy commander to lighten his burdens, but Eisenhower "wanted somebody he knew." Would Clark join him as his second in command, become the Deputy Supreme Allied Commander, and help make Torch a reality and a success?

Clark was torn by conflicting emotions. He hated to relinquish command of the II Corps, where he was indisputably the boss. Ever since he had commanded an infantry company at the Presidio, he had served for most of the past fifteen years as a staff officer, an assistant, to Bowser Bolles, Sweeney, and McNair. With Eisenhower, he would once again be the number two man. He might lose his chance eventually to command the American troops in the cross-Channel landings.

On the other hand, he had a strong loyalty to Eisenhower and a warm friendship too. He wanted to do what Eisenhower wished. They worked well together. By staying in England, Clark ran the risk of sitting out the war at the head of a training command in an inactive theater. The European invasion was postponed to sometime in the indefinite future and might never go. Torch was on and scheduled. The promise of combat in North Africa was directly ahead and attractive. Clark accepted Eisenhower's offer. He would be the chief planner for Torch and the second in command.

"I doubt the wisdom of it," Patton wrote in his diary that evening. "He may be too intrusive."

What Patton probably distrusted was Clark's lack of combat and command experience, his youth and brashness, and his quick climb to equal rank with the older Patton. Later Patton would learn the reason for Clark's sudden rise to eminence. "Clark," Patton would record in his journal, "made a big impression on the Prime Minister."

By "intrusive," Patton meant "pushy" and "not our kind," what the French called in a more general context an *arriviste*, a person who sought to get ahead by any means. There was a guarded intimation of anti-Semitism, and it was unworthy of the best in Patton.

The major object of the Torch landings was to overrun Tunisia, adjoining Libya. Because Axis airfields in Sicily, Libya, and Italy proper were close to possible invasion sites in Tunisia, the task force sailing from England was to land in Algeria; from there, the troops were to turn east and conquer Tunisia before Italian and German forces could enter the country.

The other task force, Patton's, was to land on the Atlantic shore of French Morocco and be in position to invade Spanish Morocco if Spain joined the war on the Axis side and cut the straits of Gibraltar.

With the operation tentatively scheduled for October or November, the planners in London and Washington had two or three months to prepare for what everyone knew would be an exceptionally complicated project.

It was indeed so complex as to be breathtaking. No one had any experience for getting several hundred thousand men aboard thousands of ships at different locations to sail 2,000 miles from Britain and 4,000 miles from the United States across hazardous seas menaced by enemy aircraft and submarines in order to reach separate objectives simultaneously and be ready to engage hostile forces. It was a far cry from the simple and primitive amphibious operation planned and executed by Clark when a few thousand soldiers had embarked in ships at Tacoma while the band played on the dock, then sailed along the west coast to land on the friendly shores of Monterey Bay. Had that maneuver taken place only two and a half years earlier? It was hard to believe that the state of the art of amphibious warfare had progressed so far so fast. Yet new concepts and techniques remained to be proved. To assemble all the pieces of a gigantic jig-saw puzzle and put them together on the coast of North Africa would take much imagination and hard work.

Clark returned to Salisbury to tell his principal subordinates a little of what was going on, then went to London on August 12. He established his own headquarters at the Norfolk House on St. James Square. There under his direction, British and American Army, Navy, and Air Force officers would work up the detailed plans for Torch. He moved temporarily into the Dorchester Hotel and shared an apartment with Eisenhower before taking a small flat of his own in nearby Hays Mews.

Remembering how Marshall had delegated authority to McNair at GHQ, Eisenhower gave Clark a free hand. He could make whatever decisions and issue whatever orders he wished in Eisenhower's name. Clark was to do whatever he thought necessary and simply let Eisenhower know what he had done.

On August 13, Clark started what he later called a "racehorse schedule all day." The numerous problems he had to solve made him feel as though he were "sitting on a thousand volcanoes." Every evening Clark dictated an account of whom he had seen, the subjects he had discussed, the actions he had taken. Typed during the night, the memorandum was ready for his signature the next morning. Then it went to Eisenhower for his information.

For forty-two consecutive days, Clark ran meetings, conferences, and briefings. With Gruenther his chief of staff and Lemnitzer Gruenther's assistant, Clark handled everything affecting Torch.

He carried out three major endeavors simultaneously. He built a new Anglo-American headquarters responsible for preparing and directing the invasion. He was involved with every aspect of the complex venture, from devising deception plans to determining the individual rifleman's equipment. He obtained the resources required in men, ships, planes, equipment, and supplies. That Torch in the end could go was in extremely large measure the result of Clark's perfectly cold-blooded, no-nonsense manner of dealing with people and problems.

The British proposed and the Americans accepted forming a novel organization for Torch and naming it the Allied Force Headquarters. Instead of creating a structure along the national lines of one country or the other, American and British officers of all the military services were evenly balanced in the staff positions. Giving both nationalities equal representation, AFHQ, as it was called, would mirror and enhance the close Anglo-American coalition.

Whether officers of different traditions and outlooks, practices and methods, habits and procedures could reconcile their differences and work in harmony remained to be seen. The simple fact of close proximity produced inevitable tensions. When Clark learned of a fight in a club between two aviators, one British, the other American, he inquired into the reasons for the altercation. The British officer, he learned, had said to the American, "You are not drinking our beer. Don't you like British beer?" The American replied, "You ought to pour it back into the horse."

Eisenhower resolved to make everyone serve together without friction and rancor. To this end, he scheduled an American coffee break in mid-morning as well as an English teatime in the afternoon. He would later send home an American colonel who called his counterpart a *British* son of a bitch.

As problems clarified and concepts fell into place, Clark remained hard-headed and driving. Within a week, despite continuing crises over shipping space and supply shortages, a basic plan was ready. Although Patton noted many "indefinite or undetermined factors," he felt able to depart for Washington, where he would work on his part of Torch, the landings near Casablanca. Before he went, as he wrote in his diary, he had "a drink with Clark at his flat. I do not trust him yet but he improves on acquaintance."

That was the day of the disastrous Dieppe landing. A relatively small force of Canadian soldiers crossed the Channel and came to grief on the shore. Casualties were extremely high. Whatever the reason motivating the operation—to satisfy Canadian clamors for action, to show Stalin the impossibility of opening an immediate second front in Europe, to learn through experience the requirements of amphibious warfare—the results were clear. The failure at Dieppe underlined the fragility of Torch.

Eisenhower and Clark briefed the British Chiefs of Staff late in August. There were now to be three landings. Two task forces from the United Kingdom, both composed of American and British troops, were to invade near Algiers and Oran, and Americans for the most part were to make the initial assaults. British soldiers were to follow them ashore and, under Anderson, strike eastward into Tunisia. Patton was to land near Casablanca.

An urgent telegram from Marshall got Clark out of bed at 8 A.M. on the following morning. Three landings, Marshall thought, were too ambitious for the available resources. He instructed Eisenhower to contract the operation to two amphibious assaults.

All their work seemed for naught, and Eisenhower and Clark were tired and discouraged that evening when they dined with Churchill at Downing Street. Marshall's telegram had disturbed the British planners too, and the atmosphere at table was far from cheerful. Trying to dissipate the gloom, Churchill told them about a conversation he had had with Stalin, who was insisting on the second front. "Why stick your head in the alligator's mouth at Brest," Churchill had said, "when you can go to the Mediterranean and rip his belly?"

As transatlantic messages during the last few days of August discussed cutting Torch back to two landings, to be carried out by American troops only, everything remained far from settled. Supply deficiencies hampered confident predictions. Anderson was less than sure of being able to advance from Algeria into Tunisia in time to forestall an Axis occupation. A new estimate of available air support depressed everyone. Shortages of naval resources seemed impossible to remedy.

Clark assembled 37 American and British officers to hammer out an acceptable plan. Everyone was on edge, and Clark, seeking to dissolve the tension, said, "Some of you are less confused than others about Torch. Let's all get equally confused." Laughter followed.

After interminable discussions, conferences, and transoceanic cables, agreement was reached. There would be three landings. Americans would come ashore first.

Clark wrote in his diary, "This would be an almost intolerable situation were it not for my fortunately close, personal relationship with the Supreme Commander. The cooperation we have is the result of having been old friends for a long time; the result of having worked together before on many, many problems. There's a definite advantage in having officers who know each other well working together." Clark understood what Eisenhower was thinking and saying, and Eisenhower sensed the same about Clark. They made an ideal team.

"It wasn't easy," Clark later wrote, "working with a conglomerate of Army, Navy, and Air Force officers of both countries." What made things go were "Ike's willingness to delegate authority and the Prime Minister's backing."

Churchill was particularly helpful. When Eisenhower and Clark were at a dead end, they went to him. Churchill always solved the problem if he could. When the blackout, enforced everywhere, slowed night loading for Torch at Scottish ports, Churchill ordered the lights turned on.

Clark was so busy that his aide wrote to Renie. The general, he said, never looked better. He was becoming "a regular cronie" of the Prime Minister and had dined with Churchill twice the previous week and was going again that evening. His aides were trying to get Clark out of his office early so that he could take an hour's nap, for Churchill kept his guests up until "the wee hours." Sometimes, the general had said, he pinched himself "when he looks around the dinner table and sees all the leaders of the British Empire sitting with him."

At Clark's suggestion, Eisenhower called in Clark, Spaatz, and Lee, ostensibly for a conference on general matters. The real reason was to point out to Lee how confused the logistical situation was. The figures furnished were vague, and the planners needed to know quickly and accurately what they could count on.

John Court House Lee, an officer of Patton's vintage, was a rather pompous man who, behind his back, was called, after his initials, Jesus Christ Himself. He liked comfort, and his private train and plane were fitted with such luxuries as to be almost indecent.

Eisenhower instructed Lee to clarify at once how much supply was available for Torch. Immediately after the meeting Clark took Lee aside and administered a deliberate jolt. He was apprehensive, Clark said, over the ability of Lee's headquarters to perform its functions. Shaken, Lee promised to do better.

Walter Bedell Smith, a Marshall protégé and a hard driver, arrived from Washington in September to be Eisenhower's chief of staff. Gruenther became Smith's deputy, and Lemnitzer moved to the plans and training section.

Eisenhower started the practice of presiding over triweekly Torch staff meetings in Norfolk House. To his right sat Clark, to his left Bedell Smith, and before them, at a huge rectangular table covered with pads, pencils, and ashtrays, the staff members. According to the reports, briefings, and discussions, progress was good. The major problem now was dissatisfaction with the leadership of the Oran landing.

Anxious to command troops in combat, Clark spoke privately to Eisenhower and asked to direct the Oran task force. Eisenhower shook his head. No one, he said, could handle both jobs, and no one could take Clark's place as Deputy Supreme Allied Commander.

Robert Murphy, a State Department official and the President's personal representative in French Northwest Africa, arrived from Washington. Roosevelt had sent him to London for a few days to see whether he might be useful to Torch, which Murphy knew about vaguely. Meeting with Eisenhower, Clark, and Bedell Smith, he talked about his work.

Murphy was in touch with a group of five prominent French civilians who were anti-Axis in outlook and wished to have close relations with the Allies, particularly the Americans. These men had informal ties with and access to important French military officers who had similar inclinations but who felt keenly their allegiance to the proper authorities, the Vichy government of Marshal Pétain, and, more directly, the commander of all the military services, Admiral François Darlan.

Darlan in 1939 and 1940 had been Admiral of the Fleet in command of the French naval forces. After the surrender, Darlan was Pétain's Minister of the Navy and designated successor, the number two man at Vichy. When Pétain in 1942 appointed Pierre Laval, who symbolized the policy of collaboration with Hitler, to be the Premier and head of government, Darlan resigned all of his functions except his position as Commander in Chief of the Armed Forces. Notoriously anti-British, Darlan had promised Admiral William D. Leahy, former U. S. Ambassador to Vichy France, perhaps sarcastically, to come over to the Americans if they produced half a million troops to fight the Germans. Darlan's prestige was such that if he ordered the French in North Africa to welcome the Americans with open arms, they would obey.

General Alphonse Juin was also a figure of considerable authority. Having graduated from St. Cyr in the same class as De Gaulle, Juin was badly wounded in 1915 and lost his right arm. After recovering, he was a liaison officer with the American forces in World War I. During the fighting in 1940, he was a division commander until captured. The Germans liberated him in the following year, and he became Commander in Chief of the ground and air forces in North Africa. Widely admired and respected, Juin, who saluted and shook hands with his left arm, was sympathetic to the Allied cause and hoped to fight the Germans again. But he was faithful to his chain of command and determined, in accordance with the armistice terms of 1940, to defend against invasion.

The French military establishment, Murphy continued, distrusted and disliked General De Gaulle. Austere and aloof, De Gaulle was in London, where the British supported his efforts to continue French resistance against the Axis. There were few Gaullists or "Free French" in North Africa except among students.

General Henri Giraud was another distinguished soldier. He had been wounded and taken prisoner in 1914, had escaped captivity, and returned to fight again in World War I. In 1940, he was in command of an army when he was again captured by the Germans. Escaping again, he made his way to southern France, the unoccupied zone, where he was living in hiding. He had no connection to the Vichy regime. If he were brought to North Africa, he might rally the French military to the Allied side.

Naturally, the French who proposed to cooperate with the Allies had certain demands—no infringement of French authority in North Africa, the promise of military and economic aid, and the like.

The French forces, Murphy believed, would resist Allied landings for at least 48 hours. He could persuade certain anti-Vichy groups to seize coastal batteries, radio and telegraph stations, newspaper offices, and other sensitive points of communication, and thus help the Allied forces ashore.

Eisenhower gave Murphy a sketchy explanation of Torch. He furnished a list of targets and the order of priority he desired for their destruction or capture. He provided some misinformation to pass on to the French. Although 100,000 men would land in the initial assault and they would increase to 250,000 in several weeks, Murphy could promise 150,000 men coming ashore, then rapidly mounting in number to half a million, Darlan's figure. But in Eisenhower's opinion, only French military men who were willing to cooperate could assure significant help to the landings.

Murphy returned to Washington.

In mid-September, the planners set the Torch D-Day for November 8, less than two months away. The war was going badly from the Allied perspective. Although Allied bombers were striking targets in Europe, the Germans remained masters on the continent and were advancing deeply into the Soviet Union. Their undersea and surface raiders were winning the battle of the Atlantic. Torch, if successful, would change the momentum of the conflict, swing the initiative to the Allies, and signal a new turn of events.

Clark now prepared to go to Washington with all the detailed plans, directives, and maps. Clearing out of his office at noon, he conferred briefly with Eisenhower, shopped on Regent Street for gifts for his family, then traveled to Prestwick, Scotland. When night fell, his plane took off. After several misadventures, including an emergency landing in Canada, the aircraft came to rest at Bolling Field. It was 1:30 in the morning, September 25, and Renie was there waiting.

To Clark, that day and the next were a blur. He reported to Marshall, and talked about the plans, air and naval support, political and civil affairs. Dissatisfied with the Oran task force commander, Marshall asked why Clark could not take command. Clark admitted his desire for the position and explained why it would be difficult at that late stage to designate a new man as Deputy Supreme Allied Commander. Marshall thought this unnecessary, and he dictated a cable to Eisenhower recommending Clark's appointment to command the Oran task force while he retained his post as Eisenhower's deputy.

Clark and General Thomas Handy, one of Marshall's closest advisers, thought Marshall's message too precipitous, too categorical, for it left Eisenhower no leeway. They persuaded Marshall to write a letter offering Eisenhower any officer in the United States if Eisenhower felt unable to give Clark the post. Clark took the letter to deliver on his return to London.

He discussed Torch with Secretary Stimson, who was concerned with the adverse effect on the American buildup in the United Kingdom; a European invasion would be impossible in 1943. The Secretary was also apprehensive over the many assumptions, the "multitude of suppositions," he said, that governed Torch—beliefs that the Spaniards would remain neutral, that the French would offer only token resistance, that the Germans would not move into Spain for the airfields. Clark agreed. These matters weighed heavily on everyone.

At the White House—the President was away touring defense plants—Clark had a two-hour talk over lunch with Hopkins. Clark called on Admiral Leahy, the President's chief of staff. He conferred with Handy, Patton, and others in the Munitions Building until evening.

On the following day, after meeting briefly with Marshall again, Clark discussed supplies with Somervell. He talked with Admiral King on the delicate timing of transferring command from the Navy to the Army during a landing. At lunch with Robert Murphy and General William Donovan, he went over intelligence matters. He spent the afternoon with Handy, Patton, and the principal members of Patton's task force.

"As far as I am concerned," Patton wrote in his diary, "General Clark has explained nothing. He seems to me more preoccupied with bettering his own future than in winning the war." That may have been jealousy over the important people whom Clark was seeing and the important place Clark had in Torch.

After flying to West Point for a visit with his son Bill, Clark presented the final details of the landing plans to Marshall, Dill, Leahy, King, and Admiral Sir Andrew B. Cunningham.

In London again on the evening of September 30, Clark was pleased to see Eisenhower waiting at Hendon Airport to welcome him. They went off at once to discuss what had taken place in the United States. Clark delivered Marshall's letter.

He was in his office at 8:30 A.M. when Eisenhower came over to talk about the Oran landings. They decided to ask for Fredendall, who had commanded the II Corps before Clark had displaced him. When Fredendall arrived in England in October, he officially relieved Clark of the corps command and assumed responsibility for the Oran force.

Eisenhower, Clark, and Bedell Smith were dining at Downing Street with Churchill, Prime Minister Jan Smuts of the Union of South Africa, General Sir Alan Brooke, Chief of the Imperial General Staff, and Cunningham, when a question raised by Anderson was mentioned. If Eisenhower was incapacitated, who would succeed him in command of Torch? Anderson, who outranked Clark, wondered whether the responsibility should devolve on himself. "The command," Brooke said categorically, "goes to General Clark."

Churchill read them several highly secret documents captured recently, he said, from Field Marshal Erwin Rommel's Afrika Korps in Libya. Rommel was suffering from ulcers and was on sick leave in Germany; his troops were frantic for ammunition and food.

Clark asked whether the Germans might have planted the papers to deceive the Allies.

The information, Churchill said confidently, was authentic.

The papers were, no doubt, Ultra Secret intercepts, and Churchill did not reveal the source of his intelligence. Later that month he met privately with Eisenhower, swore him to secrecy, and told him about the group of experts at Bletchley who decoded and translated highly sensitive German messages.

A few days afterward, Group Captain F. W. Winterbotham briefed Clark and a very select group of high-ranking Americans on the Ultra Secret operations. According to Winterbotham's recollection, Clark seemed hardly interested and left before Winterbotham completed his presentation.

Having surmised from Churchill's dinner conversation at Downing Street that the British possessed a special intelligence source, Clark was interested only in Winterbotham's confirmation of the fact. He had no concern with the technical aspects of the operation. Restless, with other matters on his mind, he excused himself and departed before Winterbotham finished his briefing.

Queried many years later on whether he made use of the Ultra Secret information during the Italian campaign, Clark responded, "Hell, I couldn't wait to get it."

Late on Friday, October 16, Eisenhower received an important radio message from the War Department in Washington. It paraphrased a cable sent by Robert Murphy from Algiers.

Murphy had returned to North Africa. He had met with the five French civilians and with Major General Charles Mast, Chief of Staff of the French 19th Corps. The Americans, Murphy told them, were preparing a massive operation—half a million men, two thousand planes, eight battleships, seven aircraft carriers, one hundred destroyers—for an invasion of North Africa sometime in the near future. Were there Frenchmen, he asked, who could help avert bloodshed between friends? The United States had no designs on French territory or authority.

Mast suggested appointing Giraud as a senior commander in the venture. Giraud could successfully urge the French military in North Africa to hold their fire. He could rally all Frenchmen in North Africa to support the Americans. Yet Giraud, Mast warned, opposed landing in North

Africa, for that would prompt the Germans to overrun and occupy southern France, that part of the country under Vichy rule. More productive, Giraud believed, would be an immediate invasion of southern France.

But Mast was willing to talk with American military representatives. If five officers—a senior familiar with the entire operation, plus operational, logistical, and amphibious experts, together with a Navy man—could come to North Africa secretly, Mast would gather key members of his staff for a conference. They could meet at a house near Cherchell, about 75 miles west of Algiers.

Murphy promised to inform his government. He sent his cable to Washington, and Washington forwarded a copy to Eisenhower. To him it seemed important to keep the rendezvous proposed by Mast. Torch was so risky that any possible help was welcome. Before taking action, Eisenhower decided to discuss the message with his closest advisers and to seek the advice of Churchill and his Cabinet.

Early on Saturday, October 17, Eisenhower summoned Clark and Bedell Smith to his office. He also telephoned Churchill at Chequers and asked him to call a Cabinet meeting that afternoon to take up an urgent matter. Churchill grumbled about being disturbed on the weekend but agreed to Eisenhower's request.

As soon as Clark read the telegram, he said, "When do I go?" He was the most senior officer who could be spared from Torch. He knew the plans intimately. If they accepted Mast's invitation as relayed by Murphy, Clark was the logical choice to make the trip.

The voyage was hazardous. Clark might be captured or lost. But Eisenhower agreed. Clark was the obvious person for the mission. If someone went to meet with Mast, it would be Clark.

CHAPTER 9

☆ ☆ ☆ ☆

THE PANOE CLUB

"an empty repeat empty wine cellar"

EISENHOWER, CLARK, AND Bedell Smith came to several decisions on how to reply to Murphy. They would accept Mast's invitation; the opportunity to invade North Africa without bloodshed was too precious to disregard. Clark would go as the senior officer; he knew better than anyone else all the detailed plans. If they had to accept a high-ranking French officer in the Allied command structure as the price of French cooperation and assistance, Clark would step down as Deputy Supreme Allied Commander and open that position to the Frenchman.

They selected the four officers to accompany Clark: Brigadier General Lemnitzer, the AFHQ G-3; Colonel Archeleus L. Hamblen, the G-4; Captain Jerauld Wright, U. S. Navy liaison officer with Torch since the beginning of the planning; and Colonel Julius C. Holmes, a former State Department career officer who spoke French.

To reach the rendezvous, they would have to travel to Gibraltar in two B-17 Flying Fortresses, then board a submarine for passage to the designated point, and finally paddle ashore in small boats. Because the United States had neither submarines in the Mediterranean nor small boats and highly trained experts to operate them, the British would have to furnish these.

Late that afternoon the Americans conferred with Churchill and his hastily assembled war cabinet—Smuts, Foreign Minister Anthony Eden, Deputy Prime Minister Clement Attlee, Brooke, Mountbatten, and Admiral Sir Dudley Pound, the First Sea Lord. Everyone agreed on the desirability of meeting with Mast.

"What do you want?" Churchill asked Clark dramatically. His voice was deep and sonorous as he spoke, and he obviously enjoyed the sound and the import of his words. "The whole resources of the British Empire are at your disposal."

Clark needed a submarine, several small boats, a few expert soldiers to help them ashore, plus some gold, at least 10,000 dollars, in case he had to resort to bribery in order to get out safely.

Churchill promised to meet his demands.

A message from Washington brought Roosevelt's acquiescence, together with two firm instructions. If they had to accommodate a senior French officer in the Torch structure, he was to command only French troops. Roosevelt and Churchill regarded French security as "leaky"; Clark was to hold back from Mast certain details, above all the time and the places of the invasion.

Clark himself was determined to discover whether the beaches where the Allies were to land were mined and where the French troops were normally stationed.

Word from Murphy fixed the meeting place, an isolated private house standing on a ridge behind the beach. A white light, invisible from the landward side, would be shining out to sea from a window.

As the conference broke up, Churchill turned to Clark and said melodramatically, "You can always keep in mind, Clark, that we'll back you up in whatever you do."

Early on the dreary, fog-filled afternoon of Sunday, October 18, Clark composed a farewell note to Renie. "Darling Sweetheart," he wrote, "I am leaving in 20 minutes on a mission which is extremely hazardous, but one I should do and one which I have volunteered to do...

"If I succeed and return, I will have done great things for my country and the Allied cause. Of course you know my life is dedicated to military service, and now that my opportunity has come for that service, I go forward proud of the opportunity which has been given me.

"If I do not return, know I loved you and our Bill and Ann more dearly than I could ever write. You have been an angel on earth to me, and I owe everything to you.

"God bless you all and keep you. My devoted love to my Mother and yours. I love you. Wayne.

"This is being handed to Jack Beardwood who will get it to you only in the event that I do not return. MWC."

He folded the letter, sealed it in an envelope, then wrote, "Mrs. M. W. Clark. Deliver only in event I do not return here. MWC."

At 2 P.M., two limousines stopped in front of his door to start him and his companions on their adventure. The drivers wheeled beyond Hyde Park and out of London to the northwest. Two and a half hours later they were at the Polebrook Airdrome, an American bomber base 75 miles from the city.

A pair of Flying Fortresses were ready to go and awaiting weather clearance. Clark and his party had dinner at a small secluded mess. With rain and mist still holding up flights, they turned in for a few hours of sleep. The weather improved, and at 6 A.M., they boarded, Clark and Lemnitzer in different planes, for if Clark's aircraft was forced back or downed, Lemnitzer was to continue.

Landing at Gibraltar that afternoon, the Americans met with Lieutenant General Frank Mason Macfarlane and half a dozen other British officers, including Lieutenant N. L. A. Jewell, skipper of the submarine that would take Clark and his group to the rendezvous. Jewell's honest face and solid figure typified British steadiness and reliability, and his whole attitude, Clark noted, "radiated confidence." Jewell and his crew did nothing but special and unconventional missions; they would later set adrift "the man who never was," a body with false papers designed to deceive the Germans on the invasion of Sicily.

Several cars took them to the berth of a submarine depot ship for dinner. At 9 o'clock, the five Americans and Jewell boarded the P-219, the *Seraph*. Three commandos, Captains C. P. Courtney and R. T. Livingstone, and Lieutenant J. P. Foot, assigned by Mountbatten's Combined Operations headquarters, were already there.

They traveled during the night and through the next day for the most part on the surface. The weather was good, the sea calm. Clark and his party went over plans and procedures, then played bridge to pass the time.

After darkness fell, Jewell stopped. The commando officers showed the Americans how to disembark from the submarine into foldboats, small canvas and wooden boats, each capable of carrying two men. The Americans practiced getting into the flimsy craft, pulled away several hundred yards, and tested their radios and infrared equipment.

The submarine reached the rendezvous point around 4 A.M., October 21. Satisfied that he was at the right place, Jewell submerged and took his boat out about three miles from shore. Through the periscope the crew kept the house under observation. Clark and his party peered through and made sketches of the shoreline to acquaint themselves with the terrain. The Americans packed musette bags with papers and maps. Lemnitzer distributed five and ten dollar gold pieces and several thousand francs to each member of the party, including the commandos.

Darkness came, but no light showed from the house. Clark decided against going ashore, and the submarine surfaced, moved six miles out, and charged its batteries. Clark went to bed.

He was awakened at 11:30. The prearranged light was shining. Jewell was already moving his craft closer to land. At midnight he halted two miles from shore. The moon was bright, the sea smooth.

In the early moments of October 22, Livingstone and Holmes launched their foldboat, waited until the others were embarked, then went ahead to make contact with those on the beach. Before long a reassuring signal came from Livingstone's flashlight. There was no trap. The party landed about 45 minutes after leaving the submarine.

Meeting them were Robert Murphy, his assistant Ridgway B. Knight, and half a dozen French officers, some in uniforms, others in street clothes. Among them was Lieutenant Jacques Teissier, whose father owned the house and who had sent the Arab servants away.

Gathering boats and gear, they crossed the sandy beach, passed through a small wooded area at the foot of a bluff, and climbed the steep slope to the house at the top of the ridge. They hid their equipment, then turned in to rest.

General Mast and his assistant, Major Emile Jousse, arrived around 6 A.M. Clark and Lemnitzer met them. Mast spoke English except for technical terms that Murphy or Holmes translated. The French general impressed Clark as "a man who can be relied upon."

At the outset both principals agreed to withhold no information. That was when Clark, as he later said, started "lying like hell." He could not tell the truth. Restrained by his instructions from Roosevelt, Churchill, and Eisenhower, who feared to compromise the security of Torch, Clark regretted the necessity to be less than open and frank.

According to the formal report written a week afterward, the conversation proceeded in this fashion. Apparently to test Clark's candor, Mast asked whether intelligence sources available to the Allies indicated an Axis intention to occupy North Africa. Clark replied in the negative. Mast nodded. He had the same information.

Was it possible, Mast asked, for the Americans to invade both southern France and North Africa? The primary French concern, he explained, was to keep the Germans and Italians from overrunning and occupying that part of metropolitan France governed by Vichy. Landing in the south of the country would prevent an expanded Axis occupation and expedite the liberation of France.

Logistical difficulties, Clark said, made this impossible.

What was the likely composition, Mast asked, of the invasion force?

Predominantly American, Clark replied, with British air and naval support. The Pacific war precluded the United States from maintaining sea and air forces in the Mediterranean. British ground troops would follow the initial landings and move eastward into Tunisia.

Mast stressed the need for coming ashore at first solely with Americans. What was the approximate strength of the forces? he asked.

Approximately half a million men, Clark responded.

Was sufficient shipping available to transport such a large body?

Yes, answered Clark.

Axis air forces, Mast said, could react to landings within 36 hours. It was essential to move eastward into Tunisia with all possible speed. The French military services in North Africa had few weapons, little equipment, and practically no air power for an effective defense against invasion, but they would fight strenuously even though most of the Army and Air Force, unlike the Navy, favored an American entry into North Africa.

Mast suggested bringing Giraud from France to North Africa in an American submarine. Who, Clark asked, would command the French forces if Giraud decided against coming or if he was unable to arrive in time? Mast believed that Giraud would come. If not, Mast would exercise command. Would the French accept him? Yes, he replied.

Mast needed about 2,000 rifles, ammunition, and grenades for his key personnel before the invasion. Clark promised to deliver these. Because Mast would use messengers to disseminate his orders to help the Americans ashore, he required four or five days notice of the landings.

Suppose this information fell into the wrong hands, Clark suggested.

No more than eight men, Mast said, would know. With this small group directing his organization, Mast could reduce French resistance and render the Americans substantial support.

He then presented a draft letter written by Murphy pledging the Americans to respect French sovereignty, to restore France to its prewar status, and to avoid interfering with the French administration. After the landings, Giraud was to be the commander of all the French and American forces.

Clark took exception to the last point and redrafted that part of the letter. A French commander might be appropriate at a later time, but a French general officer, presumably Giraud, could at once be named deputy to the commander in chief.

Mast approved Clark's version, and Clark reminded him of the need for the Allied Commander in Chief to accept and confirm it.

Other information came to light. Darlan, head of all the French military forces, was then in North Africa visiting his son who was hospitalized in Algiers with polio. Darlan had been neither informed of nor invited to the meeting with Clark. Mast was confident of persuading General Juin to be passive in his defensive efforts. The French Navy was sure to resist fiercely, but not for long. A frontal attack on Casablanca would be suicidal.

What worried the French most was the German occupation of all of metropolitan France. They were also concerned about Spanish Morocco and the possibility of Spain's entrance into the conflict on the Axis side.

Mast left at 10:30 A.M.

The conference was then opened to all the French and American officers, each of whom sought out his counterpart and discussed individual problems in his particular area of interest and competence. Mast and his staff had prepared plans on how the Americans could best invade North Africa, and the French handed their papers to Clark to take back to London. Except for the absence of an attack near Casablanca, their plans turned out to be similar to Torch.

The Americans learned more. Mast's men controlled the Blida Airport at Algiers and the airfield at Bone and would make them available on the first day of the landings. The locations of French units and gasoline depots, as well as specific information on harbor defenses, were other valuable pieces of information.

Mast had showed clearly his wish to be on the side of the Americans. He had proved his sincerity by passing over data on the disposition of French forces throughout North Africa. If he surmised from the speed with which his invitation was accepted that an invasion was close at hand—actually it was scheduled in two weeks—he gave no sign.

Some French officials later regarded Mast's transmission of military information to another government without authority as treasonable and despicable. To Clark, Mast's action seemed reasonable. The only hope for France to escape the German yoke was to join with the Allies. This, as well as Mast's desire to avoid bloodshed between friends, Clark decided, was Mast's motivation.

Actually, Mast's motives were probably largely personal. If the Americans came to North Africa, they would certainly win. In that case, as the leading French cooperator, as the American's man, Mast was sure to gain a high post in the succeeding French administration. He needed to meet with Clark to be absolutely sure of a wholehearted invasion rather than a raid as at Dieppe. He could then afford to take the risk of facilitating the landings. He could also persuade Giraud to become involved.

Late that afternoon came word of approaching French police. Arabs had apparently reported strange footsteps on the beach and suspicious activities, presumably connected with smuggling, in the house. Two French officers went out to intercept the policemen while Clark and his party rushed around picking up papers. Jousse jumped into civilian clothes. Clark sent a commando to the wooded area to tell Jewell by radio that the party was in trouble. Lemnitzer gave Murphy 5,000 Algerian francs and some gold pieces in case he had to buy off the police.

The rest of Clark's group, wearing their uniforms to avoid being accused of spying if caught, went down a trap door into the wine cellar, a dirty, smelly room. Someone upstairs threw a rug over the opening in the floor.

In the cellar they listened to the muffled sounds of conversation with the police. Courtney had to cough and seemed about to strangle. "General," he gasped. "I'm afraid I will choke."

"I'm afraid you won't," Clark replied.

They passed a bottle of wine around, and everyone took a swallow.

The police finally went away. The party came upstairs.

When it was dark, they left the house, carrying their gear and boats. A strong wind had come up, and the surf was unusually high and rough. Wearing a shirt, socks, and shorts, plus a Mae West lifebelt, Clark helped Livingstone shove a foldboat into the water. They waited for a lull in the waves, then dashed out and tried to get into the boat. A short distance from shore, the boat capsized. The two men rolled up on the beach. They recovered the boat intact, but Clark's trousers and shoes along with some paper money and gold were gone.

Obviously it was impossible to launch their boats and paddle back to the submarine. They dragged the equipment to a clump of trees and waited.

Despite the frantic desire on the part of the French for Clark and the others to leave, Clark instructed Jewell by radio to put out to sea until the surf quieted. If the high swells continued, Clark and his party would wait until the following night.

Around 4 A.M., the last possible moment when the foldboats could reach the submarine before dawn, someone found a spot where the surf seemed more placid. Jettisoning everything unnecessary, including tommy guns, carbines, and radios, Clark and Wright went first. Four French officers waded into the surf with them and shoved off the boat. The foldboat teetered and bounced but got beyond the breakers and headed for the submarine, a mile offshore.

Lemnitzer, who had discarded everything except the musette bag of notes on the conference and the infrared equipment necessary to locate the submarine, went next with Foot. Their first attempt capsized. Coughing and sputtering from the water they had swallowed in the undertow, they succeeded on their next try.

Every boat except Clark's overturned at least once before reaching the submarine. Everyone was thoroughly wet. The musette bags were soggy. The envelope containing gold pieces had broken, and many coins rested at the bottom of the sea. Bruised and bleeding, their clothes torn, the party entered the submarine just before daylight.

They were elated, and the rum produced by Jewell from the submarine stores quickly disappeared. In the general hubbub and hilarity of conversation and laughter was born the "Panoe Club," an exclusive group of the five Americans who had made the trip and who, after the war, would meet periodically to celebrate and commemorate their feat.

The name of the club came from a joke told while they were drinking their rum. Three wealthy businessmen went off to Canada on a hunting trip. A fourth friend was to join them later. Once they arrived in the wilderness, the three men engaged a guide and discovered that they needed three punts and a canoe. Sending a telegram to their fourth friend, they asked him to ship the necessary transportation for their outing. A day later came the reply. "Girls are on the way; am now searching for a panoe."

Jewell took the submarine down and headed for Gibraltar while Clark and his party went to bed. Awakening early in the afternoon, whiskered, bleary-eyed, bruised, and hungry, they went through their papers and missed certain documents, including several entrusted by Murphy to Holmes. Because they might be found on the beach by the wrong people, Clark ordered Jewell to surface, to break radio silence, and to send a message to Gibraltar for relay to Murphy. Would he search the beach for incriminating evidence of the conference.

Murphy would find nothing but Clark's coat and pants, and in a later cable to Clark, promised to have them cleaned and pressed and to give them to Clark when he returned with Torch.

Clark also sent a telegram to Eisenhower, reporting the coming of the police and how "our party hid in an empty repeat empty wine cellar."

On the morning of October 24, Clark cabled Gibraltar to ask for a flying boat to meet the submarine and speed their return. They spotted the Catalina that afternoon. After the plane landed, the Americans rowed over on the foldboats. The aircraft arrived at Gilbraltar that evening.

Clark transmitted Mast's request for 2,000 Sten guns and ammunition to Mason-Macfarlane, who promised to make the delivery. After dinner, Clark and his companions talked about their formal report to Eisenhower. They listened to a news broadcast and learned that Sir Harold Alexander had launched an attack out of Egypt, an effort specifically by Montgomery's Eighth Army, to draw Axis attention away from Torch. Then they boarded Flying Fortresses and flew to England.

In London on October 25, Clark telephoned Eisenhower, then drove to his country house. Eisenhower was not entirely satisfied with Clark's revision of Murphy's letter to Giraud on the place of a French commander in the Allied command organization. Once Eisenhower had secured French territory on which to base further operations against the Axis, he would be glad to turn over to the French the defense of North Africa.

From his Norfolk House office, Clark phoned Churchill over the scrambler and gave him a brief account of the adventure. Churchill invited him to dinner, but Clark declined in favor of sleep.

Clark reported the gist of his findings to the senior Torch officers assembled for their regular meeting on October 26. Then he plunged into a series of conferences to adjust plans to the information obtained in North Africa.

High praise came from Washington and London. Eisenhower proposed Clark for the Distinguished Service Medal and the others for lesser decorations. Clark commended Jewell, the commando officers, and the members of his party. Teissier, who had made available his father's house at Cherchell, would later be attached to an American headquarters as a liaison officer and would receive the Croix de Guerre with Palm. Mast would become Governor of Tunisia in 1944.

How important was Clark's conference with Mast? It confirmed Allied intelligence data, provided new information, proved the soundness of the Torch plans, gained the promise of French assistance, and obtained Giraud's support. Giraud's adhesion, Murphy believed, would "give us entry practically without firing a shot."

Word came from Giraud. He tentatively approved the agreements reached by Clark and Mast was ready to go from France to North Africa. Because he might refuse to board a British submarine, Clark arranged with Churchill to send U. S. Navy Captain Wright to Gibraltar in order to take nominal command of Jewell's submarine. The boat departed for the Gulf of Lyon to pick up Giraud.

On October 28, the principal Torch figures met for the last time in London. Fifty-four officers, Eisenhower announced, would go to Gibraltar to set up the Allied Force Headquarters. He would tell Mast on November 4 of the Torch landings scheduled for November 8, to give Mast the four days of advance warning he had requested.

Eisenhower and Clark had an audience with King George in Buckingham Palace. The monarch, according to Clark, was a small, pleasant man who stuttered occasionally and tended to keep his hand over his mouth when he spoke; he was thoroughly familiar with the invasion plans. He told how he had laughed when he read the cable from Clark about hiding in "an empty repeat empty wine cellar."

Looking ahead, Eisenhower sent a message to Marshall and gave copies to Clark and a few others. If Torch went well, Eisenhower wanted to have the Fifth Army headquarters being formed in the United States to come to North Africa. If Marshall approved, Eisenhower intended to place Clark in command. He and Clark had tentatively selected key members of the staff.

Clark, by his efficiency and energy in planning and coordinating Torch, had, in Eisenhower's opinion, earned the right to command an Army. But Marshall would first have to confirm Eisenhower's recommendation. Clark was a relatively junior major general. Patton, much more senior, had a claim on the position, and Secretary Stimson had intimated as much before Patton's departure for the Casablanca landings. Who would get the Fifth Army would depend in large measure on how Torch went.

On the last day of October, with all the preparations completed, the execution of Torch started. There was little to do in London. Eisenhower and Clark relaxed in the country.

A day later a cable from Murphy threatened to turn everything topsy-turvy. Giraud, Murphy explained, could not leave France until November 20. Could Torch be postponed?

Clark was furious. Unable to locate Eisenhower for the moment, Clark handled the matter. No change in the date of Torch, he informed Marshall, was possible. The schedules were set. Would Marshall please tell Murphy?

Distressed to learn that Mason-Macfarlane had still not delivered the weapons promised to Mast, Clark asked Gruenther whether it was possible to smuggle the arms to North Africa. Gruenther said he would see what he could do. In the end, the shipment was never made.

At a large conference late that afternoon Clark impressed upon all members of the staff the urgency of adhering to the agreements reached with Mast in order to avoid unnecessary combat.

Eisenhower and clark cleared their offices by noon on November 2, then had lunch at Downing Street with Churchill, who affectionately bade them farewell.

After conferring on last-minute details, Eisenhower and Clark went home to pack. Several close friends came to Clark's flat for a drink that turned into a small cocktail party. Then Clark drove to the little-used, out-of-the-way, and well guarded Addison Road station. There was a heavy mist, and the only lights inside came from flickering coal-oil lamps. A special train of eleven cars was waiting to take 54 officers and 2 enlisted men to Bournemouth, the first leg of their voyage to Gibraltar. British and Americans talked together cordially in the club car, where a long refreshment table ran down the middle.

A cable arrived from Murphy. Giraud would meet the submarine waiting for him in the Gulf of Lyon.

At Bournemouth, the passengers slept until 3:45 A.M., had breakfast, and entered cars and trucks that took them eight miles to a British airfield at Hurn. Six American Flying Fortresses were waiting, but the weather over Gibraltar was bad. At 7:30 A.M., they returned to the train and to London.

The weather was still unfavorable on November 4, but they traveled by rail again to Bournemouth. Vehicles took them in the darkness through a cold rain and over muddy roads to the airfield. The plane motors were turning over.

Eisenhower and Clark entered separate planes. If anything happened to Eisenhower, Clark was to assume command immediately. Jimmy Doolittle, who had led the bombing raid on Tokyo several months earlier, piloted the aircraft carrying Eisenhower. Paul Tibbetts, later involved in dropping the atomic bomb on Hiroshima, flew Clark. They arrived at Gibraltar that afternoon.

A cable from Murphy, reporting a conversation with Juin, awaited them. Juin's duty, he had told Murphy, compelled him to oppose American landings even though his sympathies lay with the Allies.

Neither Eisenhower nor Clark worried. With Giraud and Mast in their pockets, they were sure they could take care of Juin.

Eisenhower and Clark shared a small office about eight by nine feet in size tunneled into the rock. There at 10 P.M., November 5, they officially opened AFHQ and notified Washington and London. The first Torch convoy passed through the straits of Gibraltar undetected by the Germans or Italians.

So far at least, all was going well and on schedule. Everything seemed about to go off like clockwork.

CHAPTER 10

☆ ☆ ☆ ☆

THE DARLAN DEAL

"Politics isn't my line"

DURING THE TWO tense days remaining before the Torch landings, as the three task forces moved across the water to their destinations near Casablanca, Oran, and Algiers, Eisenhower and Clark at Gibraltar could only pray for good luck. Would the arrangements with Mast help get the inexperienced American troops ashore with a minimum of trouble? Would Mast and his colleagues be able to dislodge and replace the French political and military authorities who were loyal to the Vichy government and who were certain to oppose the invasion? Would Giraud reach North Africa in time to issue a proclamation and rally the French armed forces to the Allied side?

Picked up by Jewell's submarine, then flown by Catalina plane to Gibraltar, Giraud came to Eisenhower's office around 4 P.M., November 7. The landings were to begin in seven hours, and it was manifestly impossible for Giraud to get to North Africa before the troops waded ashore. But if he made a statement urging the French to welcome the

90

Americans, Eisenhower would send it to London for broadcast to North Africa. That might be enough to avoid bloodshed.

With Holmes serving as interpreter, Eisenhower and Clark talked with Giraud for three hours. A tall and forbidding officer, 63 years old, Giraud would issue no message until he was in North Africa. He insisted on being named the Supreme Allied Commander for Torch.

Eisenhower tried to be conciliatory, Clark was tough. From time to time, whether play-acting or serious, Clark stalked out of the office, shaking his head and mopping his brow, barely keeping his temper.

They sent Giraud to dinner with Mason-Macfarlane, then resumed their conversation with him afterward. Giraud was adamant.

At one point Clark told Holmes to translate, "We would like the Honorable General to know that the time of his usefulness to the Americans for the restoration of the glory that was once France is now. We do not need you after tonight." At another stage, to Holmes for translation, "If you don't go along [with us], General Giraud, you're going to be out in the snow on your ass."

Giraud did not budge.

The Torch landings started in the early hours of November 8. The first reports were good.

Further discussion with Giraud that morning found no way out of the impasse. Although Eisenhower promised to install him as civil and military governor over all of French Northwest Africa after the Allies were ashore, Giraud declined to lend his name to Torch unless he was Allied Commander in Chief, with authority to make all strategic and tactical decisions. He wanted to invade southern France immediately and to carry out landings on Sardinia and Sicily.

From the Allied point of view, his demands were unreasonable. The large and complex operation, carefully planned and prepared, was already in progress. No one could shift the thousands of components in the invasion fleet to different targets on short notice.

Still another factor prevented Eisenhower and Clark from acceding to Giraud's wishes. Giraud was outside the regularly constituted Allied chain of command. The President and Prime Minister directed the Anglo-American forces through their closest military advisers, who sat together as the Combined Chiefs of Staff. They set the objectives of the military forces in the field. The Allied authority vested in and exercised by the Combined Chiefs was not binding on Giraud. For that reason alone he could not be a top Allied commander.

Eisenhower and Clark finally brought him around, perhaps because the reports from the landing forces indicated success despite French re-sistance. Giraud agreed to go to North Africa on the following day. He would assume command of all the French military forces, become Gov-ernor of all of French Northwest Africa, and do his best to stop the fighting between the French and the Allies.

That evening good news came from Algiers. Mast's group had taken control of the city for several hours, then had been scattered. Darlan was in Algiers because his son in the hospital was believed to be at the point of death. He and Juin had agreed to a local armistice with Ryder, com-mander of the American task force. Darlan's and Juin's public explanation for their action cited the overwhelming presence of American military force. In order to give Pétain a chance to bargain with Hitler and try to prevent the German occupation of all of France, Darlan limited his au-thority to the Algiers area. The local ceasefire did not extend to the Oran and Casablanca regions, where Fredendall's and Patton's troops were heavily engaged.

To bring a cessation of hostilities throughout Morocco and Algeria was most important. Freeing the Allied troops from fighting the French would enable them to move quickly into Tunisia. That was Giraud's immediate task—and Clark's.

Eisenhower had earlier decided to send Clark to Algiers as soon as possible to act as his alter ego. "I must," he explained, "have someone who can act for me without having to confer with me or get my opinions." As Clark recalled, "Ike mentioned to me how he wished he could go but again felt that the Commander should remain at his command post."

While Eisenhower stayed at Gibraltar, where the superb communi-cations facilities kept him in touch with the fighting fronts and with London and Washington, Clark would represent him in North Africa. Clark had authority to make whatever decisions he judged necessary. His primary objective was to facilitate the movement of Allied troops into Tunisia. That was possible if he could persuade the French to stop fighting and join the Allies against the Axis. Hardly less important was getting the French fleet at Toulon to sail across the Mediterranean to the Allied side.

Giraud left for Algiers on the morning of November 9. Clark and a small party, held up by a sudden squall, departed several hours afterward. Arriving at the Maison Blanche Airport around 5 P.M., Clark was met by Murphy and Ryder, both haggard and grim with fatigue and frustration. Nothing was going right. Darlan and Juin were in control. Giraud was secluded and despondent.

Ryder had carried to Algiers terms of an armistice to apply to all of North Africa, but none of the French authorities would consider, accept, and sign the document, not even Giraud. Ryder had consequently stalled the conversations until Clark could get there. The problem was that no one was paying any attention to Giraud.

The reason for French indifference to Giraud was his lack of standing in the regular chain of military command. He was an outsider, without backing except from Mast's group, which was small and insignificant.

The only person of consequence with whom Clark could deal was Darlan. He and Juin held the reins of power. And they were playing a devious game to avoid breaking the terms of the 1940 armistice with Germany. Above all, they wanted to avoid furnishing Hitler an excuse to overrun and occupy all of France.

Clark met with Darlan that evening, and they decided to defer discussions until morning. He called on Giraud and found him depressed.

Later that night Juin talked with Giraud and convinced him that only Darlan had the authority and prestige to dominate North Africa. Giraud then decided to renounce his claim, which the Americans supported, to control civilian affairs. He would be satisfied with a military command.

Clark had already perceived the dilemma. Instead of setting up Giraud as a nonpolitical authority in North Africa, that is, an individual who was neither tainted by collaboration with the Vichy government nor colored by party affiliation, Clark would have to deal with Darlan. Having been Pétain's de facto deputy, Darlan was now, after Pierre Laval, who was notoriously pro-Hitler, Vichy's number three official. The situation was "filled with dynamite," Clark wrote in his diary. "What a mess," he exclaimed. "Why soldiers have to get into things like this when there are wars to be fought—God, it's awful."

He understood well enough the complexities facing him. As his aide Beardwood noted in Clark's diary, his "current job is almost entirely political." Combat was much more simple.

Yet the possibility of collaborating with Darlan had been raised the previous month. The highest Allied political and military authorities had given prior approval if negotiating with Darlan was necessary.

Wearing his best uniform, Clark met with Darlan on the morning of November 10. In a small room off the lobby of the Hotel St. Georges, Clark sat at the head of a table. To his left was Darlan, 61 years old, stubby, partly bald, with light watery eyes and a friendly manner, the principal to be reckoned with. To Clark's right was Juin, hardly less important, a bulldog of a man, with excitable eyes.

Seven other French officers were present. The most influential was
Vice Admiral Fenard, who had no well-defined position.

Wright and British Commodore Dick, naval liaison officers with AFHQ,
Clark's aide Beardwood, and Holmes sat at the table, as did Murphy,
who translated.

By this time, Fredendall, commanding the forces around Oran, had
overwhelmed the French defenders. Except for sporadic skirmishes, the
fighting had stopped. Around Casablanca, Patton was planning to mount
a full-scale attack on the city. Only an agreement with Darlan would stop
that action, which was sure to be costly for both French and Americans.
Of extreme importance also was the need to prevent French troops from
opposing Anderson's movement into Tunisia and to turn them against
Axis forces entering the country by sea and by air.

The meeting started shortly before 9 A.M., when Clark turned to Murphy
and said, "Explain to Admiral Darlan the necessity of coming immediately
to the point. We have work to do to meet the common enemy. Is he
ready to sign the terms of the armistice [for all of North Africa]? . . . It
is essential that we stop this waste of time and blood."

Darlan responded by saying that he had forwarded a resume of the
Allied armistice terms to Pétain. His Council of Ministers was scheduled
to meet in Vichy that afternoon to consider them. The Council would
send Darlan instructions. Darlan wanted the hostilities stopped, felt that
further fighting was fruitless, but had to await word from his government.

"I am negotiating with you as commander . . . on the ground," Clark
said. "I am not prepared nor do I propose to await any further word from
Vichy."

All that Darlan could do was to obey his government's orders.

"Then I will have to break off negotiations and deal with someone
who can act," Clark said.

He could do whatever he thought was necessary, Darlan responded.
There was no one else, as Clark well knew, who had the authority to
act. The French military would listen only to Darlan.

"Will the French troops east of Algiers resist as we pass through to
meet our common enemy?" Clark asked. He was referring to Anderson's
movement into Tunisia.

Darlan had asked Vichy to answer.

It was impossible to wait. "I will end this conference in thirty minutes,"
Clark threatened. "It will be necessary to retain you in protective custody. . . . We must move east. I propose to negotiate with someone who
can issue orders to the [French] troops." Why did Darlan have to have

the approval of Vichy? He could simply order the French to cease fighting the Americans.

Darlan lacked the authority to make such decisions. He had urged Vichy to accept the Allied terms. Pétain, he was confident, would agree.

In actuality, Darlan was playing for time. Through a secret Admiralty code unknown to Clark, Darlan was in touch with Vichy. Laval, he knew, was on his way to see Hitler, to try to keep the Germans from overrunning all of France. If Darlan acceded to Clark's wishes, Pétain and the Vichy government would repudiate him, and he would lose his control over North Africa.

Responding to Darlan's statement on his lack of authority, Clark said, "That is fine, but do you understand that we cannot sit here while governments agree and ministers debate? If the Admiral will not issue instructions for the cessation of hostilities, I will go to General Giraud. He will sign the terms and issue the necessary orders."

The troops might not respond to Giraud, Darlan pointed out.

"If you think Pétain will agree with you that hostilities must cease," Clark said, taking another tack, "why can't you issue that order now?"

If Darlan assumed that responsibility, the Germans would immediately occupy southern France.

"We all agree concerning the great danger of the occupation of southern France," Clark said, "but . . . what you are doing now means more killing of French and Americans. . . . This all boils down to one question. Are you going to play with the Vichy government or go with us?" To Murphy he said, "Be abrupt."

Darlan was simply bound by his oath of fidelity to the government of Marshal Pétain. It was impossible for Darlan to take the responsibility of ordering the hostilities to cease.

"This is the time when [we must] lean on our inclinations and not on our orders," Clark urged. "Here is an opportunity for all Frenchmen to rally and win the war. Here is your last chance."

Darlan was willing to send an urgent message to Marshal Pétain, recommending an armistice for Algeria and Morocco.

"You have already done that," Clark said.

Not in such specific terms, Darlan admitted.

"We haven't time," Clark said. "I am going to stand firm. All French and all Americans have the same interests at heart, and here we are fighting among ourselves, wasting time. I know that the Admiral wants, deep down in his heart, to stop this fighting between our troops. We all want the same thing, and we must get an order for cessation of hostilities this morning. We have the means...of equipping the French army and making this the base from which we can go into France. How anybody can fail to join us in an operation that can mean the liberation of France is against my understanding."

Darlan was completely in accord, but he could take no action until he heard from Pétain.

"Giraud will sign the terms of the armistice," Clark said.

But Giraud had no authority in French Northwest Africa, Darlan said. If Darlan could send a message to Vichy, he suggested, he might obtain a swift response.

Clark had no desire to be involved with Vichy. He was close enough to Vichy simply by talking to Darlan. "We can't put up with delay," he said. "This cannot go on. I will have to take you into protective custody without communications. We will have to do business with the commanders on the ground." He would bypass the top commanders and appeal directly to the local commanders to stop the fighting.

All the local commanders, Darlan said, were subject to his orders and loyal to him.

"We will make it as easy as possible for you," Clark said.

Darlan then asked for five minutes of discussion with the other French officers.

Clark and his group left the room. As Clark paced the lobby of the hotel, he wondered what the French officers were debating.

In the light of logic, they had to accept Clark's position. Allied forces had arrived in overwhelming strength. The French had obsolete weapons and could hardly prevent the invasion from succeeding. Continuing to fight only produced needless casualties on both sides. Further losses would surely embitter emotions and sour relations. And certainly, if their orders to oppose the Allies were clear, their sentiments tugged them the other way. Only by joining the Allies could they hope eventually to liberate France.

Yet the French could not give the Germans an excuse to overrun unoccupied Vichy France. They could not defy the regular and legal line of command that flowed from Vichy. They could not break their link to legitimacy. Throughout the two and a half years since their defeat in 1940, they had opted to sustain the Petain government as the legal and proper authority. Unlike De Gaulle, who had withdrawn his allegiance to the Pétain regime and who in London headed a "dissident," even treasonable governmental structure in embryo, the regular corps of officers had remained in the service of the state. They were now imprisoned by their choice.

De Gaulle and his adherents could and did argue the honor of their decision in terms of implacable opposition to the Nazis. Withholding their loyalty from the collaborationist Pétainists, expecting the ultimate defeat of Nazi Germany, they wished to be part of the triumphant forces. They would then create a new government for France, its empire intact, restored to its traditional virtues.

In contrast, the officers on active duty could only claim the honor of obeying Pétain, whom they regarded as the legitimate source of the state's authority. Their consciences were torn by conflicting wishes, but their duty seemed clear.

According to their outlook, Pétain was compelled to order the French to resist the Allied invasion of North Africa, for this would indicate to Hitler Pétain's continuing commitment to the terms of the 1940 armistice and perhaps prevent the Germans from overrunning the rest of France. Only then, after Pétain's decision was clearly made, could the authorities in North Africa bow to the overwhelming Allied presence and accept the inevitable. The force of Allied arms, Darlan could say without compromising Pétain, had constrained them from obeying Pétain's instructions.

But first they had to give Pétain his chance to avoid losing all of metropolitan France to further German conquest.

Whether Clark understood these nuances was hardly important. The French, he later said, placed "a high value on the true meaning of honor." Each individual had to sort out the problem in accordance with his own conscience. That, he thought, was what made the negotiations in Algiers so difficult.

But he could not wait for them to re-order their priorities or to come to an understanding with their souls. What he needed was action at once: stop the fighting between French and Allied soldiers, gain French co-operation to keep North Africa calm and orderly, facilitate the Allied movement into Tunisia to forestall the arrival of Axis troops.

These were his immediate aims. Once he secured them, he would try to obtain two others: French opposition to the German and Italian forces already coming into Tunisia; and getting the French fleet to sail from Toulon to North Africa.

The door of the small room off the hotel lobby finally opened, and Clark and the others re-entered. Darlan had found a way out. He had written a short paper summarizing several points: Darlan had abstained from declaring an immediate armistice; the Americans had rejected his refusal; further fighting was useless in view of the Allied strength; continuing the battle would ensure the loss of North Africa; to avoid severing North Africa from the motherland, the French military forces were to cease hostilities and assume a neutral attitude.

Was the document acceptable to Clark?

The conclusion was less than altogether acceptable. But for the moment neutrality was enough. "What I want is orders to the troops," Clark said. He wished specific instructions to the troop units directing them to stop fighting the Americans.

Darlan agreed to pass the order to his subordinates. He began to write, occasionally halting to ask Clark for some clarification of a detail.

Taking responsibility for North Africa in the name of Pétain, Darlan instructed all military to cease firing against the Americans—Clark requested him to insert "or their Allies" in order to include the British, and Darlan acceded—and to observe a strict neutrality. The French military commanders were to retain their positions. There would be no changes— Clark asked Darlan to add "for the present," and he did—in political and administrative officials and policies.

Each commander in the field was to decide the terms of the armistice in his area. For example, Patton in Morocco was to meet with Nogues, the Governor, and make whatever arrangements suited them.

Thus, "by a combination of diplomacy and plain straightforward bullying," as someone later said, Clark persuaded the French to end their resistance.

Darlan raised the question of Giraud's status. They would settle that, Clark said, after the fighting had stopped. There was room for everyone, he added, who could help the common Franco-American cause.

How about the French officers like Mast who had acted independently of the command structure and had helped the Americans? Darlan wanted to relieve them from their military duties. In fact, he had no wish to see them or to deal with them. His colleagues felt the same. They bitterly resented Mast's having acted on his own authority, in defiance of the chain of command. The Americans, one of them suggested, should put these treasonble officers in a safe place for their own protection.

"I don't understand," Clark said, momentarily surprised. "They helped us so much." Hadn't Mast been motivated by the desire to avoid bloodshed between friends?

Clark recovered at once. "However, I do understand your resentment against their not obeying orders."

What about the French whom the Americans had taken prisoners of war?

"We will give them all back," Clark replied. "We don't want any French prisoners."

When Darlan finished writing, Clark read the order and approved. He had the message dispatched immediately. In Morocco, Nogues was about to capitulate to Patton when Darlan's instructions arrived.

Everyone left the room except Darlan, Clark, and Murphy, and Clark proceeded to the next business. What about the French fleet? he asked. Darlan was vague and made no commitment. He had ordered the ships to be ready to move on short notice if the Germans entered unoccupied France. The French vessels, he assured Clark, would not fall into German hands. He remained silent on what was perhaps a vital point. The commander of the fleet was a lifelong rival of his.

For the moment Clark was satisfied. He cabled Eisenhower a progress report. "Just concluded lengthy conference with Darlan and his cohorts. . . . He finally agreed." Furthermore, he had arranged for Anderson to confer with French local commanders to facilitate the movement of Allied forces into Tunisia. Clark had also set up a meeting with Darlan and Giraud that afternoon; perhaps he could sketch out a modus operandi to enable the two senior officers to work together.

Clark asked Commodore Dick to send his impressions of the meeting to British officials. Dick's message concluded, "Clark was magnificent."

That afternoon in Vichy, Pétain dismissed Darlan as head of the French armed forces. He appointed Nogues to be Darlan's successor.

Learning of these developments, Clark went immediately to see Darlan and found him, he said, "dejected." Trying to shake Darlan out of his depression, Clark said, "Pétain is the mouthpiece of Hitler." Actually, Pétain, under the German threat to overrun southern France, had had to renounce and remove Darlan.

Darlan talked of revoking the order that he had signed that morning. "You're not going to revoke any order," Clark said.

Then the Americans must take him prisoner, Darlan said. To show that he had signed the order under duress.

"Now's your chance to get the French fleet," Clark said.

It was no longer his fleet, Darlan said. He had been relieved.

Returning to the Hotel St. Georges, Clark checked to see whether the French commanders had obeyed Darlan's order. He was gratified to discover negotiations between French and Allied offices in progress everywhere.

Taking Giraud with him, he went to Juin's headquarters, where he conferred with several French generals. They were gloomy. According to their intelligence sources, the Germans were about to invade unoccupied France.

That was what they had all dreaded, and Giraud spoke up on the appalling nature of the news. The French were at the end of their rope, he said. It was time for them to get together in order to save North Africa.

Darlan and Giraud first had to get together, Clark suggested. "This is a French matter," he said, "and you must work out your own cooperation."

In a cable to Eisenhower soon afterwards, Clark termed Giraud's statement the "best news I had today. Squeeze your left one until my next report."

At midnight, November 10, German and Italian troops crossed the line of demarcation and began to overrun all of previously unoccupied France. They also took control of Corsica. This gave the French in North Africa the excuse to renounce their pledge of obedience to Pétain. How could he be the source of legitimate authority when he was a virtual prisoner of the Axis? Illogically, Darlan's claim of being a prisoner of the Allies had hardly destroyed his own authority in North Africa.

By this time, Axis forces were pouring into Tunisia by air and sea in order to establish a large bridgehead covering Bizerte and Tunis, the ultimate objectives of Torch. In Libya, Rommel, pursued by British forces, was withdrawing his Italo-German army westward toward the southern part of Tunisia.

On the morning of November 11, Clark went to Admiral Fenard's house where Darlan was staying. Two items were very much on Clark's mind, and he spoke rather harshly.

"Although you have told us repeatedly," Clark said to Darlan, "that you want to free France, you have given us no visible indication or decision in support of us or the Allied cause. There are two ways you can demonstrate... first, by summoning the French fleet to a North African port, and, second, by ordering the Governor of Tunisia to resist invasion by the Germans."

Darlan demurred. He doubted whether anyone would obey him. But the French in Toulon would scuttle the ships if the Germans tried to seize them.

The Germans were moving fast, Clark warned. Perhaps the Navy would lack time to scuttle. "If the orders were issued at once, the fleet could get away."

Darlan could not tell the fleet to sail from France.

Clark then demanded Darlan to instruct the French troops in Tunisia to resist the entry of the Germans and the Italians into the country.

Darlan refused.

Frustrated and angry, Clark spoke sternly. "This just verifies the statement I made when I came here," he said. "It shows no visible indication indicating any desire on your part, despite your statements, to assist the Allied cause." Stretched to his full height, Clark glared down at Darlan. "Good day," he said and strode out of the house.

Admiral Fenard phoned Clark after lunch and asked him to come to see Darlan again. Darlan had changed his mind. He had sent a cable to Toulon inviting the fleet to sail to North Africa. He had instructed the French forces in Tunisia to oppose the Axis entry.

Although Clark had had his way, he was uneasy. He had reservations with respect to Darlan. To deal with him negated the Allied war aims of displacing enemy governments and those friendly to the Axis. Yet Darlan was the sole figure with sufficient prestige and influence not only to control the French military forces in North Africa but also to provide the internal stability needed by the Allies to prosecute the campaign in Tunisia.

In contrast, Giraud was of little use. All the principal French commanders were anti-Giraud. They regarded him at best as an interloper, at worst as an American puppet, even as a traitor to France.

Thus, Darlan was a necessary evil. Only he could guarantee French cooperation. If Clark ignored Darlan, he might precipitate a French civil war. But now he needed more than Darlan. He required a show of French unity to indicate a broad acceptance of the Allied presence and goals. Specifically, he had to have Giraud included in the agreements in order to indicate a turn toward a non-Pétainist, non-Vichy stance on the part of the Allies.

That afternoon Clark made further progress. Darlan agreed to be the French political chief in North Africa, and he accepted Giraud as the military commander. Because Pétain had designated Nogues to be the supreme military head in North Africa to replace Darlan, ostensibly a prisoner of the Americans, Clark asked Nogues to come to Algiers. That would provide Clark the occasion to make a public announcement stressing the harmony of all the various French factions now bound together in a common effort against the Axis. That the Gaullists had no representation seemed to make no difference.

The invitation to Nogues was a tactical error, as Clark would soon discover.

When he awakened on the morning of November 12, Clark learned to his astonishment that his negotiations had collapsed. The order instructing the French troops in Tunisia to resist the Axis forces had been cancelled.

Summoning Darlan and Juin immediately, with Fenard and Murphy there, Clark spoke sharply. "Both of you," he said, "keep telling me you want to save France and French colonial territory. Neither of you has given me one single indication of this except in words. All your deeds have been contrary to the aim you both volubly profess to have. Now I learn that the order for French troops to resist Axis moves in Tunisia has been revoked."

Juin explained to the translator Murphy. The order had not been revoked. It had merely been suspended until Nogues arrived that afternoon in Algiers. Juin wanted, intended to help the Allies, but he could not let the order stand until he had the approval of Nogues.

"Not once have you shown me that you are working in our interests," Clark said. If Juin was uncertain about whether his troops would obey his orders without Nogues' backing, "you are not strong enough to hold the position you do. We will get someone strong enough, someone whom the troops will obey."

Juin looked to Darlan for support, but the admiral was silent as he creased small strips of white paper with his fingers.

"I don't recognize Nogues," Clark said. "To us he is not the Commander in Chief in North Africa...we don't have to accept any individual. Those that we recognize must guarantee that they will fight on our side against Germany."

He was willing to fight the Germans, Juin said.

"You must not only say you are willing to fight," Clark said. "You must show, by your actions, that you are fighting. You haven't done that, and I'm sick and tired of the way you have been conducting yourself. I think you are weak."

Juin tried to explain. He was subject to Nogues' orders by virtue of Pétain's appointment of Nogues as commander in chief. Juin had to consult with him first. It was a matter of honor. If Nogues refused to let Juin issue the order, Juin would do it anyway. Why didn't Clark understand? Juin had first to talk with Nogues.

"I can't and don't accept such a plan," Clark said. "While we are waiting, the German troops are moving in [to Tunisia]. I want that order re-issued now. I'm not so sure that you aren't stalling just to help the Germans. Anyone who is going to be accepted by us must show concretely his willingness to march against the Germans. I asked you to do two simple things to prove you want to save France. First, I asked you to order the French fleet to North Africa. Second, I asked you to communicate with [the Governor of Tunisia]...to tell him that the Germans must be resisted. What have you done? There is no indication that the fleet is coming to North Africa. The French are not resisting [Axis] moves into Tunisia."

Darlan spoke. The fleet had received his message and would sail to North Africa if the Germans entered Toulon.

Clark let that go for the moment. But he could not pass on Tunisia. "The orders to the commanders in Tunisia," he said, "were revoked without any reference to me. That, to me, is almost treachery."

Goaded, the two French officers both turned to Murphy. Their hands were tied because Nogues was now the head man. The Germans had moved only small forces into Tunisia. The French troops there were watching and waiting, not helping.

Finally Juin shouted. The order for the French to fight the Germans in Tunisia had not been revoked; it was merely suspended until they could confer with Nogues.

"And in the meantime," Clark said, "the Germans are coming into Tunisia. Where is your logic if you profess to want to protect French soil?"

Juin wanted to fight the Germans. He would even serve under Giraud. That was the first time any French officer had overtly agreed to Giraud.

"All right then," Clark said. "I want your troops to resist at the Tunisian airdromes where the Germans are moving in. I want them to resist where they are able to resist."

The French were too weak to do much, Juin said.

"I demand that you issue orders to resist. If not, I am considering very gravely the establishment of a military government in French North Africa. I will put into custody everybody who will not come with us and help. I will set up a French official who can issue concrete orders and who has shown his willingness to march with us."

But Juin wanted to march with the Americans.

"You must prove it," Clark said. "You must issue the order to resist in Tunisia."

It was all so clear to Clark from a pragmatic American point of view, yet Juin tried to explain once more. The troops and officers were troubled by their consciences. They might refuse to obey orders from anyone but Nogues. There might be chaos. Please, Juin said, please wait until Nogues arrived that afternoon.

Clark was unmoved. "I have the means to enforce what we want and I do not intend to tolerate this delay."

Yet Clark himself had invited Nogues to Algiers, Darlan reminded him. Why couldn't Clark wait until he came before he did anything drastic?

While Darlan, Juin, and Murphy talked animatedly, Admiral Fenard, who spoke English, walked behind Clark's chair and whispered to him. Clark was making a big mistake. He was about to get what he wanted if only he would be a little more patient. He had the awesome Anglo-American political and military power behind him, while the French spoke from a position of political weakness and confusion. "Don't spoil everything," Fenard said. "You almost have a solution and a victory at hand."

Clark shook his head. Darlan and Juin, he was sure, were stalling.

Fenard made a hopeless gesture. "That's not true," he said. "I swear it. You are blind, sir, you are blind."

Juin then turned to Clark and said, "I am with you."

"No, you're not," Clark said.

"I am with you," Juin repeated.

"Then prove it by issuing the orders to Tunisia immediately."

"Wait," Fenard said, "and you will have all the factions welded together."

"You are not moving fast enough to keep the Germans from coming into Tunisia." Then to Murphy, "Tell them that unless they decide to go along with us right now, they are through, and I'm prepared to place them under arrest."

All they asked for, Juin said, was a suspension of the order until Nogues arrived. Nogues, Juin was sure, would accept Clark's wish.

Clark reiterated his intention of putting them all under arrest.

Juin finally exploded. If Nogues refused to go along with the Americans, Juin would put himself at Clark's disposal.

Giraud was going to be the overall military commander, Clark reminded him.

Then Juin would go with him.

"We want results," Clark said. Would Giraud be at the meeting with Nogues?

No, Darlan replied, forgetting his own elimination from the chain of command. Only those who were legally empowered to act would meet initially.

"Who is in power and who will be in power," Clark said, "will be decided by the United States government."

Well, Darlan said, remembering his position, he was no longer in power himself, and he had to consult with Nogues.

They were wasting time, Juin said. He wanted to do something to help.

"Then issue orders to resist the Germans."

While Juin made a volcanic outburst to Murphy and argued excitedly, Fenard walked to the head of the table and said to Clark in a low voice, "Wait. You have everybody with you. I swear it."

Clark paid no attention. He insisted on a display of cooperation.

"You are making a mistake," Fenard told him. "You will spoil everything."

Clark was adamant. Would Juin order the commanders in Tunisia to resist the Germans?

Now or after the meeting with Nogues? Juin asked.

"I mean now."

That put Juin in a terrible spot.

"I know it," Clark said, "but I'm in a worse spot."

But Nogues was Juin's legitimate commander.

Finally, Juin said that he wanted to talk with Darlan privately. The two Americans and Fenard left. Clark strode up and down. Fenard pleaded with him to wait for Nogues. "You don't understand the internal situation," Fenard said. "Everybody is behind Darlan. If you will wait, you will have everyone with you. If not, you will upset the apple cart."

The problem was, Clark said, if he waited, "I'll have Germans on top of us." But he agreed to wait for the conference with Nogues even though, he said, he was beginning to wonder who his friends were.

"Then you are blind," Fenard said. "You are making a mistake if you don't trust us. I am sure of it."

"I know that the stand I am taking is right," Clark said to Murphy.

Darlan and Juin joined them. Juin had checked to see what was happening in Tunisia. The French troops there were covering the railroads. Juin had told the commander to resist if the Germans attacked.

"Suppose the Germans come on the airports," Clark said. "What then?"

They already controlled some airports. The French should have attacked, Juin admitted, but the local commanders had orders directly from Vichy to do nothing to interfere with the Germans. Understanding Juin to be a prisoner of the Americans, they had obeyed Vichy.

"If the Germans come on to another airport," Clark asked, "are the French going to resist?"

Yes, answered Juin.

So Clark agreed to wait for the meeting with Nogues before reaching a decision. He shook hands with the French officers and left.

At a press conference with British and American correspondents, Clark explained how he had had his hands full for the past three days. He had been dealing with several aspirants for power. He was solidly behind Giraud. He had no particular admiration for Darlan, but Darlan had the authority to command all the military elements. Clark's goal was to get Darlan, Giraud, and all the factions together and working in harmony. Because the political situation was still delicate, he asked the press to make no announcement until, as he put it, an accord was reached or Darlan was in jail.

Unable to restrain his impatience while the French were meeting with Nogues, Clark inspected American troops. He remarked how refreshing it was to be among soldiers again.

Returning to his headquarters, he learned that President Roosevelt had nominated him to be a lieutenant general and had sent his name to the Senate for confirmation.

After dinner, Clark and his principal staff members, about nine officers, all spruced up and wearing side arms, went in a group to the hotel lobby. Darlan, Nogues, and several other French officers were there. Giraud and Mast stood apart from them.

An interpreter explained that Nogues and Darlan wanted a private conference with Clark because Nogues was Commander in Chief by Pétain's order.

Straightening to his full height and looking Nogues squarely in the eye, Clark said, "Tell Nogues that we do not recognize either him or Pétain."

Nogues blinked.

But after a while, Darlan, Nogues, Clark, and Murphy went into a small conference room while everyone else remained in the lobby. Nogues wanted nothing to do with Giraud. Darlan tried to find a compromise solution.

Almost an hour later, the door opened and Giraud was invited to enter. As he came into the room, the two other French officers partially turned their backs to him. Clark had them both shake hands with Giraud.

Twenty minutes later, Clark told them to compose their differences or he would set up a military government to administer French North Africa. He stepped outside so that the French could hammer out a position in private.

After ten minutes, Clark rapped on the door and re-entered the room. In fifteen minutes everyone came out. Only Clark was smiling.

The French had yet to work out their problems, but they were making progress. Clark gave them until the following day to reach agreement. He strongly suggested the following solution: Darlan to assume political leadership, the incumbent governors in Morocco, Algeria, and Tunisia to retain their positions, Giraud to organize a volunteer French army equipped by the Americans to fight alongside the Allies.

Sensing accommodation, Clark sent Eisenhower a cable. It would be desirable, he suggested, for Eisenhower to fly to Algiers on the following day.

Eisenhower did so, and Clark met him at the airport. As they rode to the city, they made their plans. Clark would talk with the French first, then call Eisenhower into the conference.

As they were finishing their lunch, a message was delivered to Clark. The French officials had agreed to accept Clark's suggestions.

When Clark spoke to the French officers, he was charming. He thanked them warmly for their cooperation and assistance. Then he called on Eisenhower, whose brief remarks stressed the need for harmony.

Immediately thereafter, Eisenhower and Clark departed for the airfield. Before Eisenhower boarded his plane, he pinned third stars on Clark's shoulders. "I've been waiting a long time to do this, Wayne," he said. "I hope I pin on the fourth star."

After Eisenhower left, Clark took off his new stars. He decided to wait for official confirmation. That came on the following day. He was the youngest lieutenant general in the Army. A War Department release cited his "brilliant service" as Eisenhower's principal assistant, his diplomatic negotations requiring "skill and courage," and his secret submarine voyage.

Newspaper correspondents at once clamored for the details of his clandestine trip. Because Marshall, on the second day of the Torch landings, had expressed his desire for press coverage of "personal items," that is, stories of individual heroism and bravery, and had suggested Clark's exploit as an example, Eisenhower gave Clark permission to talk to the journalists. Clark then met with them and gave his account of the adventure.

At another press conference, several correspondents raised the question of Darlan's political tarnish. Were the American and British people likely to accept a collaborator of Hitler as an ally? Whether Darlan was a rat or not, Clark explained, he was the only person in North Africa who was

LEFT: On October 21, 1942, from this dormer window in Cherchell, Algeria, a signal light flashed to the British submarine H.M.S. *Seraph,* commencing Clark's famous mission behind enemy lines to persuade the French army not to oppose the Allied landings in North Africa.

BELOW: Clark and a companion leave the sub in a collapsible boat, heading for the site of the secret negotiations.

RIGHT: Aiding Clark was Robert Murphy, President Roosevelt's personal representative, shown here with Clark.

BELOW: After days of grueling argument, the successful Clark shakes on the deal with Admiral Darlan, commander of the French forces in North Africa. The agreement accelerated the Allied conquest of the region.

in control, the one whom the French armed forces would obey. "I would have sooner walked into the Germans, than into these boys," Clark said. "Politics isn't my line." As for Giraud, he was politically clean and he had the full support of the Americans, but he had to be worked into the command structure slowly. No provision had been made to accommodate the Gaullists. Clark's greatest concern now was to get the French fleet from Toulon to North Africa.

On November 16, for the first time since the Franco-German armistice of 1940, French and German forces met in combat. A French battalion in Tunisia opened fire and drove back a German reconnaissance party. With hostilities thus resumed, the French in North Africa overtly committed themselves to the Allied side.

Gruenther flew from Gibraltar and brought interesting news. Clark might soon receive command of the Fifth Army and plan an attack against Sardinia or Sicily. Or he might take his Fifth Army headquarters to London and prepare the cross-Channel assault on the Continent. Nothing was settled.

Patton was at Gibraltar "to see Ike," he wrote to his wife. "He and Clark certainly need to know the facts of life. They send some of the most foolish instructions I have ever read." In his diary, he recorded, "Ike lives in a cave in the middle of the rock ... I was disappointed in him. He talked of trivial things." During that trivial conversation, "He asked me if Clark was a Jew. I said at least one quarter, probably one half."

It was idle talk. Eisenhower was bored, doing little while Clark ran the show in Algiers.

The so-called Darlan deal produced much unfavorable comment, even outrage, in the United States and Britain. Many citizens protested negotiating with an official who hardly represented the idealistic and anti-Nazi outlook of the United Nations. The outcry was so great that Roosevelt declared the arrangements with Darlan to be only a temporary expedient. Allied policy, he reiterated, abjured working with collaborators of Hitler.

Listening to remarks of this nature on the BBC, Clark realized how lucky he had been on his promotion. The public discussion might have prompted the Senate to hold up confirmation.

The clamor at home, Clark thought, was unrealistic. The Allies needed quick results as a matter of military necessity. Only Darlan could provide them. Without his cooperation, the Allies and the French might have fought on, with both sides losing men needlessly. This would have been advantageous only to the Axis. The Clark–Darlan agreement, Clark was sure, was correct.

By now Clark and Darlan were becoming friends. They talked to each other about their families. They gained mutual respect for each other. Clark began using his "rusty" French.

On November 22, they signed a formal agreement that had been drafted in London and approved by the Combined Chiefs of Staff. The French in North Africa promised to aid the Allied forces to expel the common enemy, the Allies pledged to liberate France and restore the French empire.

Clark then wrote Eisenhower a letter. "I know the hell you have been taking," he said, "sitting in that damn tunnel, but don't think I haven't had my share of it here. I have never gone through ten days like this before in my life, but I must say that we are now obtaining the best combination of results that I think were possible to squeeze out of the dirty mess we found here. I don't mind making decisions—you know that—but it is doubly hard when you make them knowing that they are another's [Eisenhower's] responsibility. I have not once asked you to come over here [permanently], for I thought that was your decision, but I do want you to know that when you do come it will certainly be a great relief to me. I think that the time has come when you should be here."

On the afternoon of November 23, the day after the formal signing of the Clark–Darlan agreement, Eisenhower arrived in Algiers. Although he and Darlan on the following day initialled five corrections in the document, Eisenhower had, whether consciously and deliberately or simply as a result of happenstance, kept himself out of and far from the negotiations of the Darlan deal. To all superficial appearances, he was scrupulously clean.

Clark had done the dirty work for him. Sometimes Clark "had the feeling," he later said, that Eisenhower "thought it best to remain where he was" at Gibraltar "and not inject himself" into the "problem." Had their positions been reversed, had Clark "been the commander, I would have left the deputy at Gibraltar." But he was unwilling to "challenge Ike's motives. I think he sincerely felt he should remain at Gibraltar, and perhaps when the Darlan thing was about to explode, thought it was a pretty good idea that he had remained there." If Clark sensed that Eisenhower had outsmarted or manipulated him, he gave no sign of annoyance or resentment.

Eisenhower's arrival in Algiers brought to a close the first phase of operations in North Africa. That period had been Mark Clark's show all the way.

CHAPTER 11

☆ ☆ ☆ ☆

THE FIFTH ARMY

"The best trainer, organizer, and planner I have ever met"

EISENHOWER WAS SUFFERING from a bad cold, and Clark remained very much in charge. Although a few officers were laying the foundations of the Fifth Army, Clark was busy with the French and with the fighting in Tunisia.

Newspaper clippings of his submarine voyage reached Algiers from the United States. The story, Clark noted, got a "terrific play." But he scarcely realized how the account tickled the public's fancy and how widely recognized his name and photograph became. He was surprised when his son Bill, a plebe at West Point, wrote him how well known his feat had made Bill. He replied, "So you have become famous on account of my exploits."

The New Yorker magazine interviewed retired Major Rafferty, Clark's cousin and lifelong friend, who said that relatives referred to Clark's adventure as "the day Wayne lost his pants." Louella Parsons, the Hollywood reporter, called Clark "America's dream hero." According to a Boston newspaper, every war produced an act of personal daring, ingenuity, and devotion that gave individuals a permanent place in history; Nathan Hale had been the first such American, Clark was the latest.

He became the object of adulation, and received gifts and letters from strangers. Parents of twin boys named them Mark and Clark. Hollywood planned a major motion picure of his exploit. A 13-year-old girl in North Carolina saw him in the newsreels and returned again and again to the movie theater to watch him on the screen.

The Amalgamated Clothing Workers of America sent a telegram to Clark's wife: "He lost his trousers honorably. He is a living example of the fact that a great hero need not lose his dignity thereby." As a consequence, "the most skilled pantsmakers in the world will be honored to make and present . . . as many pairs of trousers as he may need in bringing the war to the enemy." Would Mrs. Clark be so good as to send his measurements.

A young lady in Quebec knew Clark only from his photographs in the press, and she studied the pictures and wrote to him. He had, she said, "an energetic face that breathes moral elegance and imposes respect—a pure oval. Raven hair. Olympic brow. Deep brown eyes. The glance of an eagle. The nose of the Bourbons, mark of kindness and genius. A smile at once melancholy and jesting. Ears a little long. I have the impression that you descend from a strong race; a race that has bequeathed to you the resistance of an oak."

It was all very amusing and heady.

The War Department approved awards for the submarine adventure, and Eisenhower decorated Clark with the Distinguished Service Medal and Clark's companions with the Legion of Merit.

Far from Algiers, Patton in Morocco burned with resentment. He wrote to his wife, "I heard that Clark got a M. H. [Medal of Honor] for riding a sub-marine. I don't believe it but still it is not plesant [sic]." Patton had never won that award.

Intelligence information concerning Spanish Morocco led Eisenhower and Clark to ask Patton to Algiers for a conference. He arrived late on the afternoon of December 1. That evening, as the three officers were conversing, Eisenhower received a telephone call from Gibraltar, which relayed a message from Washington. Eisenhower listened, then turned and said, "Well, Wayne, you get the Fifth Army."

Patton was bitterly disappointed. Frankly, he recorded in his diary, "it was a shock."

Clark said, "Georgie, I am sick you didn't get it."

"I sat on for half an hour and left," Patton wrote. "I felt so awful that I could not sleep for a while."

Two weeks earlier he had written in his diary, it "looks as if Clark who has never commanded a battalion will get the Fifth Army." Now he wrote to his wife, "The Fifth Army under Clark . . . makes me mad but there is nothing that can be done about it."

According to Eisenhower, when the War Department was considering activating the Fifth Army, Clark "was very anxious to have that command instead of his then title of Deputy Commander in Chief." Eisenhower warned Clark that the Fifth Army would at first be a training organization. If Clark waited, he was likely to lead a corps in combat.

Whose corps was less than clear. There were two headquarters in North Africa, Patton's in Morocco and Fredendall's in Algiers, and neither was involved in the fighting. Was Eisenhower thinking of sending Fredendall home and putting Clark in command to campaign in Tunisia? Or, more probably, would Clark get Patton's corps if Patton headed the Fifth Army? Perhaps Eisenhower was looking ahead to the VI Corps, which was soon to sail from the United States to North Africa.

Whatever these prospects, Clark had already commanded a corps in England. He wanted an army. As Eisenhower said, "The title of Army Commander was too attractive" to Clark, and he "begged and pleaded" for it "for a long time." Had Eisenhower then succumbed, as he seemed to imply to Clark's pressure?

Eisenhower, no doubt, was torn by his loyalty to his two close friends. If he felt Patton deserving of the appointment on the basis of age and combat experience, he thought Clark worthy of it because of his contributions to Torch. Patton had covered himself with glory in the landings and subsequent fighting in Morocco, but without Clark, it was difficult even to imagine how the entire operations and the negotiations with Darlan could have succeeded. Furthermore, if the Fifth Army was to train troops at the outset, it was logical to select Clark, for in the fields of "organization and training," Eisenhower said, "I think Clark has no superior." Finally, command of a field army called for three-star rank; Clark was already a lieutenant general while Patton still wore the two stars of a major general.

Although Eisenhower had backed Clark from the first, even before the Torch landings, and although his recommendation carried weight, Marshall, who knew Patton and Clark well and appreciated their talents, made the choice.

For his part, Clark had "thought considerably," as he later said, "about what the future held for me and what course I should pursue, where I would feel more at home. I came to the definite conclusion at that time that I would not want to go through the rest of the war as a staff officer. I wanted to be on the command side and be with troops." He had been the number two man, an assistant, far too long with McNair and Eisenhower.

With Bedell Smith—as Clark called him, "a dynamic person"—now Eisenhower's Chief of Staff, Clark saw himself as somewhat of a supernumerary. He shared with Smith what he called many "overlapping duties." Eisenhower, Clark thought, "would not be happy" to lose him, but he "could get along without me" because Bedell Smith was altogether capable and strong.

"There wasn't a potential commander anywhere," Clark said, "who would not have hoped to get the Fifth Army." After serving for so many years in staff positions, after giving up the II Corps in England, Clark was eager to command troops. "As Ike's Deputy, I saw all the correspondence received from the time the Army was considered. Ike and I lived together in a house in Algiers. We discussed the Fifth Army many times, and he discussed potential commanders, and at the beginning indicated that I was one who would be considered. I never initiated any action by asking for command of the Fifty Army. He had told me I was being considered. I told him I would be most happy to have it, naturally."

The official cable from Marshall to Eisenhower—"Authority is granted you to activate Fifth Army Headquarters designating Lieutenant General Clark as the Army Commander"—reached Algiers on December 2. Eisenhower gave him the document. Elated, Clark passed it to his aide with a pencilled note, "Jack: Oh boy, put this in Archives!! MWC 12/2." He meant his personal papers.

He had already tentatively selected his key officers. Gruenther, the youngest major general in the U.S. Army, would be his Chief of Staff and principal assistant, Edwin Howard, Clark's subordinate at Fort Lewis, his intelligence officer.

The Fifth Army headquarters would come into being early in January 1943, with its initial mission to keep Spanish Morocco under surveillance, but Marshall suggested an additional function for Clark—to become the chief American military adviser to Churchill in England. From time to time Clark could fly to North Africa to look after the Fifth Army activities.

Marshall was undoubtedly looking ahead to a cross-Channel invasion. He saw Clark, who was close to Churchill, as the figure around whom the Americans could build their military strength in England. Clark's executive abilities, his broad outlook, and his tact and friendship with the British made him the logical officer to organize, then to head the American contingent crossing the Channel and landing on the European continent.

Clark was uninterested in what he termed a political–military liaison job. He regarded it as a place where he was supposed, he said, "to hold Mr. Churchill's hand." He wanted no part of it. He wished to command his army and to be with troops. American generals, he believed, should command American soldiers in battle. The thought of leading the Fifth Army in some operation in the months ahead captivated him.

No offensive launched from North Africa, he was sure, would be decisive in winning the war. A crushing blow to the Axis, he was certain, had to come from the United Kingdom. But a cross-Channel attack still lay in the distant and indefinite future. In contrast, the Mediterranean was an organized and active combat zone. He was impatient to get into action.

He would wait a long time, and then, as he was about to get his wish, he missed a great opportunity. For in September 1943, the Americans had to choose an officer to go to England and begin preparing for the Normandy landings codenamed Overlord; eventually that officer would lead the American combat forces. Patton, a contender for the post, was in disgrace because a month earlier, while visiting hospitals in Sicily, he had, on two separate occasions a week apart, slapped soldiers he believed to be malingerers. Eisenhower thought him too impulsive for a position requiring thoroughly controlled judgment. Clark, an obvious candidate, was about to lead the Fifth Army in the Salerno landings and could not be spared. As a consequence, Omar Bradley, a relatively obscure corps commander, received the assignment. He went to London to organize the First U.S. Army and the First U.S. Army Group for Overlord.

Had Clark accepted the job of being the American adviser to Churchill, he would have been in the right place; he would almost certainly have had the responsibilities entrusted to Bradley. Clark's standing was high. In a private assessment dictated to his aide in mid-December 1942, Eisenhower said, "Clark is an unusual individual and is particularly strong in his organizational ability and orderliness of his mind."

On December 23, 1942, Clark talked with Darlan. It was time, he said, for Darlan to think of resigning as High Commissioner in favor of Giraud. Darlan had accomplished a great deal. Although the French fleet had scuttled itself at Toulon, Darlan had unified the French in North Africa and had maintained an internal stability essential for Allied operations in Tunisia. Now it was better for him to step down, to remove all trace of Pétain's Vichy government. Darlan nodded in agreement.

On the following day a French student assassinated him.

The French wished Nogues to succeed Darlan, but Clark objected. To him, Giraud was the only possible choice. After seemingly endless conferences all night and on Christmas Day, except for a quick holiday dinner with Murphy, Clark had his way. On December 26, despite Giraud's own desire to remain in a purely military position, he became the High Commissioner. This expunged the Darlan deal. In the coming months, under American pressure and guidance, Giraud rescinded the objectionable Vichy racial statutes and liberalized the French administration.

What concerned Clark mainly in December 1942 was the campaign in Tunisia, which was going badly. Riding in an armored Cadillac, escorted by two armed scout cars and two jeeps, accompanied by a baggage truck, he and Eisenhower visited the front and talked with Anderson, who described his problems. Strong Axis forces blocked his push toward Bizerte and Tunis, the strategic and ultimate objectives of Torch; a slender logistical lifeline gave him no more than a trickle of supplies and equipment; the weather had turned cold and rainy. They could expect no quick triumph.

Anderson failed to mention what was apparent to Eisenhower and Clark. Unnecessary friction and bickering among the British, Americans, and French hampered a unity of effort. In part this seemed to be Anderson's fault.

To Clark, putting American units under British command was wrong. It violated the precept of national sectors so tenaciously practiced and preserved by Pershing. Eisenhower's AFHQ was Allied in composition, but Anderson's First Army headquarters was thoroughly British. Instead of being fragmented and under British control, American units would be more effective if they fought together under Clark's Fifth Army.

Clark recommended a new command structure. Activate the Fifth Army with headquarters near the Algerian-Tunisian border. Assemble the American units in southern Tunisia under him. Estabish a small AFHQ tactical command post at Constantine to allow Eisenhower to direct Anderson's First Army and Clark's Fifth.

With these arrangements in place, Anderson was to continue pressing toward Bizerte and Tunis while Clark launched an attack toward Sfax. There Clark would have driven a wedge between the Axis forces holding Bizerte and Tunis in the northeastern corner of Tunisia and Rommel's forces withdrawing from Libya into the southern part of the country. By preventing the Axis units from consolidating, the Allies would fight two battles to eliminate the enemy, the British in the north, the Americans in the south.

Eisenhower seemed inclined to favor Clark's suggestion when a cable from Marshall changed his mind. Marshall wanted Clark's Fifth Army to be ready to act against Spanish Morocco. Fredendall's or Patton's corps, Marshall thought, could command the American forces in southern Tunisia.

Eisenhower chose Fredendall's headquarters, which was closer. The II Corps began to move from Algeria to take charge of an increasingly American part of the front. French units continued to serve in both the British and American zones.

The Fifth U.S. Army came into being under Clark's command on January 4, 1943. Of all the messages of congratulation he received, none pleased him more than word from Patton, ever outwardly correct and courteous, who assured Clark, his new boss, of his loyalty.

The staff members at AFHQ gave Clark a farewell party. He wrote a nice note to thank Eisenhower for "all the success that has come to me during the past few months." Serving close to Eisenhower, he said, had been his greatest privilege. The stresses they had shared made him fully comprehend the depth and strength of Eisenhower's character. He then relinquished his post as Deputy Commander in Chief.

Eisenhower made out Clark's efficiency report and rated him superior in all categories. He was "vigorous, energetic, ambitious, imaginative, and well informed." In a letter of appreciation, Eisenhower termed Clark's performance as no less than brilliant. "There have been certain instances in which your tact, breadth of vision, and clear understanding of basic issues have astonished me." He regretted losing Clark's services.

Riding with Colonel Joseph P. Sullivan, the Fifth Army Quartermaster and a West Point classmate, Clark left Algiers for Oujda and a new career development. Although he was sorry to cut his close ties with Eisenhower, he was happy to be out of the political hothouse at AFHQ and back in a more purely military assignment. In command of a thoroughly American army headquarters at the extremely young age of 46, he would be in charge of his own domain, boss of an army in the field. Responsible for the security of French Morocco and Algeria, he had under him Patton's corps headquarters and two U.S. divisions, Ernest N. Harmon's 2nd Armored and Lucian K. Truscott, Jr.'s 3rd Infantry.

At Oujda Clark met with his principal officers, toured the area, surprised the enlisted men by sticking out his hand and saying, "I'm Clark." He had the officers in to toast the Fifth Army, "the new baby." Before long he was working sixteen to eighteen hours a day.

Patton recorded in his diary Clark's first visit to his headquarters. "I met him and had a guard of honor...took him on an inspection of all local troops and installations. He was not in the least interested. His whole mind is on Clark."

Writing to his wife, Patton said, "I took W. [Wayne] all over the place and he was not in the least interested in the docks, the camps, or the men. All the conversation was on what he had done or hoped to do and the latter was pattently [sic] insincere."

No doubt his envy was showing.

The Casablanca conference, one of the great wartime meetings, brought Roosevelt and Churchill and their military advisers to Morocco. Although Clark took no part in the strategic matters discussed, he attended dinners and talked with Marshall, King, Brooke, and other dignitaries. One day he and Patton had lunch outdoors with the President and Harry Hopkins. "Clark is trying to be nice," Patton confided in his diary, "but it makes my flesh creep to be with him." Many photographers were present, and "millions of pictures were taken...all for the glory of F.D.R. and for Clark when he could get a chance. It was very disgusting." He regretted having to share the limelight with Clark.

The conference produced decisions ranging over the whole global strategy. Three were important for the Mediterranean area.

First, after Montgomery drove Rommel out of Libya and into southern Tunisia, an event expected in February, Alexander was to leave Cairo and come to Tunisia. Under Eisenhower, the theater commander, Alexander was to command the Allied ground forces and direct Anderson's First and Montgomery's Eighth British Armies to clear Tunisia of Axis troops.

Second, once the Allies had expelled the Axis from North Africa, they would invade Sicily and try to knock Italy out of the war. Marshall chose Patton for the American part of the endeavor, no doubt because he was combat experienced and because Clark had to be ready for Spanish Morocco. Patton's corps headquarters would become the Seventh U. S. Army headquarters in Sicily, and Alexander would direct Patton's and Montgomery's armies.

The Allies could reach no agreement on what to do beyond Sicily. The Americans and British saw the necessity for an eventual cross-Channel attack for ultimate victory, but shortages in shipping made this unlikely before 1944. Until then, to give the Axis no respite, it might be desirable to initiate additional activity in the Mediterranean region.

The third decision concerned the Fifth Army. In addition to watching Spanish Morocco, Clark was to direct a gigantic training program for American, British, and French troops.

Clark set up an Invasion Training Center at Arzew Beach under O'Daniel, now a brigadier general. He established schools to train specialists in mine-laying, demolitions, communications, and the like. He organized replacement training camps for individual soldiers coming from the United States. He laid out courses for mountain warfare, airborne operations, air-ground support.

But he wanted combat, not a repetition of his experience in World War I, and he pressed Eisenhower for a battle mission. As Eisenhower recalled, Clark and some of his staff officers began to "plague" him for action. They were "most unhappy" throughout the spring. Eisenhower assured Clark of his eventual participation in a major operation.

Rommel now made his presence felt in southern Tunisia. Attacking the French, he then threw Fredendall's II U. S. Corps into disarray. In a series of swift engagements, he drove the Americans and French back fifty miles to the Kasserine Pass. Inflicting a serious defeat on the Allies, he seemed about to push them out of Tunisia and to upset the calculations made and the conclusions reached at the Casablanca conference.

Sorely troubled, Eisenhower badly missed Clark. "You will never know," he wrote, "how close I came within the past few days when the pressure on me was very, very drastic indeed to call upon you once more to come and help out when I found it impossible to be in three distinct places at once. There is no one on whom I depend more."

On the verge of suffering a serious strategic defeat, Eisenhower dispatched tough and burly Ernie Harmon to stiffen Fredendall and turn things around. Alexander appeared on the scene and imparted a measure of stability. And Rommel's attack ran its course.

In the immediate aftermath of the battle, Eisenhower sent Patton to Tunisia to replace Fredendall, who had fallen apart during the crisis. Patton, together with Bradley, who served as his deputy corps commander, quickly rehabilitated the American units. After leading the corps in a successful attack and defense, Patton passed the corps command to Bradley and returned to Morocco to continue planning for Sicily.

On the periphery of events, Clark worked on his training programs, cruised in his 30-foot motor boat, mailed Renie pocketbooks and a bracelet, feasted with native rulers, hunted gazelles, watched stunts by Arab horsemen.

Responding to his mother's query why he had dropped out of the news, he said, "I have tried to make it clear to all my loved ones that I want to keep out of the press, so please help me in any way you can." To Renie, he was pleased that she was going to parties and meeting "all those prominent people."

McNair was gravely concerned by the American defeat in the battle of Kasserine Pass. In order to judge the combat deficiencies so that he might improve his training methods and ever anxious to see things for himself, McNair came to Tunisia and observed the fighting. He was wounded slightly and hospitalized in Oran. He telephoned Clark, who flew there to see him. They had a long talk.

"The British have gypped us out of everything," McNair said in disgust. Alexander, Anderson, and Montgomery were running the show, Eisenhower was nothing but a figurehead. It was a bad practice to have American troops under British command. The Fifth Army was being wasted and should be in England to prepare the cross-Channel invasion. The planning for Sicily was absurd, for Alexander and Montgomery were both fighting in Tunisia and could give no attention to the invasion of Sicily. If successful, the campaign in Sicily would bring no great reward, for there was lilttle point in attacking islands; better to go for the Continent.

Clark was sympathetic, not only because he was listening to his old boss, but also because he shared McNair's sentiments.

It would be the last time they saw each other. The following year, in order to enhance Allied plans to deceive the Germans along the Channel coast, McNair arrived in England and took command of a fictitious army group headquarters. Late in July he traveled to France to witness an attack. During the preliminary bombing, several Allied bombers accidentally dropped their loads short and struck the American line. Almost a hundred casualties resulted, among them McNair, who had been well up forward. Hastily and secretly so as not to divulge the deception role he was playing, a small body of high ranking officers interred him. John L. DeWitt flew to England to take McNair's place at the head of the mythical army group.

The combat in Tunisia came to an end in May 1943 on a great note of Allied triumph. The Americans under Bradley took Bizerte, but that seemed to Clark to be a sideshow compared to the newsprint and radio broadcasts devoted to the British entry into Tunis.

With North Africa clear of Axis forces, the Allies firmly scheduled the invasion of Sicily for July. They could not agree on where to go and what to do after Sicily. The question had been raised at the Casablanca conference—if the conquest of Sicily failed to push Italy out of the war and if further operations in the Mediterranean seemed necessary, what should be the next step? But no answer had emerged. Beyond Sicily, the Americans favored seizing Sardinia and Corsica on the way to southern France, where landings would support the Normandy invasion. The British wished to move against southern Italy, which led to the Adriatic and Aegean areas.

Feeling that the issue now required resolution, Churchill traveled to Washington in May and conferred with Roosevelt. They were unable to decide on a suitable course. With the President's approval, Churchill, accompanied by Marshall and Brooke, went to Algiers for discussions with Eisenhower.

The campaign in Sicily, Eisenhower said, would show the condition of the Italian forces. If they seemed about to collapse, the Allies should invade the mainland of Italy. If they remained strong, the Allies should go for Corsica and Sardinia.

On this basis they reached a compromise. Eisenhower was to make ready a variety of operations. After the fighting in Sicily revealed certain military realities, he would select the ventures he thought to be the most productive.

Implementing this decision, Eisenhower directed the British X Corps headquarters to plan a landing on the Italian toe, an operation codenamed Buttress. He instructed the British V Corps to look into another invasion of the toe, this one called Goblet. He asked Giraud to prepare for the possible movement of French troops to Corsica. He told Clark to give his attention to a descent on Sardinia.

After the meetings in Algiers, Marshall visited some American installations in North Africa to observe the troops and to talk with commanders. He traveled to Clark's headquarters. Then he and Clark went to Morocco to see Patton. There Marshall and Clark listened as Patton explained his plans for invading Sicily. Patton was well aware of Marshall's high regard for Clark. "In Clark's presence," Patton later wrote in his diary, "I told General Marshall how helpful Clark has been. I am getting tactful as hell, and in this case it is true." Clark had facilitated and expedited Patton's requests for resources. But Patton could not resist adding in the privacy of his journal, "I think that if you treat a skunk nicely, he will not piss on you—as often."

Filling out Clark's efficiency report, Eisenhower rated him as "The best trainer, organizer, and planner I have ever met. Energetic, forceful, loyal."

In a private assessment, Eisenhower wrote, "He thinks in an orderly and logical fashion and is energetic in carrying an adopted plan into execution. While at one stage of the operations it seemed that he was becoming a bit consumed with a drive to push himself, all that has disappeared—if it ever existed—and he is certainly one of the very best we have. His only drawback now is a lack of combat experience in a high command position. This I tried to give him in the early days of organizing an American task force in the central Tunisian front. I still think that he could successfully command an army in operations."

As Patton's Seventh Army and Montgomery's Eighth, both under Alexander, invaded Sicily on July 10, Clark followed the operations closely. News from the British Broadcasting Corporation, he remarked, told much more about the British soldiers than about the Americans. That the American units were receiving less attention was, to Clark, unfair. If ever he commanded American troops in concert with the British, he would, he vowed, make sure of equal billing.

The invasion of Sicily revealed how weak and poorly motivated the Italian forces were. If another operation after Sicily was necessary to compel the Italians to surrender, the mainland seemed to be the best place to go. Eisenhower told Clark to drop his planning for Sardinia and to consider landings at Naples and elsewhere.

Without a precise invasion target, Clark and his staff worked hectically on all sorts of plans—to sail into the bay of Naples if the Italians collapsed, to battle ashore at Naples against strong German defenses, to come across the beaches near Gaeta just above Naples or near Salerno just below.

Of all the possibilities, Clark preferred Gaeta. The main problem was: did Allied single-engine warplanes have sufficient range to cover and protect landing forces there? American airmen assured him positively on this point. When he telephoned Air Chief Marshal Sir Arthur Tedder, who commanded the Allied air forces, he received a negative reply. Air cover north of Naples, Tedder said, was out of the question. The American air planners then backed down. Any chance for Gaeta disappeared when the Navy judged the offshore waters there to be far too dangerous. For

Clark, the meaning was clear: "Our air people, as well as our land and sea people," he wrote in his diary, "are very much under British domination and control."

With Gaeta ruled out, Salerno, despite many disadvantages, became the best location. Plans for an invasion at Salerno took the code name Avalanche.

On July 25, with great suddenness, Benito Mussolini was removed from power. Although his successor, Marshal Pietro Badoglio, publicly announced Italy's continuing commitment to Germany and to the war, the prospect of an Italian surrender grew more likely. That made invading the mainland more attractive. Avalanche, despite the risks of landing at Salerno, risks far greater than launching Buttress and Goblet on the toe, became more feasible.

As Eisenhower juggled Buttress, Goblet, and Avalanche in his mind, weighing the drawbacks and benefits of each, a fourth option emerged. All three forces would have to sail across the sea from North Africa to their destinations, whereas the Allied units enaged in Sicily were much closer to the Italian mainland. At the end of the campaign, the Strait of Messina, two miles of water, would separate them from the Italian toe. Eisenhower entrusted the idea of moving across the strait, an operation codenamed Baytown, to Montgomery.

Thus, all the landings being planned to take place on the toe, Baytown, Buttress, and Goblet, were British ventures. If Eisenhower cancelled Avalanche because of its inherent hazards, only British troops would invade Italy.

Clark was disturbed. Were the British endeavoring to monopolize the entry into the Italian mainland and into the European continent? Were they trying to freeze the Americans out of the glory? Was the patttern of the BBC reporting in Sicily to be repeated in Italy? Were the British seeking to give the impression that they alone were winning the war?

His suspicions were further aroused when Lieutenant General Sir B. G. Horrocks, who commanded the X Corps, came to lunch. Combat experienced, self-assured, and somewhat patronizing toward the younger Clark, Horrocks was there to discuss his possible role in Avalanche. Although he was planning to execute Buttress on the toe if Eisenhower so decided, he was also to be ready to serve under Clark in Avalanche. For if Eisenhower chose Avalanche, Clark was to have Horrocks' X Corps and the VI U. S. Corps under his command. Both organizations were to go ashore side by side, then head for the ultimate objective, Naples. How should the two corps be placed relative to each other?

If Baytown or Goblet or both struck into the toe, it made sense to have the British X Corps on the Fifth Army right, closer to the British forces coming up from the south. Horrocks agreed, then had qualms. If the VI Corps was on the left and closer to Naples, the Americans were likely to get into Naples first, ahead of the British.

The troops of both nationalities, Clark said firmly, would enter Naples together and share the victory.

Early in August, while the fighting in Sicily continued, Eisenhower provisionally selected Montgomery's Baytown and Clark's Avalanche for the invasion of the Italian mainland. Stressing the tentative nature of his decision, wishing to be prudent rather than rash, he refused to give definite word until the Sicilian campaign ended.

To Clark, Eisenhower's postponement of his final decision seemed to reflect a painful uncertainty, wavering, and weakness. Eisenhower was, Clark wrote in his diary, "having difficulty in deciding how to shape the campaign beyond Sicily." Alexander and Montgomery were still running the show, and Eisenhower was "not making a move without their consent and approval. In fact, he is accepting their decisions rather than making them himself."

From Clark's point of view, Baytown, crossing the Strait of Messina, was logical. The other two British operations on the toe, Buttress and Goblet, were strategically insignificant. Avalanche was bold, carried the element of surprise, and struck closer to the Italian heart.

On the other hand, Avalanche posed far more dangers to success. The voyage from North Africa to Salerno was longer, thus giving the Germans greater opportunity to discover the ships on their course, to attack them, and to damage the composition of the forces about to land; if they guessed the destination of the vessels, they could strengthen their defenses at Salerno. A ring of hills enclosed and dominated the Salerno beaches and gave the defenders excellent observation for their artillery fire, fire that might destroy the invasion at the water's edge. Salerno was at the maximum range of single-engine fighter planes; as a consequence, the aircraft could remain over Salerno for a minimum length of time, twenty minutes at most, no more than ten if they encountered German planes and had to drop their extra gasoline tanks. The Sele River separated the invasion beaches into two compartments, thereby splitting the landing forces and making it difficult for one to reinforce the other. An enemy thrust down the Sele River valley to the sea would mean almost certain defeat for the landings. After the Americans and British established themselves on land and possessed Salerno, they would find the way to Naples blocked by a mountainous mass of ground; two narrow passes pierced this massif, and they would be easy for the Germans to plug, difficult for the Allies to get through. Finally, the Allied troops at Salerno would be distant from help.

Avalanche nevertheless promised greater rewards. On that basis, whether Eisenhower would "insist on Avalanche or allow himself to be again persuaded by the British to follow their wishes" was a burning question. Under British pressure, he might cancel Avalanche because of its risks. Clark, his Fifth Army, and the Americans would then be out in the cold.

These thoughts were very much on Clark's mind when Juin came to visit. Their initial antipathy in Algiers had given way to mutual respect and liking. They talked about the problems of re-equipping and retraining the French troops in North Africa. When they reached combat readiness, Juin said, he hoped that they would be sent somewhere to fight. There was talk of forming them into a corps-sized body under Juin's command. If the Fifth Army was by then engaged in Italy, Juin would be happy to serve under Clark.

Clark was of course delighted. The possibility of having French units gave him an idea.

Traveling to Algiers, he took advantage of his close friendship with Eisenhower. He told him, according to his diary, "in positive terms and with intense feeling how important" he thought it was for "an early decision...on future operations." Avalanche was much better than the other enterprises. Yet Alexander and Montgomery seemed "dead set" to do Baytown and Buttress. If they had their way, the invasion of the mainland would be strictly a British undertaking. That would be a mistake. After landing on the toe, the British would work their way inch by inch up the Italian boot in a long and costly campaign.

Clark had an alternative suggestion. Let the British do Baytown and Buttress, but keep enough ships to land one American division at Salerno, later a second, and still later the French. That would get the Americans into Naples and possibly into Rome while the British were still fighting their way out of the toe. In the heat of his indignation and fervor, he codenamed his proposal Operation Pisspot.

Eisenhower accepted the tirade calmly. He would make no decision until the campaign in Sicily was over. He preferred Avalanche over Buttress. He even liked Clark's proposition. According to Clark's diary, Eisenhower promised to use all of Clark's arguments when he conferred again with Alexander and Montgomery.

On August 16, the day the fighting ended in Sicily, Eisenhower made up his mind. Baytown, crossing the Strait of Messina into the toe, was to go sometime early in September, whenever Montgomery judged his troops to be ready. Avalanche was to come ashore near Salerno on September 9. Thus, Clark's Fifth Army and Montgomery's Eighth Army would be involved. Alexander's 15th Army Group headquarters would direct Clark and Montgomery in Italy.

With Buttress cancelled, the X Corps and its two British divisions came under Clark for Avalanche. Because of a dearth of landing ships, the U. S. VI Corps had a single American division as its component. With the ultimate objective Naples, Clark placed the stronger British corps on the Fifth Army left, closer to the city.

Horrocks was injured during a bombing raid on Bizerte, and Lieutenant General Sir Richard L. McCreery replaced him. Older than Clark, he was, as Clark later said, straightbacked, tough, and unbending. They were never close friends.

At the head of the VI Corps was Major General Ernest J. Dawley. He too was older than and senior to Clark. He had been with Pershing in Mexico and France and was a close friend of McNair. Before releasing the VI Corps headquarters to North Africa and the Fifth Army, McNair had cabled Clark, "Will you accept Dawley?"

Clark was reluctant to do so. He hardly knew Dawley but he wanted someone younger, "more my contemporary."

Eisenhower understood. "Well, Wayne," he said, "you are so close to McNair, it's up to you. If you don't want him, I will back you up."

Clark was unable to refuse Dawley on the basis of his age, particularly when McNair and Marshall were confident of his abilities.

In North Africa, Clark found Dawley autocratic and austere in temperament. He formally admonished Dawley at least once—and it was painful to do so to an older officer—on the appearance and behavior of his soldiers who were often out of uniform, slow to salute, and deficient in mililtary discipline and courtesy. Yet when Eisenhower asked how Dawley was doing, Clark was loyal to his subordinate. Dawley was all right, he said.

Eisenhower remained skeptical. In a letter written late in August, he named the officers in the theater who in his opinion could command a corps in combat. He added, "possibly Dawley."

Under Dawley, Major General Fred L. Walker commanded the 36th Division. Walker was also older than Clark. He had been Clark's instructor at the War College, a colleague of his and one grade higher at Fort Lewis. When McNair had to replace the National Guard commander of the Texas 36th Division, Walker had been Clark's choice. Walker had achieved prominence in World War I when his battalion stopped a German attempt to cross the Marne River. The exploit would later haunt Walker at the Rapido. He would see himself in exactly the position of the Germans whom his men had slaughtered.

Ryder's 34th Division was also available. Ryder had carried out the Torch landings near Algiers and had fought in Tunisia. Had Clark had enough ships, he would have taken Ryder's combat experienced troops for Avalanche.

He chose Walker's untried 36th for several reasons. Dawley and Walker had a good working relationship. There had been some question over the 34th's effectiveness in the latter part of the Tunisian campaign. No doubt too, a successful performance by the 36th would demonstrate the soundness of McNair's and Clark's training methods. And finally, from Ultra intercepts, no one expected the Germans to oppose the landings in strength.

At the last minute, enough ships were found to transport a large part of the 45th Division from Sicily to Salerno. Troy Middleton, the division commander, was a World War I veteran, an older man who was solid.

Ridgway's 82d Airborne Division would also take part. The parachute and glider soldiers were to come to earth along the Volturno River, some twenty miles north of Naples, create a diversion, and draw enemy attention away from Salerno. To take early possession of the two mountain passes leading from Salerno to Naples, Clark obtained a ranger and commando force.

Eisenhower explained to Marshall the rationale of these arrangements. Because the British Eighth Army was to cross the Strait of Messina, he wanted an American Army headquarters on the mainland too, for parity. Patton, perhaps Bradley, were more obvious choices for Avalanche, but they had been busy in Sicily. Because the Fifth Army had been free to plan and prepare the operation, "I had no recourse but to name Clark to command that expedition." Bradley was keeping in close touch with Avalanche in order to take over if Clark became a casualty. When Bradley left for England to prepare for Overlord, Patton succeeded him as Clark's understudy.

What the invasion of Italy was supposed to accomplish was less than altogether clear. The Combined Chiefs of Staff had laid down two objectives: gain the surrender of Italy and tie down the maximum number of German troops. The first was as good as done. Secretly and unknown to the Germans, the Badoglio government had made contact with Eisenhower, was negotiating to capitulate, and would surrender on September 2. The invasion would then do little more than confirm Italy's withdrawal from the war; Eisenhower and Badoglio were to announce publicly the Italian capitulation a few hours before Clark's men landed near Salerno.

The second requirement, tying down as many German troops as possible in order to prevent their transfer to the Russian front or to the Channel defenses, was so vague as to be almost useless as a guide to action. According to Ultra secret intercepts of German messages, Hitler intended, in the event of an Italian surrender, to give up all of southern Italy and more. He would withdraw the substantial German forces in the south at once to Rome, then move them farther north, probably to a line across the peninsula roughly from Pisa to Rimini in order to hold the rich agricultural and industrial valley of the Po.

In this case, Clark would probably walk into Salerno, march into Naples, and follow the retreating Germans into Rome and beyond.

But what was Montgomery's role? He signaled to Alexander in his unequivocal fashion, "I have been given no clear objective for the operation." Alexander told him to be ready, after crossing the Strait of Messina, to push to Salerno to help Clark if unexpected difficulties arose there.

That was hardly a long-range goal. The Italian campaign, from its beginning, had no specific strategic aim. The Allies fighting in Italy would improvise. Without firm guidelines and expectations, they would react and respond to the German decisions, which would in large part determine the course of the combat. This was what was responsible for the postwar controversy.

As British and Canadian soldiers crossed the Strait of Messina into the toe against no opposition in Baytown, and as Eisenhower sent a British division to Taranto in an impromptu and uncontested landing, Badoglio worried about announcing, as he had promised Eisenhower, Italy's surrender. He feared that the statement would prompt the Germans to occupy Rome and to capture and imprison the royal family and the government. Eisenhower decided to send Ridgway's airborne division to the capital, to parachute on nearby airfields. But when it appeared that Italian military forces were unable to guarantee their possession of those airfields, Eisenhower cancelled the operation. It was then too late to reinstate the jumps along the Volturno that Clark wanted as a diversion in Avalanche.

Troubled by the loss of his diversionary effort, aware of the difficulties of landing at Salerno, but outwardly calm, Clark boarded the *U. S. S. Ancon*, the flagship of Admiral H. Kent Hewitt, who commanded the 450 vessels about to transport the invasion force to their invasion site. There Clark would receive his initiation to combat in World War II.

He and Renie made it a practice every day to read from the same book of daily prayers. The one that evening seemed particularly apt. Clark read, "With Thee I am unafraid, for on Thee my mind is stayed. Though a thousand foes surround, safe in Thee I shall be found... In the air, on sea or land, Thy sure protection is at hand."

Comforted, he slept soundly.

CHAPTER 12

☆ ☆ ☆ ☆

SALERNO

"this trying time"

"IT IS APPARENT to those close to him," an associate wrote during the voyage to Salerno, "that General Clark is feeling the strain of this period of waiting for Operation Avalanche to commence. There is nothing that he himself can do now. He has placed his troops, his officers and himself in the hands of the navy and must await their delivery upon Italian shores before he will be able again to assume active command."

Like athletes before a game or a competition, like actors and musicians before a performance, whose normal stage fright or nervousness vanishes as soon as the contest or presentation begins, Clark could not help feeling the pressures of leadership in general and his position in particular. Compared to Montgomery and to his immediate superior Alexander, he was inexperienced and had much to learn. Avalanche would prove his capacity as an army commander in battle. On him devolved the primary responsibility not only for the lives of the men under him but also for the outcome of the operation. Success would shorten the war, lead to ultimate victory, and justify the expenditure of human beings in battle. Failure would set back the Allies, make tragic the loss of life, shatter the hopes of people everywhere, and ruin him personally.

Whatever inner qualms he may have had, he could not let down Eisenhower, who had given him his big chance; he had to look good vis-à-vis his British colleagues; he had to uphold the prestige of the U. S. Army.

In addition to these normal considerations, Clark had another problem, that of exercising command over his principal subordinate commanders. McCreery, who headed the X Corps, was British, and Clark, an American, had to deal with him circumspectly, with discretion and tact. Coalition courtesy dicated that relationship.

Although the conventions of the British-American alliance permitted the leader of one nation to direct, actually to command, troops of the other, the situation was otherwise observed in practice. When a superior and a subordinate were of different nationalities, the superior maintained a certain distance. Clark had every right to inspect, observe, and supervise McCreery's actions. He could suggest and, if the occasion warranted, try to persuade McCreery to the course Clark desired. But if McCreery's performance was less than satisfactory, Clark would have to invite the attention of Alexander, a British officer, to that fact and request him to remedy the deficiency.

With his American subordinates, Clark could be more direct, even ruthless in his dealings, for the niceties of coalition politeness did not apply. He could, if he wished, stride decisively into their command posts, receive their reports, ask them questions, and issue instructions. But he had great respect for his division commanders. Walker and Middleton were both older than he and more senior in the old Regular Army. In addition, they had distinguished themselves in France in 1918 as troop commanders in combat.

He would, he later said, invariably ask for the opinions of his principal subordinate commanders. "I did not necessarily accept their advice but I gave them the opportunity of voicing their opinions and then I had to make a decision which I thought would best carry out the objectives assigned me. In the case of Dawley, I don't think he liked serving under me any better than I liked having him, and not having much faith in his capacity, perhaps I didn't lean on his advice or ask for it." Like Eisenhower, he already questioned Dawley's abilities.

Shortly before they had embarked for Salerno, Dawley had quoted to Clark a statement attributed to Fox Conner, Pershing's operations officer.

Conner had had great influence on younger officers after the Great War, and, according to Dawley, had said, "Don't bite off more than you can chew, and chew damn little." Clark interpreted this to mean that Dawley wondered whether he could carry out his mission successfully. To Clark, this was anathema.

If Clark had had nagging doubts of a less than committed and aggressive attitude on the part of the naval commanders, he was impressed by the manifest strength and order of the convoys. They steamed majestically on a roundabout route toward the bay of Salerno. The sea was calm, the weather bright.

Whatever he thought about the perils and problems that lay ahead, Clark exuded confidence. To show optimism and decision, to be strong and unruffled, no matter what his concerns, was the role of the commander.

He was very much aware of the difficulties of Avalanche. All amphibious ventures were hazardous. Ground troops on the high seas were in a strange and unfamiliar environment. As they transferred from ship to shore, they were extremely vulnerable to enemy action. Until they established themselves firmly on land and gathered strength, their situation was risky.

The enemy in southern Italy far outnumbered Clark's initial assault force. The Italians would presumably be eliminated when the government capitulated, but 135,000 Germans would meet the Fifth Army. On the first day 30,000 British and 25,000 Americans would go ashore, landing along 36 miles of coastline. The invaders would be a thin line of men stretched across the Salerno plain and exposed to the eyes and fire of defenders on towering and rugged heights ringing the beaches. If the Allies could stake out a firm beachhead, they would then have to drive quickly through two narrow gorges piercing the Sorrento massif in order to get to Naples.

Other uncertainties of a more general sort clouded the immediate future. The planners had meticulously prepared Avalanche, but the vagaries of luck, chance, divine providence, or mere accident, to say nothing of what the enemy might do, could disrupt schedules and timetables and bring the invasion to chilling defeat.

The only help that Clark could expect was from Montgomery's forces on the toe, 150 miles and more below Salerno. Were they too far away? Unless they moved quickly to Salerno, Clark's men would have to fight alone.

Aboard the *Ancon* Clark watched closely the reports of Montgomery's progress. His units were, Clark noted in his diary, "proceeding with little or no resistance . . . and presumably they are ready to help us." On the following day Clark recorded, the opposition against Montgomery appeared to vary "from light to none at all."

Yet Montgomery advanced slowly on the toe against two German divisions, who gave up ground grudgingly. Would they prevent Montgomery from getting to Salerno in time to help Clark?

But why should he need assistance? The surrender of Italy, to be announced by Eisenhower in Algiers and Badoglio in Rome, would, according to all estimates, produce great confusion among the Germans. They would be unable to react effectively against the invasion.

In that case, Clark was ready to take advantage of their bewilderment. He would send his floating reserve directly into Naples. He would dispatch one flying column eastward across the Italian peninsula to capture the airfields around Foggia. He would start another northward to seize Rome.

Unfortunately, he wrote a few days later to his wife Renie, "We had the wrong dope" on the Italian surrender.

At 6:30 P.M. on September 8, listening to the radio on Hewitt's cabin, Clark heard Eisenhower announce the Italian capitulation. Shortly afterward, Badoglio confirmed the event.

The surrender came as no great surprise to Adolf Hitler. For several months he had expected Italy to withdraw from the alliance and from the war. He was careful to avoid precipitating an Italian capitulation, for Italy as an ally was important to his war effort. Italian troops bolstered German units not only in Italy but also in the Balkans and southern France. If Italy committed what he called treachery and fell out of the war, Germany would have to fulfill these functions.

To cope with a capitulation, Hitler in May 1943 thought of taking over all of Italy. Rommel would march from Munich to northern Italy while Field Marshal Albert Kesselring defended in the south.

Perhaps Ultra Secret intercepts had relayed this intention to Washington, where Roosevelt and Churchill were meeting in May to decide on post-Sicily operations. If Hitler planned to occupy all Italy, an Allied invasion would be difficult.

Two months later, in July, Hitler admitted, "We cannot hold the entire peninsula without the Italian Army." How much he thought he could keep he did not say.

Shocked by Mussolini's downfall and anticipating Italy's defection in the very near future, Hitler instructed Rommel to be ready to occupy the north as before. But now Kesselring was to move out of southern Italy, first to the Rome area, then farther north to consolidate his forces with Rommel's. A strong defensive line somewhere in the northern Apennines was to protect the Po Valley and its rich agricultural and industrial resources.

Ultra intercepts revealed Hitler's plans to the Allies. Consequently, an invasion at Salerno would accelerate the German retirement. The Fifth Army would move to Rome on the heels of the departing Germans.

At a conference on the last day of August, James M. Gavin, a young paratrooper general who was not privy to Ultra, was surprised by the confidence expressed by the senior commanders for a quick victory. There was, he later said, "some loose talk about how long it would take to get to Rome." Clark joked about having adequate facilities for the press in Rome, and everyone, Gavin recalled, "chuckled sympathetically."

What was unfortunate about Avalanche was the timing. Coming immediately after the surrender announcement, the Salerno invasion struck before the two German divisions opposing Montgomery on the toe could get out. This compelled the German defenders around Salerno to stand and fight. For they had to keep control of the roads leading from the south to Rome to permit the two divisions to withdraw safely.

On news of the surrender, many Italian military units simply melted away. Men abandoned their posts, weapons, and uniforms, and returned home. The Germans had few complications in southern Italy. Around Salerno a panzer division took over the Italian coastal positions. There was hardly a ripple of uncertainty or confusion.

The Allied fleet arrived in the bay of Salerno after darkness on the pitch black night of September 8 and assembled a dozen miles out to sea. In the early minutes of September 9, soldiers clambered down the sides of the transports and into boats, which pulled away and headed for rendezvous areas three miles offshore. Columns of small craft finally headed toward the shoreline. Rangers and commandos hit the beach at 3:10 in the morning, the main forces arrived twenty minutes later.

Hope of happy Italians welcoming the invaders vanished at the outset. Flares illuminated the beaches, and enemy fire rained down. In both the British and American zones, the German reaction disrupted the assault waves and checked an orderly advance inland. The normal confusion of an amphibious landing intensified. Some troops met resistance a few hundred yards from the shore, others a mile and a half beyond. Yet boats continued to carry men to land, and by individual and team exertion and heroism, the assault groups made progress.

Standing with Hewitt on the bridge of the *Ancon*, Clark had a "helpless feeling—all out of my hands until we get reports." Even after daylight, which brought cloudless weather, the scene was anything but reassuring. German artillery fire continued to fall, making it impossible to land on some designated beaches. Allied boats appeared to scurry about aimlessly. Some were hit. German planes bombed the beachhead as well as Allied ships.

To Clark, who was waiting for word on what was taking place, the lack of knowledge prompted mental suffering. Messages from shore were infrequent and fragmentary. Casualties returning to hospital ships told exaggerated stories of German combat power. German tanks were in operation and seemed to be cutting the Americans and British to pieces. Smoke obscured the shoreline, reports continued to be sketchy, and wild rumors of disaster multiplied.

What was going on? For Clark, his enforced inactivity heightened his concern while his inability to influence the action promoted an acute sense of frustration. With his picture of the battle distorted, he believed the situation to be far worse than it really was.

Impatient to know, with only the vaguest notion of events, Clark sent Dawley ashore to make certain that regular reports reached Clark. Dawley had expected to take command of the American beachhead on the third day at the earliest. His staff and headquarters were scattered among several ships in the bay. With a few officers, he proceeded to land where he found O'Daniel, the beachmaster, bringing order to the landings. Joining Walker, who was cool, Dawley discovered everything going reasonably well. He too had trouble getting word to Clark.

The first detailed report reached Clark at about 5 P.M. After an agonizing day, he had good news. The Avalanche forces were holding the positions set out for them to occupy on the following morning. The invasion, then, was ahead of schedule. Rangers were dug in on high ground near the passes through the Sorrento mountain mass. The British were clearing Salerno and were close to Battipaglia and the airfield. The Americans had little contact with the enemy and shortly after nightfall none at all.

Yet there was disquieting information too. Allied pilots observed one of the two German divisions on the toe moving rapidly toward Salerno. Anticipating its arrival in the American sector, the panzer division around Salerno relaxed the pressure against the Americans and concentrated against the British. If the division traveling from the toe reached the Salerno area that night as expected, Eisenhower told his superiors in Washington and London, Avalanche was likely to be "a matter of touch and go for the next few days." Clark could only hope that the dispatch of one German division from the toe, leaving only one to oppose Montgomery, would "help bring the Eighth Army north."

As it turned out, shortages of gasoline slowed the German division traveling to Salerno. It would take the division several days to arrive.

While Dawley's forces moved easily to their objectives against little opposition, McCreery's men were unable to clear Salerno, advance two miles to the Vietri Pass on the main road to Naples, and enter Battipaglia to secure the nearby airfield.

Middleton's floating reserve landed on the American left to close the gap between the two corps and to help the British take Battipaglia. His units were in the valley of the Sele River, low ground that was dangerous. Clark warned Dawley to be alert to the situation. Working at a distinct disadvantage because only a small part of his staff was with him, Dawley seemed, at least to Clark, unaware of what he was talking about.

Things turned sour on the fourth morning. The German division coming from the toe struck the Americans hard, and the Germans at Salerno drove the British out of Battipaglia. When Clark went ashore, he found the Americans in the Sele valley, as he noted in his diary, "badly bruised." If the Germans pushed down the Sele corridor to the sea, they could then turn against the inner flank of either or both corps and roll up the Allied front. Beginning clearly to question Dawley's perceptions and abilities, Clark told him to shift American forces to his left to meet this threat. He also sent a message to Alexander and asked him to prod Montgomery into quicker progress.

Although the moment was hardly propitious, Clark decided to establish his headquarters on land. This would show the troops as nothing else his firm intention of staying and winning.

He spent most of the day in his jeep traveling around to visit front-line units while his headquarters set up shop in a mansion situated in a grove of pine trees. The location was too close to the combat. That afternoon, when eight German tanks and several hundred infantry attacked, the Fifth Army command post was in the direct path of the thrust. Naval shelling and air bombardment helped contain the German effort, but the danger was unmistakable. If the Germans overran the headquarters and killed or captured Clark, the psychological effect would be devastating. With a few key officers, he moved several miles down the road that evening and into a house concealed by underbrush.

In the United States, retired General Walter C. Sweeney recalled to a newspaper reporter how the Salerno landings, with Naples as the objective, resembled the Army–Navy joint maneuver in 1940, when Clark had masterminded the Monterey Bay landings to capture San Francisco. Clark and Eisenhower, Sweeney said, were regular guys, brilliant and hard workers. They were winners.

On the fifth day of the landings, a routine cable on press guidance from Alexander's headquarters infuriated Clark. The censor advised newspaper correspondents to "play up" Montgomery, who was dashing toward Salerno to chase the Germans away. The Fifth Army was having a "tough time." Actually, Montgomery was moving slowly.

Sensing intuitively an approaching crisis, Clark took a bold and unorthodox step. He dispatched a note to Ridgway in Sicily, where his division was unemployed. "I want you to accept this letter as an order," Clark wrote. He needed more strength in the beachhead. The quickest way he could get it was by having paratroopers jump in. "I realize the time normally needed to prepare for a drop, but . . . I want you to make a drop within our lines on the beachhead and I want you to make it tonight. This is a must." He entrusted the message to the pilot of a light plane who took off at once.

The pilot brought Ridgway's reply several hours later. Ridgway was accepting the mission. Shortly after midnight, in a dangerous and difficult operation, about a thousand men parachuted into the beachhead. On the following night, another thousand arrived in the same manner. Their numbers were small, but psychologically they bolstered the soldiers who by then were desperately holding on.

Opposing Clark was General Heinrich von Vietinghoff genannt Scheel, commanding the Tenth Army. Hitler had created the Tenth Army headquarters a month earlier, in August, for the purpose of taking control of the substantial German forces in southern Italy, including those evacuated from Sicily. He selected Vietinghoff, a solid and experienced professional soldier who had commanded a corps on the Eastern front and an army of occupation in France, for the post, called him to his headquarters in East Prussia, and personally delivered his instructions. If the Italians surrendered, Vietinghoff was to assure the withdrawal of his troops to the Rome area.

Vietinghoff traveled to Rome and consulted with his immediate superior, Field Marshal Kesselring, the German Commander in Chief. Kesselring, an air force officer with broad experience, had been in Italy since 1941. He had good relations with the Italians and was shocked by Mussolini's removal from power. He believed that Germany should defend all of Italy even without the Italians. Cheerful and optimistic, known as "Smiling Al" because of his beaming, jovial smile, Kesselring was of course ready to carry out Hitler's withdrawal orders.

Both Kesselring and Vietinghoff fought at Salerno despite Hitler's instructions for two reasons. They had to get the troops out of the toe before they pulled back to Rome. And they had a chance to defeat the Allies and throw them into the sea.

When Vietinghoff discovered the gap between the two Allied corps, he misinterpreted its meaning. He believed that the Allies were about to leave their beachhead and re-embark in the ships in the bay. In that case, he had an opportunity to crush them. He ordered his troops to launch a powerful attack.

It hit both Allied corps, and the fighting was fierce. Nowhere was the integrity of the beachhead threatened as in the Sele valley. By mid-afternoon German tanks and infantry were heading for the shore. Between them and the sea were only a few American infantrymen, two dozen field artillery pieces soon firing at point-blank range, and several tank detroyers hurried up from the beach where they had just landed. Cooks, clerks, and drivers joined them and built up a firing line.

Dawley telephoned Clark and reported the critical situation.

Well, what was Dawley going to do about it?

"Nothing," Dawley said, "for I have no reserves. All I have is a prayer."

That jarred Clark. To have made no plans in advance of possible contingencies was, to him, inexcusable.

Dawley's sin of omission no doubt led Clark, at least in part, to his next course of action. He immediately arranged to evacuate his headquarters on ten minutes' notice. In that case, he would take a PT boat to the X Corps, where the conditions were better to retain, as he said, a "clawhold" on Italian soil. He told Gruenther to start drawing plans to withdraw from the beachhead if that drastic action became necessary. Specifically, he wanted two plans, one for each corps, so that one could be withdrawn and relanded to reinforce the other.

Clark was preparing for an emergency. In case the beachhead deteriorated to the point of collapse, he would salvage what men and material he could. But there was to be no action unless and until Clark judged the moment to have arrived.

Hewitt started planning to comply with Clark's request even though he opposed the undertaking on technical grounds. Beaching a loaded landing craft and retracting it after it was unloaded and lightened were quite different from beaching an empty craft and retracting it when full.

Unlike Hewitt, who was temperamentally controlled, his principal British subordinate was violent in his objections. When McCreery learned that Clark was even thinking of giving up the beachhead and withdrawing the landing forces, he was positively furious. No doubt, the British reaction stemmed from recollections of Dunkirk.

The threat in the Sele valley was barely stopped. At darkness the Fifth Army was perilously close to defeat. Lacking confidence in Dawley, Clark personally directed minor withdrawals and unit shifts to shorten and solidify the front.

But the worst was yet to come. On September 14, what Gruenther later called "that black day," the Germans struck again. The Allied defenses bent but failed to crack.

In large measure, the achievement was Clark's. Conspicuously touring the front to encourage his troops, particularly those in the dangerous Sele sector, he exposed himself to enemy artillery and machine gun fire. Everywhere he imparted confidence and steadiness.

Displaying utter disregard for his personal safety, as the citation would later read, Clark spread an infectious spirit of determination and courage throughout the beachhead. He stopped frequently to talk with individual soldiers. At one place, where eighteen German tanks were advancing, he took charge of the defenses. American artillery knocked out six tanks, and the others turned back.

Two months later, without informing Clark, Gruenther wrote a private letter to Eisenhower. Clark, Gruenther said, had clearly earned the Distinguished Service Cross. He had maintained close personal contact with the combat units under enemy fire. His bravery was well known throughout the army. Gruenther had thoroughly investigated Clark's actions. Eyewitness reports authenticated them. The soldiers who had occupied the critical La Cosa Creek line termed Clark's presence the major factor in inspiring them to hold.

Gruenther wrote to Eisenhower unofficially because he wished to avoid embarrassing Clark. If Eisenhower felt obliged to disapprove Gruenther's recommendation, Clark would not know.

The battle was spent by the early afternoon just as Alexander, accompanied by Lemnitzer, his Deputy Chief of Staff, arrived. Impeccably attired, immensely likeable and handsome, Alexander was impressive. Although some of his countrymen later questioned his intelligence, he had a marvelous command presence that imparted calm and confidence wherever he appeared. Courteous, reserved, somewhat indolent, he was a thoroughly experienced battle commander with much prior experience in the Great War, in India, and already in World War II. He had the knack of judging instantly the morale and efficiency of soldiers and units.

Alexander was tremendously pleased. The allies had repulsed a serious German effort. The crisis, in his opinion, was past.

After studying Clark for signs of dejection and finding instead calmness, purpose, and control, Alexander complimented Clark on the fine job he was doing. Clark was pleased. He had passed his combat test.

At Dawley's headquarters, as Dawley briefed Alexander, Clark, and Lemnitzer on the situation, his voice trembled. As he pointed to a map, his hand shook. As he talked, his nervousness, Clark later said, was "quite apparent." When Alexander asked about his future plans, Dawleys' response was embarrassing. "Obviously under great strain, with his hands shaking like a leaf," Lemnitzer recalled, "General Dawley made a pitiful effort to explain the disposition of his troops and what he planned to do." The visitors perceived a lack of confidence in Dawley on the part of his staff.

Alexander said to Clark privately, "I do not want to interfere with your business, but I have had some ten years' experience in this game of sizing up commanders. I can tell you definitely that you have a broken reed on your hands and I suggest you replace him immediately."

Clark was uncomfortable. To relieve Dawley would ruin him. Clark asked Alexander to give Eisenhower his thoughts. But he wished Eisenhower to take no immediate action.

Soon thereafter, Lemnitzer saw Eisenhower in Algiers and told him what had transpired.

"Well," Eisenhower exploded, "why doesn't he relieve Dawley?"

As the German activity perceptibly declined, Clark was irritated to read an Allied press release from Alexander's headquarters. On Montgomery's front, the paper said, progress was rapid; on the Fifth Army front, heavy fighting continued.

A letter from Montgomery contained a suggestion. Would Clark push out units to the south "to meet my people"? He added, out of arrogance or simply a desire to help, "It looks as if you may be having not too good a time, and I do hope that all will go well with you. We are on the way to lend a hand."

The message exasperated Clark. Montgomery's forces were then sixty miles from the beachhead, too far away to help, too far even to anticipate or think of an early meeting. Sending American units to the south would facilitate Montgomery's advance. But the beachhead still needed consolidation. And he was hardly willing to acknowledge and to make a matter of record his dependence on Montgomery's approach to win his battle. The Fifth Army had triumphed without Montgomery's help.

Yet he could not be rude to Montgomery, not only because his stature overshadowed Clark's, but also because Eisenhower insisted on good relations between Americans and British. Clark swallowed his resentment and resorted to flattery. "It will be a pleasure to see you again at an early date. Please accept my deep appreciation for assistance your Eighth Army has provided Fifth Army by your skillful and rapid advance." If that was veiled sarcasm, it was nevertheless polite. He added, quite firmly, "Situation here well in hand."

Could Montgomery have proceeded more rapidly to Salerno? He faced extremely difficult ground on the toe, terrain favorable for defense, and the Germans had used it to advantage. Yet according to the Germans, Montgomery exerted relatively little pressure on them during his advance.

During that period, a party of seven—three British war correspondents, the Eighth Army public relations officer, and three drivers—set out in two reconnaissance cars and a jeep from army headquarters, traveled 150 miles across no-man's land, met no Germans, and, forty-eight hours later, reached the Fifth Army beachhead just as the battle at Salerno was reaching its climax. Thirty-six hours later, a small patrol from Montgomery's army made contact with Clark's men. By then the fighting had passed its critical stage.

Why hadn't Montgomery made a greater effort? He was probably looking to the east coast, where British troops had come ashore at Taranto and were increasing in numbers.

Clark wrote to Renie to tell her of "this trying time." He had not had a single minute to himself. If newspaper stories back home were portraying Salerno as a near catastrophe, she was worrying needlessly. Now there was a momentary lull, he was all right, and everything was going well. "We knew [beforehand] that this would be a great venture and a bold one." There had been "a real battle from the very minute we touched the beaches, and it continues now as I sit in my field command post in a truck which I have had made into a sort of house and office on wheels." In it he had a bunk, a desk, a place for his trunk locker, a wash basin with water coming from a tank on the roof, a closet for hanging his clothes, glass and screened windows—the mosquitoes were terrible— and blackout curtains.

Adding a few lines on the following day, he said, "We have had a tough time." But he was "not downhearted a bit."

He radioed Eisenhower to recommend relieving Dawley, who "appears to go to pieces in the emergencies." Anticipating Eisenhower's concurrence, Clark appointed Ridgway the Deputy Corps Commander. On Dawley's removal, Ridgway, Clark's classmate and contemporary, would step up and take his place.

Patton, idle in Sicily, had heard of Dawley's poor performance and asked Eisenhower for the corps. "I would serve under the Devil to get a fight," Patton wrote in his diary. "He said Clark and I were not soulmates so he could not do it."

Visiting the beachhead, Eisenhower attended a briefing by Dawley. At the end of the presentation, Eisenhower asked, "How did you ever get your troops into such a mess?" Instead of explaining why the defense had required some intermingling of units, Dawley replied vaguely and uncertainly.

Clark was disappointed when Eisenhower selected John P. Lucas, who commanded the II Corps in Sicily, to take over from Dawley. Although Clark liked Lucas, another close friend of McNair, Lucas was of Dawley's vintage, older than Clark. The disadvantage of dealing with senior officers under him would continue.

With both German divisions now safely out of the toe, the defenders around Salerno began to withdraw from the battlefield, moving slowly to the north.

A small party from the Eighth Army came to arrange a meeting with the Fifth. Always respectful and diplomatic, Clark sent Montgomery a note. "Again I want to tell you of our deep appreciation for the skillful and expeditious manner by which you have moved your Eighth Army to the north." Overlooking the periodic messages from Alexander's public information office trumpeting Montgomery's race to rescue Clark—as late as September 19, the guidance was, "Fifth Army no full dress withdrawal yet"—he told Montgomery, "We feel it is a great privilege to operate alongside your army."

A few days later, when the public information office radioed, "Play up Eighth Army, mention Americans," Clark was visibly irritated. Yet when Montgomery came to visit, Clark flattered him. "The Fifth Army is just a young Army trying hard to get along," Clark said, "while the Eighth Army is a battle-tried veteran. We would appreciate your teaching us some of your tricks." Montgomery beamed.

The battle of Salerno ended on September 20, and Montgomery's aide brought a message. Instead of moving north to Salerno, which was obviously in no danger, Montgomery's army was traveling to the east cost to take command of the British V Corps and other forces that had come into the country through Taranto. The last-minute decision to land at Taranto rather than any clearcut advance strategic planning was about to shape the Italian campaign.

Looking ahead to Naples, Montgomery explained that he would be unable to help Clark take the port city. But after seizing Foggia and the important airfields nearby, if Clark had failed to capture Naples by then, Montgomery would strike westward and help Clark into the city. "I propose to repeat the same tactics in respect to Rome," Montgomery added. "But we can discuss that later."

So far as Clark was concerned, there was nothing to discuss. He would take Naples alone, pursue the retreating Germans, and seize Rome. The Fifth Army needed no help from Montgomery.

Eisenhower informed his superiors of his impressions of Clark in combat. He lacked Bradley's capacity to win the confidence of everyone around him and Patton's quality of refusing to see anything but victory, but Clark was good and "carrying weight."

By then, Clark was looking toward Naples.

CHAPTER 13

☆ ☆ ☆ ☆

THE AWFUL WINTER

"some of the most difficult terrain and the worst weather of the campaign"

THE SALERNO INVASION brought Clark to public attention again. News stories described him as wearing a gold-braided overseas cap, pants tucked into paratrooper boots, and a shirt open at the throat; later he would tie a distinctive green scarf around his neck. His long legs carried him at a fast gait, and according to his aide, "The boss thinks quick and moves quick." He was impatient, yet had an "easy boyish manner." The assumption was, "General Mark Clark gets the tough jobs."

Leaving Gruenther at the headquarters to manage the staff and to handle the normal business, Clark traveled a great deal. He had learned from McNair to see things for himself. He spoke frequently with his principal subordinate commanders to learn their points of view and to understand their problems. He went often to the front not only to show himself to the soldiers, who were heartened by the sight of his figure among them, but also simply to be with them, for he liked and cared for them.

Alexander came on September 21 to talk with Clark about the future.

143

He was cordial, delighted with the way that Clark was commanding his army. "You are doing it," he said, "exactly as I wanted it." Then he outlined his expectations.

First, he wished Clark to have Naples by October 7.

Clark hoped to take the city somewhat sooner.

Second, with Naples in hand and operating as a base from which to nourish the troops in southern Italy, Clark was to advance about 20 miles to the Volturno River to cover and protect the port city.

Third, because the Allies expected Hitler to give up all of Italy except the northern region, Clark was to cross the Volturno River and continue north hard on the heels of the withdrawing German soldiers. In the western part of Italy, Clark was to head for Rome. Montgomery, who was moving to capture the airfields around Foggia, was to march his Eighth Army up the eastern or Adriatic half of Italy. Both armies were to maintain a continuous front across the peninsula as they moved up the boot.

If all went well, Alexander thought, the Fifth Army should be approaching Rome in about a month, sometime early in November. With Rome captured, the two Allied armies were to work their way gradually up to the last German positions guarding the Po valley.

Satisfied with these instructions, Clark was incensed on the following day when the normal censorship guidance cable arrived routinely from Alexander's headquarters. Play up Eighth Army progress, the message read. "Americans may be mentioned."

That was hardly right. Were Clark and his American troops merely junior partners in the Allied enterprise? Were he and his Fifth Army always to receive lesser notice in the press?

Miffed by the slight, intentional or otherwise, Clark determined to correct the injustice. American troops were playing a major role in the campaign. Their exertions were helping to win the war. They merited recognition and applause in the news media. The best way to attract attention was to gain victories. The capture of Naples, a city of almost a million inhabitants, the first metropolis on the European continent to come within Allied reach, would certainly receive great coverage in the newspapers. That would no doubt diminish the columns devoted to Montgomery.

Yet getting through the two narrow passes of the hill mass between Salerno and Naples was no easy matter. The Germans were tough and skillful. They occupied high ground, rained fire down on the advancing Allies, destroyed bridges and culverts on the few roads.

The essential Allied problem in Italy was the terrain, which denied maneuver on the grand scale. There was no place for the mechanized Allied forces to go except along the obvious corridors of advance. The Germans blocked these and compelled the Allies to struggle over the mountains. Combat there was a matter of small unit actions, a war waged by lieutenants and captains.

Kesselring was carrying out Hitler's policy to "fall back upon the Rome area," but he was doing it slowly. Meanwhile, he pointed out repeatedly the excellent defensive country south of Rome. Why give it up? he asked Hitler. Partially convinced, Hitler permitted Kesselring to hold "for a longer period of time" at a place of his choice.

Drawing on a map several lines across the peninsula where the Germans could make a stand, Kesselring set up a timetable. If Vietinghoff could deny the Allies Naples until at least the end of September, he would have time to build fortifications along the Volturno River. If he held at the Volturno until the middle of October, he could fortify the Bernhard Line in the mountains. If he defended the Bernhard Line for several weeks, he could construct the Gustav Line in the hills around Cassino. There, behind the water barrier of the Garigliano and Rapido Rivers, the Gustav Line would be an almost impregnable defensive system. With the weather deteriorating during the winter, they could keep the Allies out of Rome indefinitely.

The Allies understood how difficult it would be to fight in the rugged ground if the Germans contested their advance. In that case, the best way to get ahead was to go around the German defenses by water. Consequently, there was much talk of amphibious operations, "end runs," as they were called, to detour by sea around the German lines.

During the last week of September, as the Germans held stubbornly, Clark seriously considered a seaborne hook to outflank the German positions blocking the roads to Naples. By sending several thousand men across the water to come ashore near Gaeta, Clark would get behind the German defenders, threaten their escape routes, and compel them to abandon the port city of Naples.

Gaeta proved to be unnecessary because Allied troops finally broke through the mountain passes and reached the relatively flat plain of Naples.

Juin visited Clark on October 1. He was organizing several French divisions that were training in North Africa into a French expeditionary corps. Under Juin's command, this force was soon to join the Fifth Army in Italy.

To give Juin some idea of the battle conditions, Clark took him forward in his jeep. As they were touring the front, they encountered Ridgway on the main road to Naples. He was directing ranger, commando, and airborne troops, and the leading elements, he informed Clark, were inside the city.

Leaving Juin, who had no official place in the command structure, Clark climbed into an armored car. With an escort he drove into Naples. He was elated by its capture a week ahead of Alexander's expectation. He was dismayed by the devastation.

The Germans had destroyed the city. They had demolished sewer mains, power plants, reservoirs, aqueducts, factories; they had burned hotels and large public buildings; they had left delayed bombs in the post office and in houses suitable for billeting soldiers, and the explosives would kill more than one hundred troops as well as civilians; worst of all, they had ripped up railroads, choked the harbor with sunken vessels, and wrecked the port machinery.

It would take three months to restore life somewhat to normal conditions. More than a week was needed to clear the city of debris. It took three days simply to put out fires in huge piles of coal. Yet the first Allied ship docked on October 3, and two weeks later the port was working in limited fashion.

A letter came from Patton. "My dear Wayne," he had written from Sicily, "how proud we all are of the way you and your Army are getting forward. Please accept our most sincere congratulations on the capture of the biggest city ever taken by an American Army."

A message arrived from Eisenhower. "You are doing a good job," he radioed, "in exactly the way that I always knew you would."

Lemnitzer cabled, "Now you're rolling."

Stimson, Churchill, and many others sent congratulations. The President passed his name to the Senate to confirm his promotion to Regular Army and permanent brigadier general, an important step for professional officers, for his wartime three-star rank was temporary.

Clark was thinking of Renie, who was lecturing in Detroit. Having had no time to shop for presents, he sent her a wire in the grand manner of conquerors: "I give you Naples for your birthday."

To his mother he wrote, "This has been a real battle. I have to pinch myself sometimes to realize that I am in command of this show."

Affable and relaxed, Clark was agreeable to several requests. Alexander's public relations officer asked him to tell the press that British troops had entered Naples first. Overlooking the shabby reporting by the routine press advisories, he made the announcement even though American paratroopers and rangers had accompanied the British into the city.

Could he spare gasoline to help the Eighth Army? He arranged to ship 100,000 gallons to Montgomery.

Would he retain McCreery's British X Corps in his Fifth Army? It had been understood that McCreery's men would travel to the east coast and become part of the British Eighth Army just as soon as Geoffrey Keyes' II U.S. Corps headquarters and some American combat forces could be brought from Sicily to Naples. A shortage of vessels was delaying the movement. Furthermore, sending the X Corps across Italy would consume precious stocks of fuel.

Clark agreed to keep the British corps. If he wondered whether the request was a stratagem designed to get British troops into Rome and thus to share the glory of taking the Eternal City, he shook off the thought. Having the X Corps in the Fifth Army enhanced the coalition and strengthened Clark's forces. Yet the British had their own particular items of supply and complicated the Fifth Army's logistical establishment.

The Italian government, about to declare war on Germany, wished Italian troops to take an active role in the campaign and to accompany the Allied forces entering Rome. Would Clark accept Italian combat units in his army?

Their presence would further complicate the supply lines. And it certainly looked as though everyone was trying to be in on the liberation of Rome. But Clark consented. Before long he would have French divisions, which would impose additional strains on the supply system.

On the other side of Italy, Montgomery took Foggia on October 1, then went for the Biferno River by sending a small force in an amphibious landing to Termoli. The Germans counterattacked viciously, and the Eighth Army found itself under great pressure. Could Clark dispatch some troops to help? His immediate reaction was positive, and he asked his G-3, Brann, to look into the matter. The Germans then began to retire, and Fifth Army assistance was unnecessary.

The capture of Naples and Foggia on October 1 created great optimism in the Allied camp. The Germans were falling back. The Allies were about to begin a triumphant march to Rome. The Germans would probably, the Allies guessed, try to delay the Allied forces along the way, but the capital was sure to fall quickly.

On October 1, Eisenhower talked of being north of Rome in six or eight weeks. Three days later he and Alexander anticipated being in Rome before the end of the month. Eisenhower had thought of moving his AFHQ from Algiers to Naples, but now he decided to wait until he could, he said, "make the jump straight into Rome."

On that very day, October 4, Hitler was changing his mind about fighting in Italy. He told Kesselring to defend indefinitely south of Rome. To strengthen him, Hitler instructed Rommel in northern Italy to send Kesselring two infantry divisions and some artillery.

Within a few days, the Allies were aware of Hitler's decision. Whether Allied reconnaissance aircraft spotted the movement of the two divisions or whether Ultra or other intelligence revealed it, the transfer of forces to southern Italy indicated a German intention to hold rather than to withdraw. Hitler talked of the "decisive importance" of making "a decisive stand."

Eisenhower drew the inference. "Clearly," he informed his superiors, if the Germans resisted, "there will be very hard and bitter fighting before we can hope to reach Rome."

He was referring not only to the forbidding ground between Naples and Rome but also to a shifting balance of power. As the Germans built up their forces in southern Italy, the Allied resources were about to decline. The cross-Channel operation was scheduled for the spring of 1944, and the Mediterranean theater was to contribute resources to that venture. Seven Allied divisions—four American and three British, three American heavy bomber groups totalling 170 aircraft, and more than a hundred landing ships were to leave the Mediterranean area before the end of 1943 and go to England for Overlord. As Torch in 1942 had drained stocks of men and equipment in England, so now the forthcoming landings in Normandy were reversing the flow. French divisions, perhaps as many as four, were to come to Italy and, to that extent, replace the departing ground units, but the theater was losing strength and might have insufficient assets to gain a resounding victory.

Understanding the implications, Patton wrote to his wife early in October. "I am not as jealous of Wayne as I was, for I think that his party may well be an anti-climax." The shrinking Allied forces in Italy lessened what could be expected, while the growing German opposition guaranteed greater difficulties. The real glory, the real victory would come in northwestern Europe after Overlord.

Hitler's early intention to abandon Italy below Rome, revealed by Ultra, had in large part drawn the Allies into the Italian peninsula and been responsible for an optimistic outlook. Now, by changing his mind, Hitler had trapped the Allies. Whether they liked it or not, they were committed to campaign in Italy.

To what end? To get to Rome, a city of great symbolic significance. Allied seizure of one of the three Axis capitals would show the progress of Allied arms and hearten the American and British people. Additionally, the airfields around Rome were legitimate military targets, for Allied possession of them would shorten bomber runs over Germany. Were these reasons sufficient to justify fighting in Italy? A further rationale emerged to give urgency to Rome as the single meaningful objective. If the Allies captured Rome before Overlord, they would, it was said, psychologically damage the Germans defending in Normandy and thereby make the invasion easier. With this idea providing impetus, the effort to reach Rome before the Channel crossing became an overwhelming desire driving the commanders in Italy.

Clark's immediate task was to cross the Volturno River, swollen to flood stage by rains. He was eager to get across before the Germans dug in and established their defenses. To "ford a treacherous river and then scale high hills," Clark understood, was difficult, and he alternately urged McCreery and Lucas to get over as soon as they could. The weather, the rugged countryside, and the Germans delayed both corps. Clark finally directed both to cross simultaneously at night.

McCreery objected, and Clark came to visit him. Getting to the far bank of the river, McCreery told him, was the hardest job he had ever had. "We accept your order, of course," McCreery continued, "but I have to say that I am embarrassed when a young American commander gives British troops orders that we don't like."

That raised another issue. Would Clark have to have Alexander put pressure on McCreery? There was no time. His order stood, Clark said flatly. Then to mollify McCreery, he added, "I am glad you have been frank about it, and I know you realize the difficult position I am in when I give you orders that you don't like."

Under the cover of darkness and with the aid of heavy artillery support, with the Americans pulling the British along, Allied troops forced their way across the water.

The usual censorship guidance from Alexander's public relations office brought the same message: stress the British achievements, downplay the Americans.

Upset, Clark began to wonder whether the British were following a deliberate policy of self-aggrandizement. Were they letting the Americans fight while they themselves were getting—not only getting but also manufacturing through the press—the glory? Was this why they had asked him to announce British troops as the first to enter Naples? Was this why Montgomery had talked about helping Clark into Rome?

Gradually Clark came to believe in the existence of a conspiracy. The notion would rankle and goad him. There was no way he could protest openly. For that would disturb, perhaps destroy, the harmony between Allied soldiers of different nationalities. Eisenhower absolutely insisted on unity, and Clark had to keep his feelings to himself.

There grew in his mind the notion of assuring credit to American soldiers for what they did. If in the process Clark himself benefited, so much the better. But the essential concept was to demonstrate the skill, courage, and determination of the Americans. The best way to do so was to capture Rome. He became determined to get his Fifth Army into the city first, ahead of the British.

Severe fighting continued along the Volturno until October 15, when Vietinghoff, in compliance with Kesselring's timetable, began to withdraw slowly into a series of fortifications.

The Allies named these German defenses rather vaguely the Winter Line. Actually, three distinct systems existed. The first was an outpost or screen called Barbara. Behind it was the more strongly fortified Bernhard Line. And to the rear of that, the Gustav Line, anchored on the hills around Cassino and protected by the Garigliano and Rapido Rivers, was taking shape. If the Allies thought the fighting onerous thus far, campaigning in the Winter Line would be brutal.

Understanding the painful nature of what lay ahead, Clark established a special amphibious operations section in his headquarters. He put O'Daniel, ever his trusted troubleshooter, in charge. O'Daniel was to plan waterborne ventures to get the Allies around the German defenses.

The problems were difficult to solve. First, the Allies needed all their strength up front. They had few extra or idle units for an expedition by sea.

Second, losing ships to Overlord, the Allies had insufficient vessels to transport a large force to a beach behind the German lines. A small force put ashore, as Eisenhower said, "would not last twenty-four hours," for the Germans would quickly sweep the invaders into the sea. He needed enough boats to carry a substantial force of soldiers able to sustain themselves for at least a week.

Third, during that week, the forces on the main front had to move forward and join up with the beachhead. Thus the landing had to be close enough to the main front to make possible a quick linkup.

Seaborne hooks, Clark admitted, were terribly complicated, but they were indispensable. If the Allies were to move quickly and avoid casualties, they had to go around, get behind the Germans, and jar them loose from their defenses. What they had to do, Clark told his staff, was not to stress the dangers involved but instead to think positively on how to overcome them.

As officers scanned maps for suitable landing sites, their views began to converge on Anzio, thirty miles below Rome. An Allied amphibious force at Anzio would threaten the capital. Unfortunately, the Fifth Army was still more than a hundred miles to the south, far too distant to envision a quick linkup.

The Fifth Army labored to advance in what Clark lated called "some of the most difficult terrain and the worst weather of the campaign." The fighting was harrowing and exhausting. Progress was depressingly slow. Rome remained a distant objective.

Two main highways led to Rome, and both lay in the shadows of formidable hills. Before the troops could use the roads, they had to dislodge the Germans from the high places.

Clark constantly pondered how to get forward more quickly. As he bent over a map with several staff members, he pointed to San Pietro Infine, a village of stone houses that resembled a citadel on a steeply terraced hillside and dominated the approaches from the south. It was a critical objective and had to be taken. He wanted no frontal attack, Clark said. Make an outflanking movement. Swing wide to the east and go at the village from the side, across the slope instead of up it. That meant delay, for soldiers had to work their way carefully around to the flank, across gullies and draws, over razorback ridges, along precarious ledges, all the while trying to remain out of sight of German gunners.

There were dozens of villages like San Pietro and a hundred more posing similar difficulties. No doubt at all, an amphibious operation was the best way to get to Rome.

Early in November, Eisenhower came up with a rather elaborate idea. If Montgomery, now at the Sangro River, crossed and moved 25 miles to Pescara, then continued to Avezzano, which was 50 miles east of Rome, Montgomery would challenge the capital. As the Germans turned to meet Montgomery, they would have to weaken their forces facing Clark. If Clark could then break through the German systems anchored successively on Mignano and Cassino and advance about 50 miles, he would be in the Liri valley. Twenty-five miles farther to Frosinone, and he would be close enough to Anzio to warrant a landing. With both Allied armies thus threatening Rome, from Avezzano and Anzio, the Germans would have to start pulling back to northern Italy.

This was why, Eisenhower explained to the Combined Chiefs of Staff, he requested permission to retain until December 15 a total of 68 landing ships scheduled to go to the United Kingdom before that date. With them, he might be able to pull off an Allied entrance into Rome.

Getting Montgomery to Avezzano and Clark to Frosinone early enough to have enough time to use the vessels before mid-December was a tall order. But perhaps they could work it.

At about the same time, Hitler banished whatever doubts he had had about holding southern Italy. He sent Rommel to France to improve the Atlantic Wall, the fortifications guarding the Channel coastline. He told Kesselring to "mark the end of withdrawals."

When Eisenhower received permission to keep the landing ships until December 15, he immediately asked for an extension until January 15, 1944. With ships available for five weeks and perhaps four more beyond, an Anzio venture became possible. But only if the Fifth Army was close enough to Anzio to make the landing reasonably safe.

On November 8, Eisenhower and Alexander issued directives spelling out the ambitious scheme for Pescara and Avezzano, Frosinone and Anzio.

Hoping for a sudden crack and collapse in the German defenses, Clark held in reserve Keyes' II Corps headquarters, which had come from Sicily, and Walker's 36th Division, which was resting and training. If the Fifth Army surged ahead, they would be free to make the Anzio invasion.

There was nothing doing. The Fifth Army inched forward painfully.

When a high-ranking British officer inadvertently referred to the attack to Pescara, then to Avezzano, as an order for Montgomery to advance on Rome, Clark was immediately suspicious. The Fifth Army, he said, was able to get to Rome "and intended to do so."

Patton came for a visit and saw Clark, who, Patton noted in his diary, "is evidently having trouble with the British who simply don't fight. Their men are braver than ours, but their officers have no push."

The troops of both Allied armies were becoming weary. British and American units had sustained heavy casualties. They needed to rest before they burned themselves out in exhaustion. Yet they had to keep on, pounding and pushing. Although the constant fighting sapped the strength and vitality of the combat organizations, they had to advance to make Anzio feasible while landing ships and craft were still available.

The British were particularly handicapped. In contrast with the seemingly endless flow of American resources, British manpower reserves were dwindling dangerously. There was grave concern at the highest political and military echelons. To replace casualties on the active fronts, the British would soon start breaking up and phasing out some divisions and distributing the men to other existing organizations to keep them up to strength.

Furthermore, certain American items of equipment were superior to their British counterparts. The American 2½-ton trucks were mechanically more reliable than the British lorries, carried larger loads, and were able to run in worse weather conditions. American forces were relatively wealthy in bridgelaying and engineer materials, and specialized American units often helped the British.

Gradually, the Americans were becoming the dominant partner.

A British major general, designated to be the main adviser to the military commander of Rome, came to talk with Clark on the problems of governing the city. He expected, he said casually, to function there no matter which army took the capital.

The Fifth Army, Clark said emphatically, was going to take Rome.

Lacking dramatic news, the press concentrated on stories about the soldiers, how they fought, their conditions in the field. Clark's name dropped out of the headlines, and his mother wrote and asked him why. He replied, "I do hope I am left out of publicity, for I have had more than my share. Naturally, after our invasion here it was a popular subject, but now I hope it will die down."

Montgomery crossed the Sangro River late in November. The weather turned grim and erased early success. Rain raised the river to flood level and washed out all the temporary bridges. The offensive stalled. Resuming the attack, the Eighth Army fought in miserable conditions. After heroic exertion, including fierce fighting at Orsogna and Ortona, the British had to halt far short of Pescara. Avezzano, the "back door" to Rome, remained closed.

Unable to wait for the completion of Montgomery's effort because of the deadline for releasing the landing ships, Clark launched his offensive early in December. In terrain where it took eight hours to carry a wounded man off a mountain to a medical installation, savage battle resulted in a small advance.

A radio message from AFHQ asked Clark whether he could absent himself from the struggle in Italy for a day. If so, he was to fly to Palermo, Sicily, with seven officers and men who were to receive the Distinguished Service Cross. He joined the group and, when the plane landed, found Patton and several other high ranking officers on hand. Several minutes later, another aircraft settled on the field. It brought President Roosevelt, who was returning from the Cairo and Tehran conferences. Eisenhower was with him.

All who were there assembled to honor the seven men who were to be decorated, and the President pinned the medals on them. Finished, Roosevelt looked around and called, "General Clark." He motioned Clark over to him, then, to Clark's great surprise, presented him with the award for his actions at Salerno.

The President was very pleasant in his remarks to Clark. He passed over a letter he had composed in case Clark had been unable to come to Sicily. "I am very sorry to miss seeing you," Roosevelt had written, "but much as I wanted to come to Italy and see you at the front and to greet your fighting army there, I was told I just could not go. You and your Fifth Army are doing a magnificent job under the most trying conditions imaginable. Eye witnesses have told me about the fighting, so I know how tough it is. I have also been told of your personal courage in leading your forces, and especially of your gallantry.... Keep on giving it all you have, and Rome will be ours and more beyond. I am grateful to have such a staunch, fighting general."

After the ceremony, Roosevelt spoke to the senior officers and briefed them on the agreements reached by the Allied political and military leaders at Tehran. Among them was a decision to invade southern France. The President turned to Clark and said, "You, Mark, will command it."

Completely surprised, Clark knew nothing about the operation, its size, composition, or mission.

Landings in southern France were to take place just before or simultaneously with the cross-Channel attack. Thus the Germans would face two invasion thrusts into France, Overlord in Normandy, and Anvil, as it was called, on the Riviera. Patton's Seventh Army headquarters, idle in Sicily, was to plan Anvil, then execute it with Mediterranean resources (that is, with troops taken from the Italian campaign). But because Patton would probably leave the Seventh Army and take part in Overlord, Eisenhower had recommended Clark to head Anvil. Clark was to remain in Italy a little while longer, go to Sicily, take command of the Seventh Army, prepare the landing, and lead the troops ashore.

Eisenhower had suggested Clark because it was widely believed that Marshall would command the Overlord forces and because Eisenhower knew of Marshall's respect for Clark. After invading Normandy and driving eastward across France, Marshall's troops were to meet the Anvil forces coming up the Rhone valley. At that time, Anvil was to go under Marshall's command. Clark would then be one of Marshall's principal subordinates.

Flattered to be selected to serve in what would become the main arena of the European war, Clark was unimpressed with the strategy of Anvil. Southern France looked to him like a roundabout way to get to Germany or the Balkans. As he later said, he thought Anvil "a complete blow in the dark." Much more important for political and psychological reasons, he believed, was capturing Rome before Overlord, now scheduled for May 1944.

Instead of naming Marshall to command the Anglo-American forces in Overlord, Roosevelt chose Eisenhower.

Clark sent his congratulations and added two vaguely worded hopes not wholly formed in his mind. When Eisenhower left the Mediterranean theater and went to London to prepare Overlord, who would replace him in Algiers? Did Clark, the senior American commander in the Mediterranean area, stand a chance? Or would Jacob L. Devers, who commanded ETOUSA in London and who was senior to Clark, come to Algiers? If the latter occurred, Clark preferred to do Anvil and eventually to serve under Eisenhower in western Europe.

But both prospects, going to Algiers or launching Anvil, depressed Clark. How could he give up his Fifth Army? He was torn by the thought.

Eisenhower obtained permission to retain the landing ships until January 15, 1944, and as the fighting seemed to be going a little better, talk of Anzio revived. Unfortunately, all efforts to get toward Frosinone had little result.

Clark and Eisenhower met in Naples, and they had a long talk. Eisenhower filled him in on the changes about to take place. Eisenhower intended to leave for England early in January. Under him in the Overlord operation, Montgomery would command the British forces, Bradley the Americans. Patton was to relinquish command of the Seventh Army in Sicily and take command of another in England under Bradley.

In Algiers, a British officer, probably Alexander, would take Eisenhower's place at AFHQ and command the Mediterranean theater. Devers would probably come from London to be his deputy and the senior American officer in the area.

Was it possible for Clark to be the American deputy in Algiers or to step up and succeed Alexander in command of the 15th Army Group?

Eisenhower thought not. Clark was to go to Sicily to command the Anvil forces.

Could Clark be the American deputy at AFHQ and the Anvil commander at the same time?

Eisenhower was skeptical. Clark was to stay with the Fifth Army until he reached Rome. He was then to turn over the army to Lucas, move to Sicily, and begin the Anvil planning on about February 1.

He would, Clark said, make every effort to take Rome by that date.

Eisenhower refrained from telling Clark one item. The Combined Chiefs of Staff had offered to let Eisenhower remain in the theater until the capture of Rome. He saw no hope, he had replied, for seizing Rome quickly. The static battle, the winter weather, the firm German defense, the paucity of Allied resources, particularly the lack of assault ships, made an early fall of the city, in his opinion, improbable.

The only chance of getting quickly to Rome was to put on Anzio, but in mid-December, Clark reluctantly wired Alexander and recommended cancelling the landing operation. The deadline for releasing the vessels, together with the overland distance between the main front and Anzio, made the amphibious venture impractical.

Several days later Clark wrote Eisenhower of how pleased he was to have seen and talked with him. "I am quite reconciled," he said, "to accept your judgment." It would be difficult, he understood, for Clark to be the American deputy at AFHQ and at the same time the commander of Anvil.

He took the occasion to raise a question, "the question of using the Fifth Army for Operation Anvil, rather than the Seventh." If the Seventh Army headquarters came to Italy in the near future and replaced the Fifth Army headquarters, "at some appropriate time in February the shift could be made with no break in continuity." He hoped to have Eisenhower's concurrence "in my desire not only to use the Fifth Army staff in Anvil but also to have the Fifth Army name."

What he was saying was that he and the Fifth Army had become identified in the public consciousness and in his own as a single entity. He could hardly bear the thought of leaving his beloved Fifth Army and thus destroying that close bond.

Eisenhower had little interest in Clark's proposal. What Clark suggested was complicated and unwieldy, but that was for Eisenhower's successor to deal with.

Instead of moving Alexander up to take Eisenhower's place at AFHQ, the British appointed Field Marshal Sir Henry Maitland Wilson. He came from Cairo to Algiers, and Devers traveled from London to be his American deputy.

The combat in Italy continued to be agonizing. All the units were thoroughly fatigued, badly in need of rest. The men suffered from the freezing weather and the static warfare.

On Christmas Day Clark toured the two American corps areas, decorating and promoting men to keep up their morale, visiting hospitals, and showing himself in order to inspire the troops. He called on McCreery and wished him a happy holiday. He returned to Caserta in the evening for dinner.

He was discouraged. There was no solution for getting to Rome quickly. He might have to give up his Fifth Army. The year seemed to be ending badly.

Then he received electrifying news. In spite of all the obstacles and problems, Anzio was suddenly feasible.

CHAPTER 14

☆ ☆ ☆ ☆

ANZIO AND THE RAPIDO RIVER

"I am trying to find ways to do it"

WHAT MADE ANZIO possible were two events. First, when Eisenhower left Algiers for London, the Mediterranean theater of operations under Wilson would turn into a British province. The British Chiefs of Staff in London would become the executive agents for the Combined Chiefs and exercise more direct control over the forces engaged. That would give Winston Churchill primary responsibility for the area.

Second, Churchill had come down with pneumonia on his return from the Cairo and Tehran conferences, and he was convalescing in Marrakech, French Morocco. With little to do, he reflected on the recent meetings with Roosevelt and Stalin. The decisions reached at Tehran reflected the growing power of the United States and the Soviet Union, the diminishing influence of Great Britain in the alliance. Overlord, the Normandy invasion projected for the spring of 1944, as well as the subsequent campaign in northwestern Europe, was to be the main Anglo-American effort, and that was to be under American command, Eisenhower's. In contrast, the fighting in Italy had bogged down, resembled a stalemate, and, because of shrinking resources, was destined to become a subsidiary front. Was the Italian campaign doomed to remain quiet and unproductive? Could Churchill resuscitate the battle in Italy, soon to be under British control, and gain a great victory for British arms? Could he thereby restore the waning British prestige? He began to scheme.

Both Overlord and Anvil were assuming greater proportions in the unfolding Allied strategy. These planned operations were already exerting demands on the Allied men and material committed to Italy. Churchill firmly favored Overlord, where British and Americans would contribute equal forces to the initial landings in Normandy, but eventually the United States, simply by virtue of its greater manpower and industrial production, would become the dominant partner in northwestern Europe. Churchill opposed Anvil, the invasion of southern France, which was to be mainly a French and American venture.

If Churchill could restore vitality and immediacy to the Italian campaign, he would have to do so in the few months remaining before Anvil irretrievably weakened the forces in Italy and before Overlord irresistibly overshadowed events in Italy and brought ultimate Allied triumph.

"Nothing less than Rome," he concluded, "could satisfy" his wish. The best, perhaps only, way to get to Rome quickly was by an amphibious landing at Anzio. He determined to make that feasible.

Telegraphing his military chiefs in London, he said, "The stagnation of the whole campaign on the Italian front is becoming scandalous." The reason was the failure to take advantage of available shipping for an amphibious operation.

The British chiefs agreed. Amphibious equipment should have been used to promote an advance on Rome. The problem was, the available ships could carry only one division, two were minimal for Anzio.

"We must have the big Rome amphibious operation," Churchill cabled, meaning the two-division show. "In no case can we sacrifice Rome for the Riviera."

Then he moved into action. He called Alexander and several other British officers to confer with him on Christmas eve and asked what they needed for Anzio. They had to retain the landing ships, they replied, beyond the January 15 deadline for releasing them. They had to keep them for another month, for three weeks at the very least. In that case, a two-division operation could go around January 20.

Summoning Eisenhower, Bedell Smith, Wilson, and Alexander to meet with him on Christmas day, he talked of Rome as the major objective and of Anzio as the essential preliminary. Because Italy was losing men and equipment to Overlord and Anvil, if they expected to capture Rome, they had to undertake Anzio at once. If they waited any length of time, they were sure to lack the means, particularly in landing craft, to do anything at all.

He could, he was sure, obtain their requirements. As Prime Minister, he shared with Roosevelt the authority to direct the war effort. Certainly he could arrange with the President to keep for a little while longer the ships to transport two divisions.

On that basis they tentatively agreed to do Anzio. Eisenhower and Bedell Smith took no active part in the discussion. They would soon be leaving, and they were reluctant to influence a decision for an operation in which they would take no part. The only point they emphasized was their strong desire to have Anvil help Overlord. Wilson, who had just arrived, contributed little because he felt keenly his lack of detailed knowledge of the conditions. He said merely that it sounded like a good idea to go around the Germans instead of fighting them in the mountains. Alexander spoke warmly in favor of Anzio.

Sending a telegram to Roosevelt, Churchill asked approval to retain the ships until February. Otherwise, he said, "we must expect the ruin of the Mediterranean campaign of 1944." Anticipating a positive reply, he instructed Alexander to go ahead. Alexander cabled Clark that evening and electrified him by telling him to start serious planning.

Alexander came to Clark's headquarters two days later as Clark was inserting Juin's French corps into the line to replace the VI Corps under Lucas. That made Lucas and his corps headquarters available to command the Anzio force.

One of the two divisions to go under Lucas for Anzio, Alexander said, had to be British. The venture was hazardous, they had to expect heavy casualties, and both nations had to share the risks, the losses, and the gains.

Were the British, Clark wondered, intent on placing a division of their own at Anzio to ensure their participation in the entry into Rome? No matter. If Anzio succeeded, the Fifth Army would soon be in the city.

"I am enthusiastic about carrying out this operation," Clark told Alexander. "We've got to put it across."

Could Clark move through the awful German Winter Line and get at least to Cassino in a few weeks? There he would be at the entrance to the Liri valley, the best corridor for an overland linkup with Anzio. Could he be there when Anzio had to start? Could he be in Rome by February 1, when he had to leave for Sicily and start serious planning for Anvil? He would give the effort all his energy and devotion.

In Marrakech, Churchill received Roosevelt's reply. If Anzio would interfere with neither Normandy nor southern France, that is, if Anzio was to be a short operation to promote a quick Allied entry into Rome, the President saw no harm in letting the ships stay a little while longer.

As Clark worked with his planners to make Anzio a reality, the thought of leaving his Fifth Army haunted him. The invasion of southern France would certainly get him into the main arena of the war. Eisenhower's wish to have him on his team with Montgomery, Bradley, and Patton, a winning group, was flattering. If substantial French forces augmented the invasion of southern France and made an army group headquarters necessary, Clark would certainly be in the best position to command it. Despite the gleaming prospect, he was sick at heart over the idea of disrupting and dissolving what he saw as a sacred union between himself and the Fifth Army.

Could the Seventh and Fifth Army headquarters switch places? Could the Seventh take over in Italy while Clark and his Fifth did southern France? He sent Gruenther to Algiers to find out. Gruenther wired him on the last day of the year. AFHQ had disapproved. Clark had to take the Seventh Army to southern France.

Well, then, before he did that, he would give the Fifth Army the glory of entering Rome.

On January 1, 1944, AFHQ relieved Patton from command of the Seventh Army and appointed Clark the commander even as he retained command of the Fifth. Clark then sent a small planning group to Sicily to begin preparing Anvil.

In compliance with Churchill's mandate, naval planners worked at top speed on Anzio. Their estimates were discouraging. The available landing ships and craft could guarantee no more than eight days of support. They had then to be released to Overlord. This made possible the initial landing of two divisions but no subsequent buildup of the beachhead. If the original Anzio force remained isolated on a beachhead for more than eight days, that is, if the Fifth Army was unable to push the main front ahead to junction in that period of time, the amphibious force would lose its umbilical cord. Without ships to carry nourishment to the beachhead, the Anzio force would die. The naval authorities recommended cancellation.

"We are supposed to go up there," Clark explained to his staff, "dump two divisions ashore without resupply or reinforcement, and wait for the rest of the Fifth Army to join up." That was absurd. But, he said, "I am trying to find ways to do it." He added, "I am convinced that we are going to do it, and that it is going to be a success." But he was concerned about "leaving the two divisions in question out on a very long limb."

Alexander arrived to consult with Clark and was surprised to learn from him of this new threat to Anzio. Clark wrote in his diary, "None of those [on Christmas Day] who thus light-heartedly decided on the Shingle operation"—the codename for Anzio—"understood the details of shipping and of loading necessary to put ashore the requisite force and maintain it when once ashore."

Wiring immediately to Churchill in Marrakech, Alexander asked for "help and assistance." Anzio, he warned, was about to be stillborn. He and Clark, he said, were "willing to accept any risks to achieve our object," for "surely the prize is worth it."

Churchill overrode the naval authorities. Anzio could go, he informed Alexander, if it started on January 22.

Spurred by this news, Clark turned to solve the other vital problem. He had to crash through the German Winter Line and get into the Liri valley before that date. He had to get to and across the Garigliano and Rapido Rivers in the shadow of Monte Cassino by the time the Anzio landing was scheduled to go. He had less than three weeks to do all this. But by superhuman effort, he resolved to make it all work. It was their last chance.

He and Alexander agreed in their views. Anzio might jeopardize southern France, but Anvil might never go. Churchill strenuously objected to Anvil, and perhaps he would have his way. Overlooking the intense desire of the French to return to France, Alexander and Clark preferred, like Churchill, to invade the Balkans after capturing Rome. In any event, if Anzio brought Rome quickly, it would have no impact on Anvil.

But Clark had no illusions about the difficulties of Anzio. To give the VI Corps a better chance of survival at Anzio, he intended to blast into the Liri valley several days before the invasion in order to draw enemy units to that front and to "fix them there." Thus, the whole Fifth Army was involved in the Anzio operation, the landing, the push overland to the beachhead, and the drive to Rome.

Alexander appeared listless, and Clark wondered whether he was badly disappointed by the decision to keep him in command of the army group in Italy. Was he distressed because Wilson had come to command the theater and because Montgomery was to participate in Overlord? After

Alexander had gone, Clark's aide wrote in his diary, "General Clark said, as he repeatedly has in the past, that General Alexander was [acting like] a peanut and a feather duster."

Had the British relegated Alexander to second-class status by denying him the places taken by Wilson and Montgomery? Was he little more than a sweet and handsome man without the moral force and personal push to get his way? Did he lack the intellectual capacity and concentration, the hard-headedness that Clark had in abundance, to understand thoroughly and concretely the requirements, including tonnages, sailing and turn-around times, and all the rest of the multiple complexities involved in the amphibious venture?

Clark's own thoughts were somewhat confused. His loyalty remained with the Fifth Army and the Anzio concept. Anvil was an annoying complication. The terrible outlook was that if he relinquished the Fifth Army and took charge of the Seventh, the war might come to a sudden end and someone else would lead his Fifth Army into Germany.

Churchill scheduled a final meeting at Marrakech on January 7, 1944, to reach a decision on Anzio. Busy with his plans to advance toward the Liri valley, Clark remained at his headquarters. He sent two of his logisticians to attend. He warned them that unless the Navy could guarantee the retention of a certain minimum number of landing ships after the initial landing for an indefinite period, Anzio was impractical. They must not let Churchill cajole them out of that view. If they were unable to obtain what was absolutely necessary, if Anzio was out of the question from a supply point of view, Clark was thinking of making a shallower envelopment by sending a single division to land at Gaeta.

At the conference in Marrakech, all the experts in logistics, shipping, and intelligence raised hard and thorny issues. They stressed the dangers of Anzio.

Devers, who had just come from England, saw no problems. He wondered why the discussion was held at all. Anzio seemed to him, he said, "correct," a simple military decision of yes or no and let the staff work out the details.

There was another meeting on the following day, when command of the Mediterranean theater and responsibility for the Italian campaign passed to Wilson. Despite the acknowledged risks, the decision for Anzio became final. They were going to land at Anzio and get to Rome in a hurry.

Churchill had his way. He disregarded the advice of the specialists and technicians who questioned the details, who believed the margin of success to be too slim, who preferred to avoid counting so heavily on good luck. Churchill vanquished and overcame their doubts by the force of his position, character, and will.

Alexander immediately cabled Clark. They had to land at Anzio on January 22 to allow the release of the ships in a reasonable time.

Writing to Clark, Churchill admitted the hazards, but "I am deeply conscious of the importance of this battle [for Rome] without which the campaign in Italy will be regarded as having petered out ingloriously."

Although Clark thought three divisions instead of two were necessary for Anzio, he kept his reservations to himself. Replying to Churchill, he said, "I am delighted with the opportunity of launching Shingle Operation. I have felt for a long time that it was the decisive way to approach Rome. This is the first time the means... have been assembled." To show his optimism and confidence, he added, "I hope you will visit the Fifth Army in Rome before returning to the United Kingdom."

Clark now had to get to Cassino. There he would be up against a river line. He would then have to cross the water to enter the Liri valley.

In January 1944, while Lucas and his VI Corps prepared and rehearsed the Anzio landing, Clark sent his three other corps forward in a massive attack. McCreery on the left battered ahead toward the Garigliano River. Keyes in the center advanced toward the Rapido River. Juin on the right fought in the mountains. After great exertion and a liberal use of artillery and air support, the Fifth Army approached the water line barring entrance into the Liri valley.

From the Allied perspective, the waters resembled the letter "T" upside down. The Liri River flows from the north and joins the Rapido River coming from the east; together they become the Garigliano, which goes westward to the sea. Immediately behind the continuous Rapido–Garigliano water line that stretched across Clark's front, two mountain masses form the walls of the Liri valley. On those heights overlooking the rivers were the Gustav positions, Hitler's final defenses below Rome. To get into the Liri valley, Clark had to cross the Rapido between Monte Cassino, crowned by the Benedictine abbey, on the right, and what was called the Sant'Ambrogio massif on the left.

Clark instructed McCreery to cross the Garigliano River near its mouth on the night of January 17 and again, upstream, two nights later; Keyes was to go over the Rapido on the night of January 20 and get into the Liri valley. Then Harmon's tanks were to rush to Frosinone and beyond to make contact with Lucas, who was to have come ashore on January 22.

Aware of the difficulties, Alexander offered Clark more troops. The Eighth Army, now commanded by Lieutenant General Sir Oliver Leese, had no vital objectives, was hampered by the winter weather, manned a quiet front. Alexander could draw on Leese's reserves and give Clark a New Zealand division. When Keyes opened up the Liri valley, the New Zealanders could push to Frosinone, then to Anzio.

Clark demurred. He judged Harmon's tanks able to drive more quickly up the valley. Moving the New Zealanders across the Apennines and inserting them into battle positions would take too much time and delay the schedule.

Alexander did not insist.

Men of McCreery's corps battled across the Garigliano and established a bridgehead on the far bank of the river. That enormous achievement broke a hole in the Gustav Line.

Vietinghoff considered the breach a serious threat to the entire defense. If the British expanded their bridgehead into the Sant'Ambrogio massif, they might work their way into the Liri valley. That would put them behind the German positions along the Rapido. In that case, he would have to abandon the Gustav Line. Telephoning Kesselring, he reported the situation and asked for two additional divisions to help him contain the British and drive them back.

Kesselring had two divisions in reserve near Rome. They were resting and training, also guarding against a possible Allied airborne or amphibious attack near the capital. Knowing nothing about the imminent Allied landing at Anzio, Kesselring acceded to Vietinghoff's request in order to preserve the Gustav Line.

The two German divisions began to move down the Liri valley toward the Gustav positions. Their departure from the Rome area cleared the coast for Lucas.

Clark was meeting with newspaper correspondents who wanted to know what the Garigliano crossing meant. Was it designed to hasten the fall of Rome? Every operation, Clark replied, had that end in view.

Churchill was writing to Wilson on a delicate matter. "No one is keener than I," he said, "in working with the Allies in closest comradeship. I am however anxious that Operation Shingle"—the Anzio landings—"should be a joint concern and not, as it may be represented, a purely American victory.... It will lead to bitterness in Great Britain when the claim is stridently put forward, as it surely will be, that 'the Americans have taken Rome.'" He wanted Wilson to make sure of sharing the credit fairly.

Devers came to see Clark. A large and somewhat inarticulate man with a bland and cheerful smile, a shambling gait, never seemingly in a hurry, Devers appeared to be something of a big kid. Some thought him devious. Others saw him as simple, direct, and forceful. A classmate of Patton's, Devers had taught mathematics at the Military Academy. Clark had been his student and had done poorly. Devers had been close to Marshall, who used him as a trouble-shooter to solve problems and get complex jobs done quickly. Before Eisenhower's appointment to command Overlord, when everyone expected Marshall to have that responsibility, Devers was a candidate to replace Marshall as the Army Chief of Staff. Now he was number two man to Wilson, and the senior American officer in the theater. His star seemed on the wane.

Although Clark remained directly under Alexander for operations, he was directly under Devers for administration. Devers was his immediate American boss, his point of contact for Marshall, the War Department, and the Joint Chiefs of Staff. Devers' reports to Washington on a variety of subjects, including his judgment of Clark's efficiency and stamina, would in large part determine how the President and his advisers saw Clark's performance.

He intended, Devers said, to recommend Clark to command Anvil.

Clark was somewhat irritated. Everyone, it seemed, was trying to separate him from his Fifth Army.

He had already been notified of his selection for that command, Clark replied.

Their meeting was less than warm and friendly. With reservations about serving under Devers, Clark sent Eisenhower a message that evening. "I hope that this other affair"—he was referring to Anvil—"goes through as you had anticipated and that I may have the opportunity before long to again come under your command."

To his mother, who was being asked by magazine writers for a boyhood story, he implored, "I sincerely hope that you will not give it. I well understand what the public wants, but there are many people in the Army who resent these things, and there is no use antagonizing them, so please do as you have done and refrain from giving any publicity on me."

McCreery's attempt to force a second crossing of the Garigliano close to Keyes' II Corps area in order to help the Americans over the Rapido was a failure—mainly because of a lack of amphibious trucks called DUKWs. Near Naples, Lucas had conducted a dress rehearsal for Anzio and, during that practice operation, the Navy had lost more than 40 DUKWs, as well as two dozen artillery pieces, in the sea. Because Lucas absolutely had to have the DUKWs for Anzio, McCreery and Keyes depleted their stocks and sent the equipment to Lucas. McCreery, Clark noted in his diary, "needed them badly in the Garigliano crossing."

So would Keyes when he sent Walker's 36th Division across the Rapido. "I can not furnish the 36th Division with the 12 dukws which they need so badly in their crossing of the Rapido," Clark noted in his diary. The climax of the Fifth Army attack, the Rapido operation was to open the Liri valley to Harmon's tanks. But the inability of the British to provide assistance by a second crossing seriously jeopardized the Rapido effort.

Ultra intercepts told Clark how successful he had already been in pinning down the Germans and in attracting additional German forces. The two divisions moving from the Rome area had uncovered Anzio. But Clark had to cross the Rapido and open the Liri valley for a rapid linkup with Lucas' forces soon to land at Anzio.

The Rapido is a small stream, 25 to 50 feet wide, 9 to 12 feet deep. In January 1944, it flowed swiftly and was a definite military obstacle. What made it a problem above all was the attitude of the 36th Division commander, Walker.

Having punished the Germans in 1918 when they had attempted to cross the Marne River, Walker saw himself at the Rapido in the same position as the Germans. "Have been giving a lot of thought to plan for crossing Rapido River some time soon," he wrote in his diary early in January. "I'll swear I do not see how we can possibly succeed in crossing."

Walker voiced his misgivings to Clark and to Keyes, but mildly. When Walker met with Keyes on the day before his attack, he was apparently confident of getting across the stream.

Late in the afternoon of January 20, just before his assault, Walker wrote in his diary, "We might succeed but I do not see how we can. . . . So I am prepared for defeat. . . . However, if we get some breaks we may succeed."

The outcome hinged in large measure on what the engineers did. Theirs was a massive and multiple task. They had to clear a profusion of German mines in the flats adjacent to the river, first on the near side, then, when the infantry got across, on the far bank; provide pneumatic and wooden assault boats and paddles and run a ferry service across the water; put up catwalks and footbridges, later Bailey bridges for tanks and artillery pieces, and construct and maintain bridge approaches and exits—all in darkness.

The entire effort turned into a nightmare. Almost everything that could go wrong did. As more than ten thousand soldiers moved toward the river, mishaps and misfortune dogged them. Men lost their way and wandered into minefields. The Germans shelled the flats and inflicted casualties, knocked out footbridges and boats, and disrupted the attack.

Confusion and terror developed at the river's edge. Mounting hysteria led to panic. "Everything became disorganized," a report said. In the "maze of roads and pathways...nervous uncertainty prevailed." The "men were not keen for this attack." Like Walker, they expected to be slaughtered.

A handful of brave and intrepid soldiers managed to get across. The Germans quickly surrounded and isolated them. Walker thus had to try to cross again in order to rescue them. "I expect this attack to be a fizzle just as was the one last night," he wrote. Without the conviction that success was possible, dreading the losses to be inflicted on his division, he lacked the personal force to inspire his men and the ruthlessness to drive his units, and thus he transmitted his doubts to his troops and ensured failure.

During the 48-hour operation, the 36th Division lost almost 1,700 men killed, wounded, and, by far the greatest number, missing, presumably captured. His division, Walker noted, was "wrecked."

Busy with the landing at Anzio, Clark learned of the debacle on the following evening. "As was anticipated," he wrote in his diary, "heavy resistance was encountered in the 36th crossing of the Rapido River."

A day later, he met with Keyes and Walker. He opened the conversation by saying, "Tell me what happened up here."

Walker was apprehensive. The failure was his. He felt uncertain about how well he had exercised leadership. He had remained in his division headquarters during the attacks. Should he have been forward at the crossing sites to hearten and to push his men?

Writing in his diary later that day, he said, "I fully expected Clark and Keyes to 'can' me." That they did not fire him seemed to justify and excuse him. They were "not in a bad mood." They made no attempt to blame him or anyone. And gradually Walker came to see all three of them as partners in the fiasco. As the junior, he was less responsible than the others.

"It was," Walker heard Clark say to Keyes, "as much my fault as yours."

What Clark meant was that he and Keyes should have supervised Walker more closely to ensure success, to make certain of drive and determination in that vital endeavor. For to the Germans defending along the Rapido, the American attack was inconsequential, turned back easily.

Walker misunderstood Clark's words. "Clark admitted," he wrote, "the failure... was as much his fault as any one's."

The disaster and the tragedy affected Walker deeply, and he saw in Clark's words exoneration of himself as well as an admission of Clark's error. "The great losses of fine young men during the attempts to cross the Rapido to no purpose and in violation of good infantry tactics are very depressing. All chargeable to the stupidity of the higher command."

To Walker the incompetence of his superiors was the reason for the defeat. He was unaware of the connection between the Rapido crossing and the Anzio landing—should Clark and Keyes have made sure that he understood? Walker was ignorant of the need for haste to get into the Liri valley and to make contact with the Anzio beachhead before the release of the landing ships—should his superiors have told him? With Clark altogether involved in the Anzio preparations, was Keyes remiss? Lacking knowledge of the big picture, Walker believed Clark's impatience to get across the river stemmed from his exaggerated personal ambition to take Rome.

Unknown to Walker, several officers from Texas met a few days later in secret. Judging Clark's inefficiency to have been responsible for the high and, to them, unnecessary losses along the Rapido, they decided to request a congressional investigation of the battle and of Clark's leadership after the war.

As early as January 9, Clark had expected the 36th Division to "be badly worn down by their crossing of the Rapido." But the attack was necessary to gain entrance into the Liri valley for the eventual linkup with Anzio.

After talking with Keyes and Walker, Clark set down his thoughts. "In deciding upon that attack some time ago, I knew it would be costly but was impelled to go ahead... [to] draw to this front all possible German reserves in order to clear the way for Shingle [Anzio]. This was accomplished in a magnificent manner. Some blood had to be spilled on either the land [meaning the Gustav Line] or the Shingle front, and I greatly preferred that it be on the Rapido, where we were secure, rather than at Anzio with the sea at our backs."

He never again referred to the Rapido operation in his diary. He regretted the losses and the failure, but the need to assist the Anzio landing was, to him, "more than sufficient justification" for the river assault.

The motive remained. "We must [still] get a bridgehead over the Rapido in order to permit the debouchment of our tank forces into the Liri valley." Because the 36th Division seemed incapable for the moment of further effort, Clark told Keyes to send Ryder's 34th Division across the Rapido upstream, above the town of Cassino. Clark had to get into the Liri valley and up to Anzio, where Lucas and the VI Corps had landed.

The Anzio concept had changed in the course of development. From a raid-like and subsidiary operation of 24,000 men making a shallow envelopment around the left flank to a beachhead just ahead of the Fifth Army front, Shingle grew into a major landing of more than 110,000 men deep in the German rear. Instead of assisting the advance of the main forces through the Gustav Line, as Clark saw it, the landing had in some minds, among them Alexander's, taken on an independent life of its own.

Precisely what the landing was supposed to accomplish was never fully clear. Alexander failed to specify his wishes in an order or directive. Clark went his own way. There was no doubt of the necessity to take the port of Anzio and to stake out a beachhead to protect the harbor, which ensured the lifeline from the Fifth Army by sea. Was anything more expected?

Alexander anticipated a twenty-mile advance inland from Anzio to the Alban Hills. A huge and towering volcanic formation overlooking the Anzio plain, the feature dominated the two principal highways leading to Rome. Alexander wanted Lucas to gain the heights. That would "cut the enemy's main communications," the two roads, and "threaten the rear" of the Gustav Line. The landing and the advance to the height, he believed, would force the Germans to turn their main attention to Anzio. That would weaken their Gustav defenses and make it possible for Clark to break through and link up quickly with the Anzio forces.

Agreeing that Allied possession of the Alban Hills would compel the Germans to abandon the Gustav and withdraw altogether from southern Italy, Clark believed an advance from the beachhead to the Alban Hill mass to be well beyond the capacities of the Anzio force. With merely two divisions, Lucas would be unable to hold the ports of Anzio and Nettuno, to seize and occupy the heights, and to protect the twenty miles between the sea and the hills. The Germans, as Clark envisioned the situation, would have to react in strength to the landing and make what he called a "ruthless" concentration against Lucas. By so doing, in Clark's opinion, the Germans would have to weaken the Gustav positions. That would allow the Fifth Army main forces to rush forward overland from Cassino to Anzio. After making junction with Lucas' beachhead, the main forces would take the Alban Hills.

Thus, for Clark's purposes, a landing and a firmly held beachhead against strong German pressure were enough. Furthermore, he was uncertain how long it would take him to get through the Gustav Line and up the Liri valley to Anzio. Unwilling to issue a categorical order, Clark sent Lucas deliberately ambiguous instructions.

Lucas was, Clark said, "To seize and secure a beachhead," which was clear enough. He was then to "Advance on" the Alban Hills, which was fuzzy. Was he to go toward the hills or to them? That would be up to Lucas. If the Allied invasion at Anzio prompted a German retreat out of southern Italy, Lucas was, of course, to head for the heights. But this seemed so doubtful to Clark that he had no desire to order Lucas to follow a risky course of action that might lead to the annihilation of the VI Corps.

If Lucas met slight opposition and if Clark's main forces were speeding up the Liri valley, Lucas could, if he wished, move to Albano or to Cisterna to cut Route 7; he could then go beyond Cisterna to Valmontone and cut Highway 6 at the northern end of the Liri valley. This was in line with Alexander's view. But Clark believed that Lucas needed at least three divisions to carry out these actions.

The divergent outlooks and concepts held by Alexander and Clark would lead to confusion. They should have been resolved at the outset. It was the responsibility of Alexander, the superior commander, to make his desire clear and prevailing. Instead, because of his own lack of decision or because of his inhibitions in the coalition command, he allowed the venture, like the entire operational strategy in Italy, simply to develop. In the case of Anzio, Lucas would find himself in the middle of and eventually the victim of opposite expectations.

A solemn gray-haired man who smoked a corncob pipe, Lucas had always looked older and smaller than he actually was. He was steady and calm, but fighting in the mountains of southern Italy for three months had tired him.

At first flattered to be chosen to lead the expedition, Lucas soon lost his enthusiasm. He began to see the assumptions as dangerous. The operation was, he said, "such a desperate undertaking that it should not, in my opinion, be attempted." Knowing a little of how Churchill had restored the undertaking, he wrote in his diary, "This whole affair has a strong odor of Gallipoli and apparently the same amateur is still on the coach's bench." The final rehearsal of the landing on a beach near Naples confirmed Lucas' pessimism. Everything went wrong.

Increasingly, Lucas found himself out of sympathy with Anzio. "The general idea seems to be that the Germans are licked and are fleeing in disorder," he wrote. "We are not (repeat not) in Rome yet. They will end up by putting me ashore with inadequate forces and get me in a serious jam. Then, who will take the blame?"

As he boarded the vessel for the trip to Anzio, Lucas was in an ambivalent frame of mind. "I have many misgivings," he wrote, "but am also optimistic." With several days of good weather, "I should be all right. . . . I think we have a good chance to make a killing." With no right of access to the Ultra intercepts, with no knowledge of the absence of German forces near Rome—should Alexander and Clark have told him?—he wished that "the higher levels were not so over-optimistic."

Two days later, when the initial waves swarmed ashore at 2 A.M., no opposition awaited them. "We achieved what is certainly one of the most complete surprises in history," Lucas wrote. "I could not believe my eyes when I stood on the bridge and saw no machine gun or other fire on the beach."

Alexander and Clark visited Lucas during the day. Alexander was very cheerful. Clark was somewhat subdued, for he was depressed by reports of the Rapido action. After expressing their satisfaction to Lucas, both commanders left without recommending what Lucas ought to do.

Would he choose to be bold or prudent? With no Germans present, the road to the Alban Hills, even to Rome, was open. Audacity promised an overwhelming victory. Yet to abandon the ports of Anzio and Nettuno and his lifeline to Naples, to drive to the Alban heights or to Rome might lead to disastrous defeat. If the Germans kept the door to the Liri valley closed, they might destroy his corps. Because the Fifth Army was hardly dashing up the Liri valley, Lucas decided to gather his resources on the shore, build up his strength in the beachhead, and provide a sound basis for survival. Then he would see about the Alban Hills.

Alexander and Clark had already decided to reinforce the beachhead. The only way to loosen the Gustav defenses was to threaten the Alban Hills. And for that Lucas needed more strength. His two divisions were hardly enough to frighten the Germans off the Gustav Line.

As soon as Kesselring learned of the landing, he started, with Hitler's approval, to move substantial forces to Anzio—from Genoa, Rimini, Leghorn, and other parts of northern Italy, from southern France, the Balkans, and Germany. He instructed Vietinghoff to send back the two divisions recently dispatched from the Rome area to the Gustav Line, plus two divisions from the Adriatic front. All were en route by evening, and the semblance of a defensive line was taking form around the Anzio beachhead.

Writing in his diary on January 23, Clark said, "Lucas must be aggressive. He must take some chances." He had to appear to threaten the Alban Hills. To that end Clark would augment the beachhead to the maximum that logistics and his Cassino front permitted—about a division and a half. Lucas' first efforts, Clark understood, had to be concerned with stability. But, eventually, Lucas had to strike out.

Lucas expanded the ground he held, established dumps and depots, and brought more men ashore. By the third day, he had a beachhead seven miles deep, a front of sixteen miles. As ships plied between Naples and Anzio, he built up his resources methodically. Refusing to be hurried into an advance "on" the Alban Hills, he waited to be ready beyond all doubt before he pushed out seriously. For the main Fifth Army forces were making little progress as they struggled to get into the Liri valley.

Clark confided his thoughts to his diary. Moving closer to Alexander's idea, he wrote that when Lucas had enough strength, "I will then strike out and cut the German lines of communication, forcing his withdrawal out of the Cassino area. Then, I will turn my attention to Rome."

With portions of eight divisions enclosing the Allies at Anzio and parts of five others on the way, the Germans prepared to launch a decisive attack and eliminate the beachhead.

"To extend the beachhead a little," Lucas sent his troops toward Albano and Cisterna to cut Highway 7. They were unable to reach their objectives. "I must keep my feet on the ground and my forces in hand and do nothing foolish," Lucas wrote. His beachhead was about ten miles deep. He refused to be "stampeded."

Clark came for a visit and was impressed by the orderly way in which Lucas was developing his logistical structure. He talked of the continuing battle around Cassino, where the combat was fierce, the conditions were frightful. Ryder's 34th Division was taking a battering without result.

From Clark's description, Lucas had the impression that "the bloodiest fight of the war is in progress." How long would it take the Fifth Army to break into the Liri valley and link up with him?

Alexander showed up and complimented Lucas. "What a splendid piece of work," he exclaimed. But he began to question Lucas' caution. Only if Lucas actively threatened the Alban Hills could he resolve the impasse at the Gustav Line.

Clark agreed.

On edge, Clark was vexed and frustrated, in a bad mood when Jumbo Wilson, large and urbane, came later that day to see him. When, Wilson asked sympathetically, did Clark think he could leave Italy and devote his full attention to southern France?

Was he asking whether Clark was ready to give up his struggle to get to Rome? Were they trying to get him out of Italy?

He thought he could leave, Clark replied, about the middle of March, perhaps later.

Wilson understood the strain on him. He wanted Clark, he said, to remain in Italy as long as possible.

"I told him I wanted to speak frankly," Clark dictated into his diary later that day, "that the Fifth Army had landed at Salerno, taken Naples, and battled its way to the north through hellish terrain and with bloody losses and that it was entitled under my command to take Rome—that if on the 15th of March I was battling at the gates of Rome, under no circumstances should I be pulled out.

"He assured me that under no conditions would he do so.

"I also told him that if under certain conceptions Anvil should become a 'fart in the dark' of one division spawning the Mediterranean with no intention of landing any place, I wanted no part of it.

"He assured me that it was his desire that I stay with the Fifth Army and never even look at Anvil."

That suited Clark just fine. He would find a way out of the discouraging situation. He would never give up. Rome was the only objective of importance. Churchill, Roosevelt, Marshall, everyone wanted Rome. He would get there. No one else was going to do it.

CHAPTER 15

☆ ☆ ☆ ☆

THE DARKEST HOUR: MONTE CASSINO

"so preoccupied and harassed"

HAVING PROMISED ALEXANDER to go to Anzio and prod Lucas, Clark arose at 3:45 A.M. on January 28 to start what was to be a harrowing day. With Brann and his aide, he drove to the mouth of the Volturno River and embarked in a storm boat, which struck a sandbar and splashed water over him. He was soaking wet and chilled to the bone when the three officers boarded two PT boats waiting for them.

In order to get out of the cold and piercing wind, Clark sat on a stool in the prow beside the skipper, a young ensign named Benson. They occasionally passed Allied ships. Some challenged them, and they responded with Very flares and signal blinkings. Five minesweepers working together asked for their identification.

Half an hour later, about seven miles from Anzio, an Allied vessel two thousand yards away requested their identity. Clark stood up and moved a few feet away to get a better view. The PT boats fired green

and yellow flares and blinked appropriate signals. Instead of acknowl-
edging, the ship began to fire at them.

One round struck the deckhouse and exploded less than two yards from
Clark. Another knocked over the stool where he had been sitting. The
opening salvo wounded five of the crew, four on deck, one below in the
tiny mess.

Picking up a Very pistol, Clark fired the correct flares, but the shooting
continued.

Ensign Benson, knocked from the wheel, was down on the deck,
wounded in the legs. Clark bent over him and asked, "What shall we
do?"

"Don't know."

"Let's run for it," Clark said.

Helping Benson to his feet, Clark held him up to the wheel. As shells
crashed around them, they turned and sped away.

After propping Benson up, Clark turned his attention to the wounded.
Finding a first-aid kit, he poured sulfanilamide into their wounds.

They reached the group of five minesweepers, identified themselves
again, and pulled alongside a British vessel. A doctor was aboard and,
with some difficulty, they transferred the injured men to the larger ship.
Two of the wounded soon died.

Although Brann tried to dissuade Clark from continuing to Anzio
because of the danger, he insisted on proceeding. He had to take his
chances too.

Going aboard the other PT boat, the party went toward Anzio. They
located the ship that had fired on them, identified themselves, then came
alongside and asked what had provoked the attack. The skipper had been
alerted to hostile boats in the area. The PT craft had been traveling fast
in the slanting rays of the early morning sun. They had appeared to be
Germans in attack formation.

Clark and his party ran into the Anzio harbor just as an air raid started.
Turning quickly, they headed out to sea. They cruised around while
German planes bombed the port and the ships offshore. When the aircraft
flew away, they came in. It was just pass noontime. Clark went immediately to Lucas' command post.

He had shipped Lucas more troops, another infantry division and half
an armored division—the other half waited near Cassino for an opening
into the Liri valley so that the tanks could drive overland to Anzio. By
augmenting Lucas, Clark then reduced the forces at the Cassino front.

Maintaining a precarious balance between the two would probably prevent a decisive victory at either place.

Now that Lucas had three and a half divisions, Alexander thought him able to seize Cisterna and go on rapidly to Velletri in the Alban Hills. In view of the German buildup around Anzio, Clark considered Cisterna far enough. Taking Cisterna would cut Highway 7 and deny the Germans use of the road. Complimenting Lucas on his thoroughness, Clark urged him to take "bold and aggressive action" to Cisterna.

He told Lucas of his intention to set up a small Fifth Army advance headquarters on the Anzio beachhead, which he judged more dangerous than the Cassino front. With a small place of his own, he could see personally what needed doing and how he could help.

Re-embarking in the PT boat, he returned to his headquarters, which had moved that day from the palace grounds at Caserta to a hillside just below the mountain town of Presenzano.

Lucas was sure of his course. He had secured a proper beachhead and was trying to keep the Germans off balance. To him, Clark seemed "gloomy," preoccupied by his attempt to get into the Liri valley. The longer it took him to crash through the Gustav Line, the more vulnerable to disaster the Anzio forces became. A defeat at the beachhead would be calamitous. But in compliance with Clark's wish, Lucas planned an offensive to threaten the Alban Hills.

"You can imagine how busy I have been with this new operation," Clark wrote Renie, "and now, instead of one front on my hands, I have two and, naturally, plenty to think about." Telling briefly about his experience in the PT boat, he said, "I was very fortunate."

Before going again to Anzio, Clark visited Keyes. A month earlier Keyes had impressed Clark as an outstanding commander, "likeable, a hell of a good soldier, with a good mind." Keyes always had accurate and detailed knowledge of his tactical dispositions.

Now Clark was disappointed. Busy with Anzio, he had asked Keyes to coordinate American and French forces in the hills around Cassino, normally Clark's task. Keyes had been unable to mesh the Franco-American efforts. Critical of Keyes' initiative, Clark spoke bitingly to him.

Everyone was on edge. Opening up the Liri valley seemed to be impossible.

At Anzio Clark went to his new command post in a pine grove on the palace grounds of Prince Borghese. Bad news awaited him. The rangers, elite troops, had spearheaded the attack to Cisterna very early that morning. Marching forward quietly in a large ditch leading to the town, they hoped to gain surprise. Instead, at daylight the Germans ambushed them. Of the 767 rangers who had set out, six returned; the others were captured or killed.

Clark was, he wrote, "distressed." Having the rangers lead the way was to him "a definite error in judgment"—whose, he did not say.

He was discouraged when he wrote in his diary. His original estimate had gone awry. Unable to get into the Liri valley, Clark had to do something positive at Anzio. He swung increasingly toward Alexander's concept and began to consider an advance to the Alban Hills. There the Allied forces would be off the floor of the Anzio plain and on high ground. They would thus deny the Germans their exceptional view of the beachhead, which permitted them to rain accurate and deadly fires down on Lucas' installations and troops.

But getting to the Alban Hills, Clark realized, was probably too much to expect. The Germans had gathered substantial strength around Anzio.

"I have been harsh with Lucas today, much to my regret," Clark wrote, "but in an effort to energize him to greater effort."

Lucas saw himself as "engaged in a hell of a struggle." The future was "crowded with doubt and uncertainty."

Clark stayed overnight. On the following day he inspected the positions, talked with key subordinates, cheered the soldiers. As he became familiar with the conditions, he saw no hope for getting to the Alban Hills in the near future. That realistic appreciation darkened his prospects.

"I don't blame him," Lucas wrote in his diary, "for being terribly disappointed. He and those above him thought this landing would shake the Cassino line loose at once, but they had no right to think that."

What no one mentioned was the marvelous chance Lucas had had to achieve a magnificent triumph. Having gained surprise in his landings, facing no German opposition at the outset, he could have reached and taken commanding positions on the Alban Hills. According to German reports, he could have gone all the way into Rome untouched.

But such a course of action required a daring and unorthodox leader with dash and flair and the ability to risk losing all. By giving up his port, cutting his ties to the rear, and fighting on his own, he had to be able to face with equanimity the constant threat of annihilation.

Lucas was anything but that kind of commander. Why, then, had he been selected to carry out the Anzio operation? No other corps commander had been available.

Would Allied forces on the Alban Hills have frightened the Germans into abandoning the Gustav Line? Given Kesselring's nerve and Vietinghoff's skill, the Germans might well have trapped the Allies on the Alban Hills or in Rome and completely destroyed more than 100,000 soldiers.

Lucas had played it safe and sound. He had chosen the conventional military option. He had ensured his survival, the first rule. And in so doing, he had guaranteed a protracted struggle for Rome. The quick capture of the capital, the hope behind the Anzio landing, glimmered and vanished. Only the nagging thought of what might have been remained.

At the time, Alexander thought Lucas had been wrong to sit tight. But after the war, according to General James M. Gavin, Alexander, looking back, felt Lucas had been right to wait and consolidate.

Alexander talked with Clark about resolving the impasse. Clark recommended, whether seriously or sardonically, another landing at Civitavecchio, 65 miles above Anzio. That would really loosen things up.

According to Clark's diary, Alexander was "taken aback by the suggestion." Anzio was posing enough logistical problems. Another landing would present them with additional difficulties.

"Overcome them," Clark offered.

But the proposal, in Alexander's opinion, was too wild for serious consideration. Another landing would further disperse and fragment the Allied strength. The two vital points were Anzio and the Cassino front, and solutions could be found only at one place or the other.

Before leaving the beachhead, Clark apologized to Lucas for having harassed him.

"I am glad he did," Lucas wrote in his diary, "as I really like him very much."

"I have been tremendously busy lately," Clark informed Renie, "hovering between my two battle fronts." He was tired and "could use about a week's rest," but it was impossible for him to do so, for something was "boiling every minute."

At the beachhead again, Clark found the British and American divisions so depleted by casualties and tired that he wondered whether they could withstand a German blow.

One came on the following evening, starting with an intensive bombing and shelling of the Allied positions. Near Clark a British ammunition truck received a direct bomb hit. Rushing to the aid of the badly wounded driver, he took personal charge of the efforts to extricate the soldier, give him first aid, and get him to a hospital.

The battle raged for three days, and Clark's presence, which inspired the defenders, helped keep Lucas' men from being swept out of the beachhead. Lucas wrote in his diary, "Things get worse and worse." But Clark's calm confidence, his frequent appearances among the combat troops, and his stability and leadership maintained the solidity of the positions. More than a year later he was awarded the Bronze Star for his actions.

Alexander had meanwhile come to a decision. Because he could expect nothing more than a successful defense at Anzio, he had to make things happen around Cassino. For that he needed more troop strength. To that end, he instructed a New Zealand, an Indian, and a British division to move, in that order, out of the British Eighth Army on the Adriatic front and across the mountains to the western side of Italy. If these fresh soldiers replaced some of Keyes' and Juin's units in the high ground around Cassino, specifically on the approaches to Monte Cassino, they might force an entrance into the Liri valley.

To keep these three British and Commonwealth divisions together and under central direction, Alexander created a provisional corps under Lieutenant General Sir Bernard Freyberg, a crusty and opinionated New Zealander. Highly decorated in World War I, Freyberg had more recently commanded the forces in Crete and had participated in the desert fighting under Montgomery. He was an impressive figure with a reputation for being hard to handle.

With respect to the command arrangements, Alexander had three alternatives. He could move the boundary line on the map separating the Eighth and Fifth Armies to the west and thereby still keep the provisional corps under the British Eighth Army, commanded by Sir Oliver Leese. But that would disrupt unity of command. The efforts west of the Apennines consisted of a single enterprise, and all the parts functioned best when an overall commander directed them. To give Leese control of the provisional corps would remove Clark's authority over a critical portion of the battlefield.

Or Alexander could place the provisional corps under Clark's Fifth Army. That would retain the unity of outlook. But Freyberg was temperamental and headstrong, and perhaps Clark would be unable to work effectively with him. Besides, Clark already commanded four corps— Lucas' at the beachhead, McCreery's, Keyes', and Juin's around Cassino. To add Freyberg's would give Clark a larger than usual span of control.

Alexander's third possibility was to establish the provisional corps as an independent organization directly under his own command, under neither Fifth nor Eighth Army. That too would violate unity of command, but Alexander was more concerned with Freyberg's personality. Certain of his ability to direct the difficult Freyberg, he decided to follow the last option.

To discuss the details of inserting Freyberg's provisional corps into the front, Clark, Alexander, and Freyberg met at Caserta. The New Zealanders and Indians were arriving, the British division would come later.

Alexander had asked Freyberg to recommend where and how to employ his corps, and Freyberg understood that he was to operate under Alexander's direct control. He thus drew a tentative plan without conferring with Clark.

Clark regarded this as an invasion of his authority, prerogatives, and territory. He found it distasteful, even unethical. Unable to comprehend Alexander's wish to keep the corps independent, he thought that all the forces on the front around Cassino comprised a seamless whole. He urged Alexander to put Freyberg under Clark's control, and, reluctantly, according to Clark's impression, Alexander agreed.

Eight months earlier, Eisenhower had set down his appraisal of Alexander. Remarking Alexander's "winning personality" and "sound tactical conceptions," Eisenhower continued, "The only possible doubt... with respect to his qualities is a suspected unsureness in dealing with certain of his subordinates. At times it seems that he alters his own plans and ideas merely to meet an objection or a suggestion of a subordinate, so as to avoid direct command methods."

Alexander had held a loose rein over his subordinate Montgomery in North Africa, Sicily, and Italy. Now he followed the same course with Clark.

They decided to put the New Zealanders and Indians into the front near the town of Cassino. Freyberg at once expressed his confidence in moving quickly across the Rapido River and into the Liri valley.

Dictating for his diary, Clark said, "Freyberg is sort of a bull in a china closet. He feels he is going to win the war, and [instead] with his 15,000 vehicles"—more than normal for a division—"is going to clutter up the entire Liri valley area. He immediately clashed with Keyes when he indicated where he was moving artillery, his New Zealanders, his Indians, and other impedimenta. I turned it over to my staff, telling Freyberg that he could move into no areas until he had coordinated with all Fifth Army activities." That was the advantage of having Freyberg under him.

But he advised Keyes how important it was to maintain friendly relations with Freyberg. The New Zealanders, Clark said, always expected special consideration.

Clark was nervous and fidgety, under great strain, when he answered a letter from Renie. Traveling under War Department auspices and talking to large audiences around the country to stimulate war bond purchases, she was a member of a team of celebrities on tour; for one period of time, she appeared with the well-known band leader Glenn Miller. Her performance was a talk about her husband, what kind of soldier he was. She turned out to be an effective public speaker, humorous and compelling. During one appearance, when a man promised to buy a $1,000 bond if he could kiss her, she invited him to come up on the stage and do so at once. The Treasury Department awarded her a distinguished service citation for selling well over $25 million in war bonds.

She was so good on the platform that the Redpath Bureau, a firm managing public lecturers, signed her. Although she continued her war bond drives, she also toured for Redpath. She spoke about her husband's submarine trip, billed as "one of the great adventure stories of all time," and read excerpts from his letters. In the process she created resentment among some Army wives who thought it wrong to earn money by exploiting her husband's position.

Her efforts gained Clark a continuously good press. She described him "working coolly" in "his tent virtually under enemy guns," preferring his van to living in the royal palace. She pictured him as a simple field soldier. At a luncheon meeting in Indianapolis with 1,200 ladies of the Scottish Rite, where she spoke of a spiritual reawakening in the country, of brotherhood and peace, she characterized her husband as athletic and hard working. He accompanied her when she bought her hats and helped her choose them. He was, she said, an "awfully good man, rather a religious man."

Unaware of the controversy she was promoting in some quarters, Renie was busy. She spoke five nights a week for nine months in 1943 and would do the same in 1944. She met important people. She reserved Sundays for Ann and visited Bill at West Point as often as she could.

"You had heard of our new landing," her husband wrote, referring to Anzio. "However, you said practically nothing of it." He was hurt and disappointed. He wanted her concern and support. "You seem to be so engrossed in the details of your trip, which is natural. I had hoped, however, to get your reaction."

He was, he said, "tremendously busy with two fronts, running from one to the other. We are having severe fighting in both places. I hope for the best."

But he was worried. "As I have told you many times, my greatest ambition has and always will be to command an American Army in combat, and preferably the Fifth Army. I aspire to nothing greater."

The survival of the Anzio beachhead was a matter of touch and go, while around Cassino the men of Ryder's division burned themselves trying to get on the heights overlooking the Liri valley.

As Freyberg looked ahead to relieving the exhausted Americans, he began to feel uneasy about the Benedictine abbey at the top of Monte Cassino. It dominated, both physically and psychologically, the approaches to the Liri valley. He spoke to Clark, and Clark recorded Freyberg's "apprehension that the monastery buildings would be used by the Germans and stated that in his opinion, if necessary, they should be blown down by artillery fire or bombardment."

This was a delicate subject. Allied policy sought to respect and preserve "all religious institutions" and all "local archives, historical and classical monuments and objects of art," unless "military necessity" required their destruction. Alexander and Clark had warned their subordinates to take "every precaution...to protect these properties" except in the case of "military necessity." What was militarily necessary was, of course, a matter of judgment. Specifically, the Fifth Army warned the air forces "to avoid bombing [the] abbey on Monte Cassino."

Already the Vatican had complained of damage to the abbey by artillery fire. The rounds striking the building had been unintentional and accidental. German defensive positions were so close to the abbey walls that an occasional stray Allied shell struck the shrine.

The Germans were also concerned with preserving religious and historical monuments, and Vietinghoff forbade his soldiers to enter the monastery. But it would be impossible, he told Kesselring, to keep the abbey free from harm because "it lies directly in the main line of resistance."

When Freyberg expressed interest in taking the abbey deliberately under fire, Clark authorized him to do whatever he wished if, in his opinion, military necessity dictated the action.

The Indians were scheduled to attack Monte Cassino, and as the division commander, Sir Francis S. Tuker, a British officer, viewed his problems, he came to see the monastery as the single most formidable obstacle to success. He wanted the building destroyed before his troops went forward, and he asked Freyberg to arrange for an air bombardment.

Accordingly, Freyberg telephoned the Fifth Army headquarters at 7 P.M. on February 12. Clark was at Anzio, and Gruenther took the call. He recorded the conversation immediately afterward.

"I desire," Freyberg said, "that I be given air support tomorrow in order to soften the enemy position in the Cassino area. I want three missions of twelve planes each, the planes to be Kitty Bombers carrying 1,000-pound bombs."

Thirty-six bombers dropping a total of eighteen tons of high explosive was hardly an exorbitant request. Unfortunately, Clark had obtained the promise of a concentrated air effort at Anzio in order to break up German troop concentrations. Gruenther doubted whether the air forces could provide all the planes Freyberg wished.

He would like whatever "he could get," Freyberg replied.

Gruenther would, he told Freyberg, "go into the matter at once."

Checking with the air forces, he secured a partially favorable response. They could furnish 36 bombers carrying 500-pound bombs for a single mission.

Gruenther called Freyberg and informed him. What, he asked, did Freyberg want the aircraft to strike?

"I want the Convent attacked," he said. He meant the Benedictine abbey.

Earlier that day, Freyberg's headquarters had routinely submitted a list of targets for air bombardment if planes were available. Gruenther had the paper in his hand and looked at it. The monastery, he told Freyberg, was not included.

"I am quite sure it was on my list of targets," Freyberg said, "but in any case I want it bombed. The other targets are unimportant, but this one is vital. The division commander who is making the attack feels that it is an essential target and I thoroughly agree with him."

In the absence of Clark, Gruenther said, he was unable to authorize the bombing. He promised to call Freyberg back.

After trying vainly to reach Clark at Anzio, Gruenther called Alexander's chief of staff, now Sir John Harding, and explained the situation. In Clark's opinion, Gruenther knew, there was no military necessity to bomb the monastery. Keyes and Ryder agreed. But in view of Freyberg's special position, Gruenther asked whether he ought to accede to his request.

Like Gruenther, Harding lacked the authority to make such a decision.

He had to talk with his boss. He would call Gruenther back.

While waiting, Gruenther got through to Clark. Seeing no reason to destroy the abbey, Clark was embarrassed because of, he said, "the extremely strong views of General Freyberg." Gruenther told him of passing the request to Alexander.

Still waiting for Alexander's response, Gruenther phoned Keyes. Keyes saw no necessity to destroy the abbey. Several thousand civilians had taken refuge in the building. No Germans were inside, although many were very close to the outer walls. Destroying the monastery would probably enhance its value as a defensive installation, and the Germans after bombardment would feel free to use it as a fortress.

Harding phoned back. Alexander had decided to bomb the monastery if Freyberg considered its destruction a military necessity. Regretting the action, Alexander had faith in Freyberg's judgment.

Gruenther told of his conversation with Clark. If Freyberg were an American officer, Gruenther said, Clark would refuse permission for an air strike.

Harding replied coldly. Alexander had made his position "quite clear."

Gruenther then telephoned Clark, who asked him to request Freyberg to reconsider. Clark was willing to defer to Freyberg's judgment, but Freyberg had to be sure. If he still wished the bombardment, Gruenther was to order it no earlier than 10 A.M. on the following morning. That would give Clark time to talk with Alexander beforehand. If he persuaded Alexander to change his mind, they could cancel the bombing.

Gruenther telephoned and advised the New Zealander of Clark's reluctance to authorize the bombardment unless Freyberg was absolutely certain of it as a requirement for the attack.

Freyberg had no doubt. It was a military necessity.

The magic words having been categorically spoken, Gruenther authorized the air mission. He so informed the bomber command.

An hour or so later Freyberg called Gruenther. They had to postpone the bombardment. The bombs would endanger the Indian troops who were too close to the target and could not move out of harm's way in time.

Gruenther sighed in relief.

Returned from Anzio on the following morning, Clark talked with Alexander on the telephone and explained why he did not favor the bombing. German troops seemed not to be using the monastery. Women and children were taking shelter there. It would be shameful to ruin a property of such religious and historical value.

All this was so, Alexander agreed. But if Freyberg wanted a bombardment, Alexander would have to give it to him.

Yet Alexander was uncomfortable, and he telephoned the theater commander. Wilson concurred in Alexander's logic. If Freyberg thought bombing necessary, they had to bomb.

Now the air force commanders became interested. Having never before employed a large fleet of heavy or strategic bombers against a battlefield target, they saw an opportunity to prove the value of air power. Could planes accomplish what soldiers could not? By flattening the monastery, aircraft would smash the German defenses and enable the Allies to enter into the Liri valley. If destroying the religious and historical property was bothersome, the importance of linking up with and rescuing the Anzio beachhead was undeniably a military necessity. If German troops occupied the monastery, that fact provided further justification for bombing.

To discover whether Germans were using the abbey for observing and controlling artillery fires, Ira C. Baker, who commanded the Mediterranean air forces, and Devers, Wilson's deputy, flew in a Piper Cub over the building on February 13. Their flight was comparatively safe; the Germans rarely fired on small planes to avoid exposing their antiaircraft gun positions. The two American general officers identified what they believed was a military radio aerial in the inner courtyard and thought they saw several German soldiers moving in and out of the monastery.

Now there was no doubt about the propriety of bombing. Tuker, the Indian division commander, had initiated the request, Freyberg had transmitted and supported it, Alexander and Wilson had authorized the bombardment, and Eaker and Devers escalated the decision. Freyberg's modest proposal of 36 planes mushroomed into an all-out effort of 250 aircraft. Freyberg began to talk frankly and enthusiastically of levelling the monastery.

Although the basic motive was to get Indians and New Zealanders into the Liri valley, a new intent had come to the forefront. The air forces were about to demonstrate the power of the bomber.

Someone thought of the monks and the refugees, and on the evening of February 14, planes dropped messages warning the occupants to leave. The abbot sent his secretary to arrange the departure with the Germans. They decided to vacate the abbey at 5 A.M. on February 16.

That was a day too late. For on the morning of February 15, waves of bombers flew in awesome formation over Monte Cassino, dropped almost 600 tons of bombs, turned the top of the mountain into a smoking mass of rubble, and demolished the monastery. The earth trembled. Men watched with mixed emotions. Some exulted over the spectacle. Others like Clark were sick at heart.

The bombers broke neither the will nor the defenses of the Germans. The Indians and New Zealanders were unable to pry their way into the Liri valley. After several days of savage fighting, the battle around Cassino subsided. No swift linkup with Anzio could be expected.

To find out whether the Germans had occupied the abbey before the bombardment, Clark had his counter-intelligence agents investigate. They discovered that the Germans had scrupulously refrained from entering the monastery before the bombing. Afterward they turned it into a fortress.

Meanwhile, disaster stalked the Anzio beachhead. Hitler expected the Allies to cross the Channel and invade Europe in the spring or summer. If he could eliminate what he called the "abscess" at Anzio, he could, he believed, compel the Allies to postpone their landings on the continent. With German divisions from northern Italy, Yugoslavia, and elsewhere now massed around the beachhead and outnumbering the Allies, Kesselring scheduled an all-out attack.

As the bombers were obliterating the Monte Cassino abbey, Alexander cabled Brooke in London to complain about Lucas, who, he said, was tired and negative, lacked drive and enthusiasm and initiative. Lucas seemed unable to master the situation. His staff was depressed. His corps headquarters was dug into deep wine cellars connected by tunnels, and he rarely appeared above ground. What was needed at Anzio, Alexander said, was "a thruster like George Patton."

Brooke, Chief of the British Imperial Staff, immediately informed Eisenhower, and Eisenhower told Patton to be ready to fly to Italy. Patton, who was training his Third Army in England for the forthcoming invasion of Normandy still several months away, was excited. A year earlier, after the battle of Kasserine Pass, Eisenhower had summoned him from Morocco to go to Tunisia and take command of the II Corps. Now apparently he was indispensable again. With great anticipation, Patton prepared to travel at once. Whether he would take command of the Fifth Army or of the VI Corps was unclear, but it made no difference to him so long as he was engaged in fighting. Within a few days he received disappointing news. His trip was cancelled.

For on February 16, while Devers visited Lucas and found his logistical arrangements impressive, Alexander and Clark met and talked. Both were sober and grave. The Indians around Cassino were locked in deadly combat, and the beachhead forces, struck hard by the Germans, were fighting desperately.

"You know," Alexander said, referring to Anzio, "the position is serious. We may be pushed back into the sea. That would be very bad for both of us—and you would certainly be relieved of your command."

If that seemed like blackmail, Clark chose to disregard the inference. He agreed with Alexander to replace Lucas. The troops needed a dashing figure to inspire them. They decided to appoint two deputy corps commanders, a British officer who would help Lucas with the British units, and an American who would eventually take over, for the VI Corps was an American headquarters.

Clark had a long talk with Devers on February 17. First, they decided to relieve Lucas as soon as the battle was over. They would replace him with Truscott, who was young and dashing. Succeeding Truscott in command of the 3rd Division would be O'Daniel, Clark's old friend.

Second, Clark let off steam about the difficulties of working with the British. Devers was sympathetic.

Third, Devers passed along his views on Anvil. There was still no firm decision to invade southern France. Marshall and Eisenhower wanted Anvil; Churchill and Brooke opposed it. Even if the operation materialized, it would probably not amount to much. He thought Clark ought to stay with the Fifth Army. Enchanted with the advice, Clark dictated later for his diary, "I have no other desire than to command the Fifth Army in battle and to the successful conclusion of this war."

Fourth, Devers transmitted some disturbing news. There was talk of having Alexander's 15th Army Group headquarters take direct command of the beachhead forces while the Fifth Army retained control of the Cassino front.

Was Alexander trying to dissociate the Fifth Army from Rome? Was Alexander maneuvering to lead the Allied forces into the city? Was he trying to turn the capture of Rome into a British victory?

Managing both fronts, Clark admitted, was a tremendous burden. But he hated to give up command of the Anzio forces. He much preferred keeping the beachhead, which was closer to Rome, and letting the Eighth Army take over the main front around Cassino.

Finally, they touched on the basic problem confronting them as Americans in Italy. "Devers seems to understand," Clark wrote in his diary, "the difficult position which we find ourselves in with the entire Mediterranean now in British hands." The Americans were outsiders under

British orders and subject to their methods of running the war.

Tense and nervous, Clark was up very early on the morning of February 18. Reading the latest dispatches from the beachhead, he found the news so bad that he decided to go there at once. He flew in a Cub plane escorted by two Spitfires. The airfield at Anzio was under artillery shelling, but his pilot landed safely. He spoke with the principal commanders, who were all under great pressure. The forces were in Lucas' final beachhead line, and beyond that they could not withdraw. Otherwise, the front would disintegrate.

Lucas was tired, "very tired," Clark noted, "but I did not take him out because it was in the middle of a battle." Besides, Truscott "was not sufficiently" acquainted with the big "picture to take over."

Four Spitfires escorted his Cub plane on his return trip. It was a long and lonesome flight. Clark contemplated his problems. Rome was still distant. There was a distinct prospect of defeat on both fronts. His career was in jeopardy. The British were running the campaign and trying to squeeze him out of his legitimate functions.

He talked with Freyberg and asked him to continue attacking in order to help the beachhead. "I urged him to speedier action," Clark wrote in his diary, "knowing it would be to no avail. You can't hurry these Britishers."

He was positively depressed. "I have been so hamstrung and jockeyed by higher headquarters that the Fifth Army has lost a great deal of its power to control its own tactical operations, but I will insist, as long as I am Commander"—was he wondering how long he would retain his position?—"on presenting my views and demanding their execution as far as possible."

It was difficult to be harmonious and polite in a time of adversity, and when Wilson came to call, "I had a very frank conversation with him. He is always considerate, and I feel wants to be helpful."

Everyone, Clark told him, had a commitment to Anzio. The beachhead needed wholehearted support. Yet the naval forces, headed by John Cunningham, were holding back, acting in high-handed ways without concern for requirements, trying to cut the tonnages allocated, and closing the port of Anzio from time to time for no good reason.

Wilson was affable and sympathetic. He agreed with Clark on the necessity of seizing Monte Cassino before sticking their heads into the Liri valley, on the futility of trying to take the Alban Hills for the moment. He had no other comfort to offer.

Clark was anything but in a happy or buoyant mood when he dictated a letter to Renie, who had written from Dallas. "Although I am in pretty much of a tailspin," he said, he was glad that "I stand pretty well in Texas" and that Renie was doing a splendid job selling bonds, visiting hospitals, and cheering the wounded. He was pleased to know that the men to whom she spoke "feel proud of the Fifth Army and its Commander."

There was severe fighting, he continued, at Anzio, and the battle around Cassino, "as strong a position in the mountains as I have ever heard of in my study of military history," was "desperate also." He was squeezed between the two. "As I have written you so many times, if I can just bring a victory for this Fifth Army, that is all I want."

As for her complaints that his letters were "cold," he always felt restrained by the censors. He was unable to be enthusiastic or spontaneous about writing something they would read. In addition, he was "so pre-occupied and harassed at the present time that I have little thought for anything except winning the battle."

He was surrounded by the British. Italy was a British theater of operations, Anzio was Churchill's original venture, and Clark was subject to Alexander's wishes, hampered by Freyberg's stubbornness, at the mercy of Cunningham's lack of cooperation. Except for Devers' dubious assistance, Clark was all alone, trying to maintain American prestige and to gain an American victory.

Devers in Algiers seemed to Clark to be of little help. He was too distant, in terms of both geography and personality. If anything went seriously wrong in Italy, it would be Clark's head. He wondered whether Devers was sending the War Department a true picture of developments, whether he was portraying Clark's difficulties sympathetically. He thought not. "In fact," he wrote, "I am convinced of that."

If Clark understood Churchill's desire for a British triumph, he paid it no heed. He felt deeply his responsibility to the soldiers of his Fifth U.S. Army, particularly to the Americans in the organization, even more to the isolated and battered troops at Anzio, as well as his obligations to the American people. So he pushed tenaciously for what he thought was right and proper. Otherwise, the battleground would become completely a British arena, and the British, who lacked drive and push in combat, were likely to outmaneuver the Americans and make any victory appear to be theirs alone.

He was down, but he was not yet out.

Actually, the darkest moment had passed. A basis existed for renewed hope in eventual, if not immediate, success.

CHAPTER 16

☆ ☆ ☆ ☆

A TIME OF FRUSTRATION

"high-handed methods"

WHEN THE GERMAN attack ended at Anzio with the Allies bruised but holding their final beachhead line, Clark relieved Lucas and placed Truscott in command of the VI Corps. Clark sent Lucas to Sorrento for several days of rest, kept him as deputy Fifth Army commander for three weeks, then dispatched him to the United States.

Around Cassino and the Gustav Line, the Allied resources were growing. The British 78th Division had come across the Apennines from the Eighth Army to join the Indians and the New Zealanders in Freyberg's provisional corps. A third French division was arriving to bolster Juin's corps, and a fourth would soon be there. Two new American divisions were in Italy, and a third was on its way. Perhaps the weight of these additional forces would turn the balance.

Seeking even more strength to crack the Gustav Line and get into the Liri valley, Alexander thought again of bringing most of the Eighth Army to the vital area west of the Apennines. If he did so, he would have to reorganize the forces and split Clark's zone between him and Leese.

Clark had protested this course of action earlier, and he remained vexed. "It really shocked me," he dictated for his diary. "There is nothing in it that I agree with." What he objected to was the time it would take to bring the units over the mountains, to reshuffle the front, and to insert the new forces into the line. To Clark, Alexander's intention showed his "willingness to delay this operation indefinitely." He was referring to the burning need to break into the Liri valley and link up with the troops at Anzio.

When they met to discuss the matter, Clark "anticipated a stormy session, but it worked out all right." He raised several minor objections, and Alexander had his way.

Before moving the Eighth Army across the mountains, Alexander decided to let Freyberg try once more to break the Gustav defenses and to penetrate into the Liri valley. If that failed, there would be, he said, "a certain pause in land operations." During that interval, while leaving a few British units under the V Corps on the quiet Adriatic front, he would transfer the rest of Leese's Eighth Army to positions in front of Monte Cassino and the Rapido River. Alexander would disband Freyberg's provisional corps and move McCreery's corps to Leese's control. That would give Leese four corps—a Polish, a Canadian, and two British corps. He would shift Clark's Fifth Army to a relatively narrow zone on the west coast. Clark would then have Keyes' II Corps and Juin's French Corps, plus Truscott's VI Corps at Anzio.

The more Clark thought about Alexander's concept, the more he liked it. With the exception of two British divisions at Anzio, the Fifth Army would have American and French units, and Leese instead of Clark would have to deal with McCreery and Freyberg, both difficult subordinates.

At the end of this large-scale adjustment, Alexander would have six corps across the western part of Italy, all in narrow sectors facilitating depth and punch.

But first the New Zealanders and Indians were to attack again. The most promising approach now seemed through the town of Cassino, and Freyberg asked for and was promised a heavy air bombardment to help his advance.

"Freyberg may be an extremely courageous individual," Clark dictated for his diary, "but he has no brains, has been spoiled [by the British], demands everything in sight, and altogether is most difficult to handle."

Clark hoped for an attack in three days, "but of course it may be delayed."

Freyberg wanted at least three successive days of good weather so that his tanks would operate on dry ground. Instead, freezing rain, snow, high winds, and the paralyzing grip of winter imposed a halt. The effort was postponed.

The air forces, disappointed by the bombardment of Monte Cassino, now looked forward, as someone said, to "really make air history" at Cassino. They would "break up every stone in the town behind which a German soldier might be hiding." They paid little attention to warnings of debris created by the bombs, obstacles sure to hamper the attacking men and tanks.

Still waiting for the weather to clear, still concerned about troops at Anzio, Clark vented his wrath on the naval forces, particularly the British. Dictating for his diary, he said, "Evidence continues to accumulate that Admiral Cunningham and his Navy are in no way cooperating with me. He does not come direct to me but insinuates to everyone he sees that he has been hoaxed into the position which makes it necessary for him to maintain my forces in the Anzio bridgehead. He not only does not cooperate in the supply setup but with his naval gunfire. He imposes so many restrictions and makes it so difficult that it is easier in most cases to do without his naval gunfire support than to accept the restrictions he imposes. He continually screams about [enemy] gunfire in the harbor, knowing full well that there is nothing that can be done on this situation that is not already being done."

It was, fundamentally, a matter of point of view. For Clark, the presence of warships at Anzio gave him additional artillery support. The big naval shells crashing into enemy troop concentrations discouraged the Germans and heartened the Allied soldiers. On the other hand, if the vessels came too close to shore, they became targets of long-range German artillery pieces, and that of course went contrary to the naval tradition of protecting the ships against damage or destruction. To Clark, this signified a reluctance on the part of the Navy to take risks for the support of the ground forces.

But the worst part, Cunningham "has set an arbitrary limit of 2,500 tons [of supply] per day, which not only is not sufficient to maintain my forces but thereby precludes the essential buildup for any counteroffensive."

Cunningham, of course, had a point. Anzio had developed quite differently from the original conception and imposed heavy requirements on him. As he wrote to Churchill, "The situation...bears little relation to the lightning thrust by two divisions envisaged at [the meetings early in January at] Marrakech."

Instead of nourishing two or three divisions in the beachhead for a limited period of time, Cunningham had to support a force that had grown to the equivalent of five and a half divisions for an indefinite period, with no end in sight. Even though strict control of ammunition expenditures in the beachhead, great care in laying out and camouflaging dumps and depots, and austere living conditions among the troops—no laundries or canteens and rigid checks to prevent pilferage and waste—kept requirements down, the supply effort put a heavy strain on naval resources, which Cunningham sought constantly to economize. A daily delivery of 2,500 tons of supply was possible unless a major disaster occurred in the Anzio harbor.

Clark wanted at least 2,700 tons of supply per day, because he had to build up his ammunition and other items for an ultimate attack out of the beachhead. Yet Cunningham ignored Clark's requests. Neither Alexander nor Wilson was willing to speak with Cunningham on Clark's behalf.

Frustrated, Clark threw up his hands over the British system of command. Unity was absent because the British Army, Air, and Navy were independent entities.

"I know how you have worried at the news from my beachhead," he wrote to his mother, "and of course you must realize how I have worried too...we have accomplished all that could have been expected. It is no picnic for the Germans either." In the midst of his concerns, he was heartened by hundreds of letters he received from unknown people all over the United States who were proud of the Fifth Army and were "praying for us."

The situation at Anzio flared up at the end of February, when the Germans struck again in the midst of rain, this time in the Cisterna area. Under great pressure, the Allied line held. When the sun came out on the following afternoon, Allied planes hammered the attacking forces. The Germans fell back.

The success was in the main Truscott's. But Clark was having trouble with Truscott too, for Truscott's radio messages seemed to have a "whining attitude," as though he was uncertain of Clark's understanding or support. Was Truscott trying to put everything into the record so that he could not be held to blame if a setback occurred?

Clark appreciated Truscott's difficulties. He would have to let him know that he, Clark, accepted full responsibility for whatever happened at Anzio.

In the course of what would turn out to be the final German attack, shells struck two landing ships in the harbor, killing several men. The Navy then issued what Clark considered to be "high-handed orders without reference to the Army." Cunningham curtailed the use of landing ships in the supply runs from Naples and prohibited their employment to evacuate the wounded. Clark raged against the "high-handed methods pursued by Admiral Cunningham and his subordinates." They took "drastic action to protect their shipping without giving the least thought to the results of such action upon the ground battle in the bridgehead."

He was also indignant because Allied ships fired on Cub planes even though the Fifth Army headquarters always informed them of courier flights. The Navy's response was, "planes must keep their distance or be fired upon."

A welcome letter came from Wilson on the last day of February. The Italian campaign, Wilson had written, was too important to burden Clark with the details of Anvil, the invasion of southern France. Firm planning had to start at once and in earnest. Therefore, Wilson had decided, and Devers had concurred, to retain Clark in command of the Fifth Army and to relieve him of responsibility for the Seventh Army and Anvil.

Clark dictated for his diary, "This is a great relief to me, for I have no time to give any thought to any other subject except the battle."

Ever conscious of public opinion and seeking to counter the prominence of the Americans in the newspapers, Churchill directed Alexander to rename the troops at Anzio. They were to be referred to as the "Allied Bridgehead Force" in situation reports, communiques, and press stories.

Clark was, according to his aide, "greatly annoyed." Churchill's action was "part of a steady effort by the British to increase their prestige in the Mediterranean area," another attempt "to exalt in the public mind the part that the British, as contrasted to the Americans, are playing there."

He requested Alexander to modify the Prime Minister's order and call the troops "The Fifth Army Allied Bridgehead Force."

Going to Anzio and narrowly escaping death or injury when his jeep went through an intersection just before a salvo of four shells struck the road, Clark lectured Truscott on his attitude and behavior. Then he commended Truscott for stopping the German attack.

Nineteen officers of the Operations Division in Washington arrived to acquaint themselves firsthand with conditions in the theater, and Clark briefed them. They questioned why Lucas had not seized the Alban Hills at once. Lucas, Clark said, "was quite correct." Had Lucas moved to the "tremendous ground mass," he would have been reckless. Without a secure base, the troops would have been doomed to destruction.

For Freyberg, who was waiting near Cassino for good weather, forecasters finally had good news. Their prediction of three days of clear skies starting on March 15 made the New Zealand attack possible.

On that morning Clark went forward to witness what would be up to that time the greatest massed bombing in direct tactical support of ground forces. Joining Devers, Alexander, Eaker, and Freyberg, he watched Cassino, visible little less than three miles away. What sounded like a drone of locusts was the first intimation of the approaching planes. The noise became a murmur then a pulsing throb. Finally the aircraft appeared as specks in the sky.

Their 1,500 thousand-pound bombs struck and demolished the town of Cassino, crushing buildings, toppling walls, cratering streets and covering them with debris. Stabbing flashes of orange flame raised billowing clouds of smoke and dust. The ground shook violently.

With Cassino pulverized, Freyberg expected the enemy strongpoints to be destroyed, German communications disrupted, hostile artillery neutralized, heavy casualties inflicted, and the survivors stupefied, dazed, and demoralized. Surprisingly, according to a report, "plenty of defenders remained; plenty of fight, plenty of guns, ammunition, observation points, and plenty of perseverance." When Allied soldiers tried to enter the town, they found their progress blocked not only by gunfire but also by huge bomb holes and broken masonry.

That afternoon, despite the prophecy of clear weather, the rains came. In the torrential downpour, the battle became confused. After three days Freyberg seemed bewildered. His "enthusiastic plans," Clark noted, "are not keeping up to his time schedule." Freyberg had looked for his men to walk through the town, and his "handling of the ensuing attack," Clark judged, "has been characterized by indecision and lack of aggressiveness." He was terribly disappointed, for Freyberg's failure postponed a linkup with Anzio.

Writing to Renie, he tried to explain the conditions at Cassino. "If you could just see the mountains here and the terrain, you would realize what a fortress it is and how heavily defended it has been made by the Germans through concrete tunnels, pillboxes, tank emplacements, mines, etc. Our air did a lot to help blast him out, but no air blast has ever driven all the infantry out of its positions, and, in my opinion, never will."

He mentioned having visited an exposed and dangerous forward position to see for himself exactly why progress was slow. "I must get information firsthand," he explained, "if I am to know positively what the situation is. I pray for results today and tomorrow. We just have to get through it."

Renie begged him not to visit risky places. He answered brutally: "You turn your lamb chops on the stove, and I'll run the Army."

After more than a week of strenuous effort, Alexander and Clark halted Freyberg's attack. "I hate to see the Cassino show flop," Clark noted, but the New Zealanders and Indians were exhausted.

Having tried and failed three times to break into the Liri valley, the Allies would now wait until May when the weather was clear and the ground firm, the troops were rested and the forces augmented.

Postponing further battle until May jeopardized a major hope of the campaign, reaching Rome before the cross-Channel attack. Although Overlord, the Normandy invasion, would be delayed a month—to some extent because the need to continue using ships on the Naples–Anzio run made it impossible to release them to England for the Channel crossing. But even June seemed too soon to expect the fall of Rome. This was disappointing.

The operational lull in Italy also affected Anvil, the plan to invade southern France. There was much confusion about whether the Allies would actually carry out Anvil. American and British leaders debated its merits, it seemed, endlessly; the Americans for it, the British against. But one thing was certain: if Anvil received approval, the Mediterranean theater was to furnish the resources for the Riviera landings. That is, AFHQ was to invade the south of France with forces then engaged in Italy. When should Wilson and Devers bring these units out of the line in order to rest and train them for the amphibious venture?

Originally conceived as a strategic diversion for Overlord, Anvil was supposed to go just before or at the same time as the cross-Channel operation. If that schedule was honored, the troops had to be disengaged from Italy in the near future. That would weaken the Allied forces in Italy and make more difficult, if not entirely impossible, a linkup with the Anzio beachhead and a subsequent drive to Rome.

Under American pressure, the Combined Chiefs of Staff decided tentatively to carry out Anvil. As a result of British insistence, the Americans agreed to defer the operation until the junction of the Cassino and Anzio fronts and the capture of Rome.

When might the long-awaited linkup occur? Wilson asked Clark.

A large-scale effort at the beginning of May, he thought, would require about three weeks to reach Anzio. With Rome still to be taken, the timing was probably too late "to contribute much to Overlord." But that, Clark said, was "a matter beyond my scope."

As soon as Rome fell, Wilson and Devers planned to pull the VI Corps headquarters and several American divisions out of Italy for Anvil.

Clark was resigned to the eventual loss of these troops. He was interested in Rome, and what happened afterwards, at least for the moment, was of little consequence. Getting to Rome in a hurry, he told Devers, was wishful thinking.

Looking ahead to Alexander's big attack by the Fifth and Eighth Armies in May, Clark saw little hope for the Eighth Army to break into and advance up the Liri valley where the Germans had their strongest defenses. The Polish and Canadian contingents in the Eighth Army, he was sure, would bear the brunt of the fighting. The Fifth Army was to have only "a subsidiary role," but Clark expected to "carry the ball through the mountains as usual." The British would lag "except as assisted by the Fifth Army attack." If Juin and his French corps could break through relatively lightly defended mountains and occupy high ground overlooking the upper Liri valley, they would force the Germans to withdraw from the Cassino area. Expecting this as likely, Clark instituted special mountain warfare training for several American units which, using pack mules, would fight alongside the French in virtually impassable hills traversed by primitive roads, paths, and trails. They might thus outflank the Germans in the Liri valley, the natural passageway to Rome.

Eric Sevareid, the news broadcaster and commentator, interviewed Clark on April 1, and the personal chemistry between them was bad from the outset. They talked about 45 minutes. Sevareid's lack of understanding of the problems astonished Clark. Sevareid saw Clark as a self-important figure motivated by personal ambition.

The war in April was a matter of small probes, patrols, and raids, as both sides rested and waited for good weather.

Badly worn out, Clark spent several days resting at Sorrento and Capri. Marshall then summoned him to Washington. President Roosevelt, Marshall explained, wanted to hear from Clark about the coming drive to Rome.

That may have been nothing more than the excuse to reinvigorate and restore Clark. Possibly a visitor to Italy, perhaps John E. Hull, a member of the Operations Division who had spent several days with Clark, had alerted Marshall to Clark's frayed nerves, his short and explosive temper,

George Patton's tight expression in this photo, taken in North Africa in 1942, may reflect his resentment that Clark, younger than Patton and formerly junior to him in rank, was now his superior.

More glory: Clark receives the Distinguished Service Cross for valor at Salerno from Roosevelt in December 1943.

ABOVE: January 22, 1944: Clark on the beachhead at Anzio on D-day.

RIGHT: Shortly after this visit to Clark in Italy, Winston Churchill appointed him commander of Allied ground forces in Italy. Churchill had nicknamed Clark "the American Eagle."

On June 5, 1944, the liberator of Rome (at left in leading Jeep) finally entered the Eternal City.

October 1944: On a hillside in northern Italy, British general John Harding (pointing) discusses with Clark (standing) and other American generals the obstacles to the Allied advance on Bologna.

his feeling that no one was doing all he could to resolve the operational impasse. Maybe Gruenther thought Clark was falling apart. The strains of Anzio and Cassino had been heavy.

Clark left with his orderly, Technical Sergeant William C. Chaney, his good friend, Charles E. Saltzman, who was Gruenther's deputy, and his aide. They arrived in Washington at three o'clock in the morning. Renie and a staff officer met them at the airport. Clark's presence, he learned, was top secret. Not even his mother knew of his trip. Marshall had arranged for Renie and her husband to stay at his house at Fort Myer, and a car took them directly there.

She was shocked at how "thin and tense and tired" he looked. He appeared, she said, "haggard."

On the following morning in Marshall's office, Clark listened as the Army Chief of Staff gave him instructions. Clark was to have a few days of rest at the Greenbrier Hotel in White Sulphur Springs, West Virginia, where part of the large establishment was a governmental hospital, another part accommodated interned German and Italian diplomats. Clark dictated a note to his mother, Marshall interrupting every now and then to tell him how to word the message. Beckie was to get her hat and meet her son and Renie and Ann at the airport.

What were the chances for capturing Rome before Overlord? Marshall asked. Everyone expected the seizure of Rome, he said, to hearten the French Resistance.

Clark briefly explained the plans.

Then he and his family flew to West Virginia. They lived in seclusion at a guest house. He and Renie flew to Bernard Baruch's place in Georgetown, South Carolina, where the President was staying. Roosevelt was eager to know the battle plans and, as Clark showed how the Allies expected to drive to Rome, indicated a surprising knowledge of the terrain and the forces.

After two weeks, Marshall instructed Clark to return to Washington and permitted him to spend a night at his apartment—reluctantly, as Clark's presence in the United States was still secret. A car drove him home and into the basement garage; a secret service man was in the elevator.

He met with Marshall and a select group of congressmen and senators at a small seafood restaurant, probably the Alibi Club, hired by Marshall. While all ate oysters and threw the shells into a great bowl in the center of the table, they talked frankly about the plans for Rome.

On the following day, he and his party departed. Clark took with him his dog, a small cocker spaniel named Pal. In Italy, spring was in the air.

Alexander's massive regrouping had taken place and the Eighth Army had come over the mountains to the Cassino front; as Clark traveled around his new Fifth Army area in the coastal zone, he felt much better. Improvements in road maintenance and in troop appearance pleased him.

Writing to Renie, Gruenther said that her husband's visit to the United States had relaxed him. "He is a hard-boiled soldier, of course, but he does get homesick every now and then." His dog Pal would be good company for him. "The Fifth Army is simply devoted to Wayne. He is a real leader who inspires the greatest confidence in every one of his subordinates. All of us consider it a great honor to be serving under him. Personally it is the finest experience that I ever had, and I never want to leave him."

Ernie Pyle was one of four correspondents who had dinner with Clark and several of his staff officers. "I found General Clark very congenial," Pyle wrote, "and straightforward too. He impressed me as a thoroughly honest man." Clark was not at fault, Pyle said, for the slow progress in the Italian campaign. The conditions were indescribably heartbreaking.

Alexander scheduled his big attack for May 11. His concept was clear. Uninterested in Rome at the outset, he sought to fashion a trap to catch as many Germans as possible. Leese's British Eighth Army was to go north up the Liri valley to Valmontone; while this attack was in progress, at a time to be determined later, Truscott's VI Corps was to thrust east from Anzio to Valmontone. The meeting of these forces would block German escape routes, particularly Highways 6 and 7. With the Germans enclosed, squeezed, and eventually eliminated, the roads to Rome would be open. Clark's Fifth Army had the relatively minor task of keeping up with the Eighth Army, thereby protecting its flank.

Clark was dubious whether Alexander's plan would work. The Eighth Army confronted the same obstacles that had prevented the Fifth Army from getting into the Liri valley. During the past month, the Germans had increased and strengthened their fortifications barring entrance, for the valley was the obvious Allied route of advance. Perhaps the Fifth Army, specifically Juin's French corps, could make better progress across the mountains.

Alexander's intention to send Truscott from Anzio to Valmontone bothered Clark, for that direction took the VI Corps away from Rome. He had instructed Truscott to be ready to strike toward any one of several objectives, north to Rome, northeast to the Alban Hills, east through Cisterna to Valmontone, and south to facilitate juncture with the Fifth Army. Clark rationalized his order on the ground of having plans for all eventualities. He wanted, he said, to keep his options open, his mind free from definite prior commitment. He wished to be able to take quick advantage of fast-breaking opportunities. He was, of course, thinking of Rome.

By going to Valmontone, Truscott's corps would expose its left and rear to a German attack from the Alban Hills. Even if the VI Corps and Eighth Army met at Valmontone, they would be unable to trap a substantial number of Germans, for there were many escape routes, too many roads leading out of the Liri valley.

What Alexander really wanted Truscott's thrust to Valmontone to do, Clark thought, was to loosen up the German opposition ahead of the Eighth Army. A VI Corps attack to Valmontone would threaten the German rear and thereby permit the British Eighth Army to make quicker progress with fewer casualties.

As Truscott in accordance with Clark's instructions worked on preparations to go wherever he might be ordered to move, Alexander visited him. Alexander informed him of his intent to send Truscott to Valmontone. Truscott reported the conversation to Clark and asked whether there was any point in drawing plans for the other attacks.

Clark interpreted Alexander's action as an infringement on Clark's prerogatives. Truscott was Clark's direct subordinate.

"I know factually," Clark wrote in his diary, "that there are interests brewing for the Eighth Army to take Rome, and I might as well let Alexander know now that if he attempts any thing of that kind he will have another all-out battle on his hands, namely, with me."

He had it out with Alexander, who was surprised. He had no desire, he said, to undermine or usurp Clark's proper relationship with Truscott. And thus, by inference, he lost the right to control the direction of the VI Corps effort.

Mollified, Clark acceded to Alexander's desire and told Truscott to give first priority to Valmontone but to be ready to go elsewhere too.

On the day before the attack, Clark's aide recorded a statement of Clark's thinking. "It was his prime desire to vindicate the beachhead, and if it was the last thing he did, he would do it." Clark was no doubt referring to the original concept of the Anzio operation, an attempt to take Rome quickly. To that end, the men at Anzio had carried out a dangerous venture, then had suffered through an agonizing ordeal. He would redeem their sacrifice by using them to get to Rome, the ultimate objective.

If Alexander reserved for himself the right to tell the VI Corps when to attack, Clark would retain for himself the right to tell Truscott which way to go. For the corps belonged to him and his Fifth Army. Anzio was a British project executed in large part by American effort and blood. Determined to make Anzio an American victory, Clark would do so by capturing Rome. Furthermore, he would do his utmost to get to Rome before the Normandy D-Day.

As Clark frankly said later, "We not only wanted the honor of capturing Rome, but we felt that we more than deserved it . . . nothing was going to stop us on our push toward the Italian capital."

He wished two things, to be first in Rome and to be there before Overlord. To follow Alexander's plan would deny the Fifth Army the first goal and probably the second. "I was determined," Clark said, "that the Fifth Army was going to capture Rome, and I was probably overly sensitive to indications that everybody else was trying to get into the act."

Several months earlier, Alexander had expected Anzio to be the prime instrument to compel a German withdrawal from Cassino; Clark in contrast had regarded Anzio as little more than a threat, a subsidiary operation, while the important battle took place at Cassino. Now their anticipations were again reversed and still contrary. Alexander looked for the decisive battle at Cassino while Clark saw the vital action as coming at Anzio.

Alexander's big attack opened at 11 P.M. on May 11, as 1,660 guns fired along a 25-mile front from Monte Cassino to the sea. Allied soldiers of both the Fifth and Eighth Armies then moved forward.

CHAPTER 17
☆ ☆ ☆ ☆
ROME

"by right of eminent domain"

THE OPERATION STARTED slowly. Polish forces fought up Monte Cassino, but the Germans refused to give way, and the Poles had to fall back. Keyes' American corps in the coastal sector gained little ground.

Elsewhere, progress was better. The British crossed the Rapido River and constructed two vehicular bridges over the stream during the night. When tanks, artillery pieces, and trucks entered into the Liri valley in the morning, they came at once under German fires directed from Monte Cassino. As the German defenses on the valley floor congealed, the British mechanized units had nowhere to go. Traffic congestion became a nightmare, and the initial British momentum bogged down.

The spectacular break occurred in the French zone. Juin's men surged forward into the relatively trackless mountains behind the Garigliano River. In three days of fighting, they advanced six miles through terrain that the Germans had regarded as a wasteland impossible for military operations; as a consequence, few German units and obstacles were there.

203

The ardor and skill, as well as the success, of the French were surprising. Having significantly penetrated the Gustav defenses, the French on high ground overlooking the adjacent forces on both sides, along the coast and in the Liri valley, compelled the Germans to abandon the Gustav Line.

After a week, with the French almost twenty miles from their starting positions, Kesselring pulled his troops back.

As the German defenders of Monte Cassino abandoned the hill, the Poles marched to the top and took the monastery. The British drove forward in the Liri valley, the Americans along the coast. The French in Clark's Fifth Army had won the initial battle and had pulled along both the Americans and the British. But the French were unable to descend from the high ground, for Alexander had reserved the Liri corridor for the British, who were making the main effort.

If all elements continued to roll, junction with the beachhead was only a matter of time. In several days, a week at most, the main front would join the troops at Anzio. At what point should Truscott's forces attack and put the finishing touches on the German defeat? And which way should they strike?

Clark talked with Alexander about these matters, and Alexander remained, Clark noted, "adamant" on having Truscott head for Valmontone "regardless of the enemy situation." That might be the wrong direction, Clark warned. There were no natural paths of advance, and Truscott's units would have to cross high and broken ground. Only foot soldiers accompanied by mules carrying weapons and equipment could fight their way to Valmontone. Taking a map and showing it to Alexander, Clark drew a circle around Valmontone and asked in effect, Okay, where should the VI Corps go from there?

Fast, mobile patrols, Alexander said, should cut all the roads leading north and east.

Could riflemen, tired by their effort to get to Valmontone, launch fast and mobile patrols?

"He brushed this aside," Clark wrote.

Then Clark resorted to guile. Juin's French corps, he said, more than ten miles ahead of the adjacent British Eighth Army, could threaten the rear of the German forces holding up the British and thereby loosen up the opposition.

Alexander was obviously delighted. And that to Clark made evident Alexander's principal motive for the Valmontone operation, to help the British forward.

Later that day Alexander sent Clark a message and accepted his suggestion. If, as seemed likely, he said, the Eighth Army was unable to keep abreast of the Fifth, specifically the French forces, Clark was to have the French jostle the Germans in the Liri valley facing the British.

It was Clark's turn to be delighted. If the French cut off the Germans below Valmontone, there was little point to sending Truscott's VI Corps to cut them off again at Valmontone. Truscott could head for the Alban Hills and Rome.

That evening, his wedding anniversary, as he wrote to Renie to tell her how happy she had made him in their years of marriage, he was in good spirits. He was, he said, unable to write at length because he was in the middle of "a great and decisive battle" in which "my Fifth Army is doing well."

The French were doing so well that Clark no longer needed to hold a division in reserve for emergencies. He decided to send the troops by sea to Anzio. The climax of the combat was approaching, and Truscott would soon be able to break out of the confines of his beachhead. Clark told him to be ready to attack in six or seven days through Cisterna to Valmontone. Clark was unable to be guilty of insubordination to Alexander, but he was beginning to think of sending only part of the augmented VI Corps to Valmontone. The rest he would point toward Rome.

The Gustav Line had collapsed, but there was no sudden German rout or disintegration. Kesselring had erected new defensive positions called the Caesar Line to protect Cisterna on Highway 7 as well as Valmontone on Highway 6. Units falling back entered these fortified places.

Lemnitzer, Alexander's American Deputy Chief of Staff, delivered a categorical message to Clark on May 19. Alexander wanted Truscott to start toward Valmontone on the night of May 21 or on the morning of May 22.

"I was shocked," Clark wrote in his diary, "that a decision of this importance should have been made without reference to me. I sent that word back to General Alexander, who made the weak excuse that he felt that we had discussed it for the past three days."

What shocked Clark was the peremptory nature of Alexander's order. Clark thought it premature for Truscott to attack. The additional division he was sending to Anzio had yet to arrive, and his main front was still distant from Anzio. What was important above all was the timing of Truscott's attack, and he expected Alexander to consult with him on the best moment to disrupt the German defenses. Determining Truscott's direction could wait.

This Clark told Lemnitzer. Alexander and Clark should review the situation carefully every day to be sure of the right moment for the attack. To create the proper conditions, the Fifth and Eighth Armies had to put strong pressure on the Germans to prevent them from reacting against Truscott's thrust. If both Allied armies were heavily engaging the major German forces, Truscott had a good chance of breaking out. The problem was, the British were failing to put enough push into their efforts.

Alexander withdrew his order.

"Our battle goes well," Clark wrote to his mother. "We have made fine progress.... It is time this fine Fifth Army had a break. We hope to keep on going."

When on May 20 the French occupied the high ground dominating the Liri valley at its narrowest point and thereby threatened the rear of the Germans opposing the British, Clark could envision the fulfillment of his most important desire, making contact with the beachhead. Anzio was now about fifty miles ahead of his main front, and union between the two seemed at hand. He told Keyes to keep driving hard.

Alexander and his chief of staff, Sir John Harding, came to see Clark. They were somewhat embarrassed. Lemnitzer had transmitted to them Clark's message on the need for both armies to attack forcefully. Leese, who commanded the Eighth Army, was unable to do so. The British were taking heavy casualties. Leese could resume the offensive only after three days and only with a single Canadian division.

"He"—Alexander—"asked me hesitatingly," Clark recorded, "if I could attack and outflank the Germans, making it unnecessary for the Eighth Army to attack. He said he desired to conserve losses."

The major British difficulty, Clark knew, was declining manpower resources. During the previous November, the British Army Adjutant General, Sir Ronald Adam, had visited Clark to inform him of British deficiencies. The British were disbanding about one division approximately every two months, then sending the troops as individual replacements to the units engaged in the active theaters of operation. Again in April, Alexander had reminded Clark of the problem. He had asked Clark to use the two British divisions at Anzio sparingly for minor activities because Alexander was unable to obtain new troops for the dead, wounded, and injured. Because the British were gathering men in England for Overlord, they could spare few soldiers for the Italian campaign.

Clark remained implacable. "I told him to conserve losses in one place we would have them in another; namely, the Fifth Army sector." To Clark, that was inadmissible. "I strongly recommended that Leese speed up his attack and that both armies attack all-out at the same time."

British manpower shortages were hardly Clark's concern. The Eighth Army, he thought, was intentionally slow. The British were willing, indeed hoping, to let the French carry the major weight of the battle. To Clark, the Americans and the British were the senior partners in the Italian enterprise and, as Alexander had said during the planning for Anzio, they had to share the risks and the gains and the losses.

Yet Clark understood the difficulties facing the British in the Liri valley. The Germans had placed mines, guns, and troops in great depth on the best approach to Rome. "I do not believe," he wrote in his diary, "Eighth Army would advance through Liri valley unless French cover the mountains on Eighth Army left." He told Alexander that he would have Juin's corps threaten the Germans in the Liri valley and thus force them to relax their opposition against the British.

Alexander, according to Clark, "apologized." He regretted the inability of the British to apply the pressure expected in the main effort. The Fifth Army, he acknowledged, had broken the Gustav Line. He had "never dreamed that we could make the progress that we have through the mountains."

By that admission, Alexander lost control of the battle. By cracking the Gustav Line, Clark won the upper hand. He could in large measure disregard Alexander, and Alexander would raise no objection. With a free hand, Clark could determine not only the timing but also the direction of Truscott's attack out of the beachhead.

Yet Clark remained suspicious of British efforts to outwit him and to gain the credit and the glory of the battlefield victory that now seemed assured.

From Anzio he talked sharply over the telephone to Gruenther. "You go all-out," he said, "in seeing that there is no restriction placed on my whereabouts. I have always traveled at will in my Fifth Army sector, and, when appropriate, it has been announced, and I do not intend to have any restrictions placed on that now. You tear anybody to pieces who attempts to change this. The censor here, due to some damn fool idea, thinks that my presence . . . cannot be mentioned. You must act on this promptly. . . . Be sure that . . . this is a Fifth Army show. I do not want the first announcement of this to come out to the effect that Alexander's troops have attacked from the beachhead."

The beachhead troops were Clark's. He wanted everyone to know and to understand that fact.

He told Truscott to be ready to attack through Cisterna to Valmontone as Alexander wished but to be prepared to shift toward Rome.

Kesselring began systematically to withdraw the German units out of the Liri valley on May 22. The troops falling back occupied the Caesar Line, concentrating at Cisterna and Valmontone.

With the Germans retiring, with Keyes on the coast about to enter Terracina, thirty miles below Anzio, with the Canadians about to attack in the Liri valley to hurry the German withdrawal, the proper moment in Clark's opinion had arrived for Truscott's move. The VI Corps attacked on May 23 and struck toward Cisterna. Clark, who had arisen at 4:30 that morning, joined Truscott at a forward observation post. The fighting for Cisterna was fierce, but the town remained in German hands at the end of the day.

On the main front, Keyes continued his advance. He had imbued his men with the idea of "rescuing" the Anzio beachhead. The long awaited junction would surely occur soon.

Looking ahead to the meeting of the two fronts, Clark phoned Gruenther. Who was going to release the news when Keyes' II and Truscott's VI Corps joined? he asked. Clark was averse to letting Alexander make the announcement because it was, he said, "primarily a Fifth Army matter." If Alexander refused to give Clark authority to issue the statement, "you make damn sure that their communique is properly worded, making it a Fifth Army show, for that is exactly what it is."

The linkup, bringing the long ordeal of the beachhead forces to an end, occurred shortly after 10 A.M. on May 25. Alexander and Clark released the news to the world simultaneously four hours later. Alexander's special communique handsomely announced the contact as the culmination of a spectacular Fifth Army advance covering more than sixty miles in fourteen days. The Navy issued its own statement and emphasized the naval support that had made it possible for the beachhead to endure for four months.

The historic junction made, Clark now turned his attention to Rome. Why lead the VI Corps away from the city? Why encourage British competition? He decided to split Truscott's forces. Alerting Truscott to the idea, Clark outlined his concept. Two and a half divisions were to keep going toward Valmontone while three divisions were to head for the Alban Hills, at first to protect the left rear of the Valmontone forces, eventually to drive to Rome.

Then he left for Borgo Grappa to be present at the place of linkup. About 25 news correspondents and photographers accompanied him to cover the dramatic event. To Clark, the accomplishment was satisfying, even emotional. Joining the main and beachhead fronts, he wrote in his diary, "meant more to me than anything since our success of Salerno." His feeling of responsibility for the troops in the beachhead, isolated and battered, had been almost unbearable.

Wishing to counter the prominent news dispatches relating the successes of "General Mark Clark's Fifth Army," Churchill asked Alexander to say something publicly about the British achievements in the battle. Alexander complied as best he could.

As the British surged up the Liri valley in the wake of the German withdrawal, Truscott finally captured Cisterna. Clark then told Truscott to carry out the thrusts he had outlined. He made known his decision to Gruenther and said, "We are shooting the works."

Clark's formal directive to Truscott, ordering the new attack to Valmontone and to the Alban Hills, eventually to Rome, appeared on May 26. A copy of his order went routinely to Alexander's headquarters and apprised him of Clark's action. At 11:15 A.M. that day, Alexander, accompanied by Lemnitzer, arrived at the Fifth Army headquarters. Clark was at Anzio, and Gruenther received the two officers.

Alexander had come for clarification of Clark's intent. Would Clark keep driving toward Valmontone?

"Certainly, sir," Gruenther replied. He explained the two-pronged action in some detail.

Alexander seemed satisfied. He thought it a good plan. "I am for any line of action," he said, "which the Army Commander"—Clark—"believes will offer a good chance to continue his present success." But he wanted to be absolutely "sure that the Army Commander will continue to push toward Valmontone, won't he? I know that he appreciates the importance of gaining the high ground [nearby]."

Gruenther reassured Alexander. Clark, he said, had Valmontone thoroughly in mind.

When he reported his conversation to Clark, Gruenther added his impressions. Alexander appeared to have had no mental reservations about Clark's course. He seemed to be well pleased with the entire situation. He was complimentary in his references to the Fifth Army and to Clark.

As for Clark, he wrote in his diary to explain what he considered to be Alexander's obsession with Valmontone: It was a "long-standing . . . preconceived idea . . . based upon the false premise that if Highway 6 were cut at Valmontone a German army would be annihilated. This is ridiculous, for many roads" led out of the Liri valley. The Germans could easily bypass a trap at Valmontone. To Clark, Rome remained the vital objective.

Actually, Churchill nourished and reinforced Alexander's hope of destroying a substantial number of Germans at Valmontone. With the Germans swept off the field of battle, both Fifth and Eighth Armies could march triumphantly into Rome.

The Germans refused to let go. They held firmly to their defenses and balked at Allied efforts to get to Valmontone or to the Alban Hills.

Alexander traveled to Anzio, and Clark briefed him, then took him to see Truscott and the battlefield. They gazed at Cisterna, wrecked, abandoned, in shambles, with German equipment strewn along the sides of the roads. They visited several division headquarters and talked with the commanders.

"Have been all around the front with Alex," Clark told Gruenther on the telephone, "and he seemed greatly pleased and very flattering in his remarks of the Fifth Army."

A reassuring message came from Lemnitzer. He was maintaining close watch over the communiques and press releases issued by Alexander's headquarters, for he wanted to be certain that the Fifth Army received "credit for its share of the work—which is a very, very great share indeed."

Moving Keyes' corps headquarters to take control of the thrust to Valmontone, directing Truscott to the Alban Hills, Clark expected desperate fighting and quick success. Only the first estimate was correct. The Germans stayed tough on the approaches to Rome and to Valmontone.

"Most of my worries," Clark confided to his diary on May 30, "have nothing to do with the immediate battle. They are political in nature...

"First, the British have their eyes on Rome, notwithstanding Alexander's constant assurances to me that Rome is in the sector of the Fifth Army.... The Eighth Army has done little fighting. It has lacked aggressiveness and failed in its part of this combined Allied effort." The Fifth Army deserved the honor of Rome. Yet when Clark asked Alexander to move the boundary between the two armies slightly eastward and to the right, thereby underlining the notion of reserving Rome for the Fifth Army, he was "met with a reply indicating that the Eighth Army must participate in the battle for Rome."

Second, he was concerned about the French corps. By its brilliant achievement in the mountains, it had earned the right to enter Rome too. Yet it was being pinched out of the action by the converging advances of the adjacent forces. "A more gallant fighting organization never existed," Clark wrote, "yet my offer for it to attack Ferantino, provided it could use Route 6," which belonged to the Eighth Army, "was promptly turned down. General Alexander indicated that he would be delighted for me to take Ferantino to facilitate the advance of the Eighth Army but that after taking this point my [French] troops must withdraw" from the British sector, "this in spite of the fact that the French Corps, after taking Ferantino, would be 30 or 40 miles in advance of the leading elements of the Eighth Army."

Frankly willing to violate Alexander's instructions "in the interests of the battle" and to reward the French for their great accomplishment, Clark told Juin of two alternatives. He could let French troops "spill" over into the zone reserved for the British. Or he could move a French division into the Anzio area, put it into an American corps, and ensure its entry into Rome.

"He told me his government would be most reluctant to consent to the latter solution," meaning that De Gaulle, who headed the French Provisional Government in Algiers, was against having a French division separated from the French forces and under American command; he wanted all the French divisions under Juin. He was, no doubt, thinking ahead of pulling the French units out of Italy for Anvil, the invasion of southern France.

Clark then called off Juin's Ferantino operation and directed him forward in a narrow and constricted zone limited to a single mountain road, which connected with Highway 6. "I then, by right of eminent domain, will 'slop over' into the Eighth Army area, usurp Route 6, and put him [Juin]...headed for Rome."

But Clark was uncomfortable, and sought to justify his action. "I feel there is some inclination on the part of Alexander to commence alibiing for his Eighth Army....Alexander is worried that I have sabotaged his directive to attack Valmontone. I have not done so."

His purpose was clear. "I am throwing everything I have into this battle, hoping to crack this key position which will make it necessary for Kesselring to withdraw both of his armies to the north of Rome."

If Clark was unable to break the Caesar Line in three or four days, he thought of waiting for the Eighth Army to come up so that both armies could launch a coordinated attack, "but I fear the same results from the Eighth Army. It will not put in its full effort, for it never has."

At a press conference on May 31, Clark explained off the record what was happening. The VI Corps, with five divisions, was driving directly toward Rome. The II Corps, with two and a half divisions, was trying to cut Highway 6 near Valmontone in order to trap the Germans. Using a map and a pointer, he showed the correspondents why he had little hope of surrounding the Germans. There were too many roads; the Germans could easily escape. Once at Valmontone, maybe the II Corps would also turn to the north toward Rome. If both II and VI Corps went for the city, he had no idea which would enter first. But he was less interested in Rome than in pursuing the Germans beyond.

Then he told Truscott and Keyes to give the troops another shot in the arm. For, he noted in his diary, "There is much pressure upon me, although it is not being applied directly, to have the Eighth Army in on the battle for Rome." To Gruenther, he acknowledged his overall mission as destroying the Germans "rather than busting into Rome." That may have been a concession to Alexander.

A remarkable feat by Walker's 36th Division brought Rome much closer. Walker's men climbed Monte Artemisio during the hours of darkness, reached the top, surprised the Germans, and took possession not only of dominating ground but also of the road leading directly from Velletri into Rome. The act, Gruenther remarked while reporting it to Clark, "has caused all of us to turn handsprings."

On June 1, American troops crossed and cut Highway 6 just beyond Valmontone and seized the high ground that Alexander wanted. Most of the Germans were gone.

The presence of Americans at Valmontone, the head of the Liri valley, blocked the Eighth Army's main road to Rome. His access to the city obstructed, Leese sent a liaison officer to the Fifth Army. If Clark could take Rome without Eighth Army assistance, he, Leese, would bypass the capital and head for Tivoli. That seemed to settle one terrible question in Clark's mind.

The other, whether he would reach the capital before Overlord, continued to haunt him. None of his subordinates realized as intensely as he their race against time. The Normandy landings were set for June 5, although Eisenhower would postpone the invasion for one day. As Truscott battled up Highway 7, Clark turned Keyes north from Valmontone to drive for Rome along Highway 6.

"Mother dearest," he wrote, "I know you have been pleased with the progress of the Fifth Army during the last three weeks. We have achieved glorious results. The fighting is severe now, but...I pray for decisive results soon." Referring to his trip to the United States in April, he said,

"I am glad you gave nothing to the reporters with reference to my visit home. Again, by virtue of events of the Fifth Army, I am in the public eye, and we must be careful that I do not overdo. I have told Renie the same thing."

Alexander and his chief of staff Harding came for a visit on June 2. "They were quite meek," Clark noted. If Clark was unable to get into the city, Alexander said, he would bring the whole Eighth Army into the battle. Clark assured him that the Fifth Army was moving.

They then discussed how to announce the capture of Rome. As soon as Clark's soldiers were in the streets of the city, they decided, Clark would radio Alexander, "Fifth Army troops have entered Rome." On receipt of the message, Alexander would release the news.

Still suspicious, Clark talked with Gruenther on the telephone later that day. He wanted Gruenther to be sure that the press announcement contained the words "Fifth Army troops" rather than "Allied troops."

Harding called Gruenther and passed along Alexander's highest praise for Clark's conduct of the operations. Clark was directing the battle in masterful fashion. The compliment, Harding said, was sincere. Alexander had absolute confidence in Clark's actions.

With both American corps competing in a race to Rome, the excitement in the Fifth Army mounted. "The CP has gone to hell," Gruenther said on June 3. "No one is doing any work here this afternoon."

Clark let the entry into Rome unfold without direction. Satisfied that both corps were driving hard to be first into the city, secure in his knowledge that no one competed with the Fifth Army for entrance, he was doing nothing, he told Gruenther, to shape the maneuver; God and the Boche, he said, would decide that.

Every national contingent in the campaign wanted to be represented in the triumph at Rome, and Alexander, harking back to the British victory at Tunis, was thinking of a parade about a week after the city fell. Clark planned no formal ceremony. If Alexander wanted to stage a celebration later, that was all right with Clark, so long as all the Allied units participated.

"Let's get through [the city]," he told Gruenther, "and exploit our success to the north...before we think of parades." So far as he was concerned, "The kill is here, and I have just issued instructions to all of my subordinate commanders to pursue relentlessly and destroy the enemy and not think of Rome. There is still tough fighting."

That evening Hitler gave Kesselring permission to vacate Rome. There was to be no combat in the city. The Germans began to depart, but they left rearguard units to keep the Allies out until the bulk of the troops were gone and on their way to the north.

Lieutenant Colonel Henry E. Gardiner, a veteran of the fighting in North Africa and Italy, commanded a tank battalion in the 1st Armored Division. At first light on the morning of June 4, he and his tankers were ready to dash to Rome. Joining them were tough Canadian and American soldiers of the First Special Service Force, a highly trained and elite combat unit of about 2,000 men who had battled in Italy and more recently at Anzio. They climbed aboard the tanks. Everyone was excited.

"We went right down Highway 6 to the edge of Rome proper before encountering any opposition," Gardiner wrote in his diary a day or so later. They had just passed a large white sign with blue reflecting dots that spelled "Roma" and marked the city limits, when an antitank gun knocked out the leading tank, "quite a fight developed, and the infantry took some casualties. Found myself in a hot spot and had to take to a ditch." The men jumped from the tanks and took cover as a firefight developed with artillery and tank shelling, as well as the rattle of small-arms fire.

Soon afterwards, the commander of the First Special Service Force arrived. He was Brigadier General Robert T. Frederick, a quiet daredevil who resembled a handsome Hollywood actor. He was in command of the tank-infantry column and, as was his normal practice, he was up front. He stopped in the road and listened to the sounds of the battle. Just ahead of him was the white and blue Roma sign.

A few minutes later, Keyes, the II Corps commander, came up in his jeep. "What is holding you up here?" he asked Frederick.

"The Germans, sir," Frederick replied.

"How long will it take you to get across the city limits?"

"The rest of the day," Frederick estimated. Several self-propelled antitank guns, he explained, required an outflanking movement.

"That will not do," Keyes said. General Clark had to be in the city at four o'clock.

"Why?" Frederick asked.

"Because he has to have a photograph taken."

Frederick stared at Keyes. Was he serious? Or joking?

Keyes' face remained impassive. Whether his remark was simply intended to be humorous or a frank desire to hurt Clark, he too was suspicious of Clark's haste to get into Rome.

A cavalryman like Patton, formerly Patton's chief of staff, Keyes was devoted to Patton. Just before Keyes took his II Corps headquarters from Sicily to fight under Clark in Italy, Patton had advised him. "I told Geoff," Patton wrote in his diary, "to be careful never to mention the Seventh Army" or his experience with Patton, for Clark, he thought, was jealous of Patton's reputation.

Several minutes later Clark appeared. He had left his headquarters at 8:30 A.M. Accompanied by Brann and two aides, in a convoy of two armored cars and six jeeps, he headed for Rome. He reached the place in the road where Keyes and Frederick were talking. He had to stop too, for an occasional round of enemy fire sent them all periodically to cover. When he made known his desire for the blue and white Roma sign, Frederick had a man go forward the few yards to take down the trophy and give it to Clark.

When the gunfire subsided, Gardiner walked back to report what was going on. He joined Clark, Keyes, and Frederick and described the situation.

Because there would be no swift entry at that location, Clark departed.

Frederick then asked Keyes why Clark was so impatient to get into Rome.

"France is going to be invaded from England," Keyes answered. "We've got to get this"—the capture of Rome—"in the newspapers before then."

That afternoon, around dusk, all German resistance stopped. Allied troops, by far the greater part American but including an occasional contingent of French and British, together with a stream of newspaper correspondents, slipped into the streets of Rome. Most of the combat units headed for the bridges over the Tiber. They found all the structures standing and intact. That made it possible for them to continue through the city in pursuit of the Germans.

The objective of the bloody and agonizing campaign had finally fallen. At 1:30 A.M., June 5, in the Piazza Venezia, soldiers raised simultaneously the union Jack and the Stars and Stripes on the two flagpoles on the Monument to King Victor Emmanuel II. Several weeks later Clark sent the British flag to Churchill, the American to Roosevelt.

Clark made his entry on the morning of June 5. At 7:30 he left his command post and flew by Cub plane to the outskirts of Rome. A vehicular column was quickly formed, and Clark, accompanied by Gruenther, rode in a jeep. They penetrated into the city on Route 6, went past the Colosseum, headed for the city hall on Piazza de Campidoglio on Capitoline Hill, and got lost.

Driving haphazardly through streets flanked by frenzied crowds of

Italians who were cheering and waving flags, they finally came across a priest who said in English, "Welcome to Rome. What can I do for you?" He gave them directions to Capitoline Hill, and when he learned who was in the jeep, he announced Clark's name to the people. A young boy on a bicycle then preceded the jeep, shouted that Clark was coming, and led them to the city hall.

There at 10:30 he met his corps commanders, Truscott, Keyes, and Juin. They made small talk for the benefit of photographers and newsreel cameras. But there was another reason for the conference. The situation had been so fluid during the race for Rome that Clark needed an update on the locations of his forces and their directions of advance. He also learned from his principal subordinates that all the bridges across the Tiber were under guard; and that Allied troops were advancing beyond the city to the north on the heels of the retiring Germans.

The moment was a great personal triumph for Clark, but he shared it with his major commanders who had all helped to overcome trials and tribulations along a bloody trail. Rome was, above all, an Allied victory and a Fifth Army success.

The capture of Rome brought Clark many messages of congratulations. The one he liked best was Alexander's, which, Clark replied, "deeply moved" him. "The success of the Fifth Army would not have been possible without the unstinting assistance received from the Eighth Army and your understanding guidance of the combined effort."

If the words were hypocritical and perhaps guilt-ridden, they were also generous. Rome dissipated the rancor and suspicion, at least for the moment. Sweet victory overcame the sour taste, at least temporarily. After the fact, on the surface, and for the record, the alliance was as harmonious and as strong as ever.

In the United States, many photographs in the press showed Clark at the Colosseum, driving through the streets of the city, at the Vatican.

Clark and several members of his staff had an audience with the Pope, who talked of his interest in all mankind, of his gratification with Allied arrangements for feeding the poor and needy civilians in Italy, of his last visit to America.

"Isn't it wonderful," Clark wrote to his mother, "that I can say we are in Rome? I feel I must pinch myself to realize it is true . . . my men have performed like inspired soldiers. They have done magnificently. I sure am proud of them." A few days later he wrote, "Our capture of Rome . . . has been a great victory and we deserve it after the hell we have been through for so many months."

In the Church of Santa Maria degli Angeli in Piazza Esedra, along with 10,000 officers and men, plus members of the United Nations diplomatic corps accredited to the Holy See, Clark attended a solemn mass of thanksgiving conducted by the Fifth Army chaplain.

As for the glory of taking Rome, it was sweet but fleeting. For one day the seizure of the city filled the newspapers. And on the following day, headlines proclaimed the Normandy landings. That invasion, the major strategic Allied thrust, immediately overshadowed the Italian campaign and reduced the war in Italy to subsidiary significance.

Had Clark been right in his obsession for the city? Alexander thought not. In his memoirs, he wrote, "The battle ended in a decisive victory for us, but it was not as complete as might have been." He regretted Clark's failure to drive wholeheartedly for Valmontone.

Had it been possible for Clark to put all his forces into the thrust toward Valmontone and had he done so, he would probably have lost the opportunity to take Rome before Overlord as Roosevelt and Marshall wished. As for trapping the Germans, a blocking position at Valmontone would have brought small result. Operationally, the Alban Hills were a more important objective. After that dominating ground was in Allied hands, the Germans gave way.

Hardly insensitive to the personal fame involved in taking Rome and disappointed in its immediate displacement by the Normandy invasion, Clark made Rome a symbol of American military prowess. He had gained a great American victory, won a triumph for the Fifth Army, and deprived the British of what Churchill had endeavored to promote, a brilliant success for British arms.

But Clark had had an additional motive in driving to Rome. His strongest loyalty was to the men and women who had suffered far too much and far too long in the Anzio beachhead. He felt an overwhelming sense of responsibility for their isolation, their dangerous vulnerability, their ordeal. He owed them Rome. They had earned it. Rome was a tribute to their courage and sacrifice.

Long after the war a British infantry officer, E. B. Haslam, wrote, "We lost a lot of good men in the mud of the trenches at Anzio. At the end of May in the Anzio Beachhead we were absolutely tired out. We needed a rest and we needed a morale booster. In my view, Mark Clark was absolutely right to take Rome. That was our triumph; we had deserved it."

For Alexander, Clark had been difficult to handle. Perhaps that was why he had never issued Clark a written order for Valmontone, why he never gave Clark an ultimatum. Alexander accepted Clark's methods and plans because Alexander himself was uneasy over his own fundamental motivation, his desire to help the Eighth Army up the Liri valley. He overruled Clark only after the war.

The preponderance of American power in Italy created its own prerogatives, and Clark had his way. The British, denied the glory of capturing Rome, looked to the Normandy beaches where the strengths of the Allied partners were still, for the moment, equal.

CHAPTER 18
☆ ☆ ☆ ☆
THE NORTHERN APENNINES

"caught in the British Empire machine"

THE COMBAT TROOPS of both the Fifth and Eighth Armies pursued the retreating Germans beyond Rome. "The past few days have been the same," Henry Gardiner wrote in his journal, "fighting, moving, and driving on and on." The mass movement was by necessity largely unorganized and improvised. The forward elements searched for uncontested roads, tried to avoid costly battles, skirmished when necessary, endeavored to press on. They advanced so rapidly that Clark was out of telephonic communications with the leading units until June 17, when the Fifth Army headquarters moved to Tuscania, 70 miles north of Rome.

Allied progress then petered out. The drive had been exhausting and had worn out men and machines. The farther the Allies went into northern Italy, the lengthier and more stretched their supply lines became. Naples and Anzio on the west coast, Bari and Taranto on the east were increasingly distant from the front. Hampered by shortages of gasoline, ammunition, and other items, the Allies, after the initial bound through

Rome, found it difficult to push the Germans hard. About 85 miles above Rome, the troops ran into Germans defending a temporary line and had to halt.

Kesselring conducted a masterful withdrawal. After retreating for two weeks, he had his forces stop and dig in along a line centered on Lake Trasimeno. They held for ten days, then pulled slowly back about thirty miles to the Arezzo Line. There they stayed for ten days more before moving back once again. This time they were on the Arno Line, from Pisa to Florence and across to Ancona on the Adriatic shore. Essentially a screen, these defenses were twenty miles forward of the Gothic Line, Kesselring's final and strongest positions about 150 miles above Rome.

Ordering his subordinates to retard the Allies by carrying out sharp rearguard actions and by destroying bridges, culverts, and tunnels, Kesselring was deliberately using up the summer. He settled his units along the Arno Line about the beginning of August. If he could keep the Allies there until September, he would have the advantage of autumn rains. If he could delay the Allies even longer, he would have the additional benefit of winter weather, cold and freezing rain as well as snow in the high altitudes. At the Gothic Line in the northern Apennines, a wide belt of prepared fortifications in the mountains, Kesselring would try to block the Allies from entering the Po valley.

Whether Alexander, Clark, and Leese understood Kesselring's intention from Ultra intercepts and other intelligence information, there was little they could do except to follow the Germans as hard as they could. When Leese asked permission to use a road reserved for the Fifth Army, Clark told him to go ahead even though he had to stop Keyes temporarily. "Our interest," Clark said, "is to facilitate whipping the Boche in his demoralized condition, regardless of who does it."

If the Allies had indeed demoralized and whipped the Germans, they ought to exploit their success. And just when it seemed to Clark that they were likely to win complete victory in Italy, Anvil reared its head.

Whether the Allies should invade southern France had long been argued. Churchill opposed the operation as an unjustifiable diversion of forces, while Eisenhower, with Marshall's support, insisted on Anvil as a necessary adjunct for Normandy. Although the issue had yet to be settled, the Combined Chiefs of Staff instructed Jumbo Wilson, the Allied commander of the Mediterranean theater, to prepare the landings immediately after the fall of Rome. In compliance, his deputy, Devers, directed Clark to release Truscott's corps headquarters and three American divisions in mid-June and Juin's French corps headquarters and all four French divisions a month later.

In Clark's eyes, the immediate withdrawal of the Americans and the eventual loss of the French seriously reduced the Fifth Army forces just when the pursuit of the Germans promised a stunning triumph. Whether the Fifth Army at full strength could have pushed harder and farther in view of the declining flow of supplies was, of course, uncertain.

Major General Willis Crittenberger's recently arrived IV Corps headquarters replaced Truscott's, and a few new organizations were later scheduled for the Italian campaign. But even with an eventual improvement in logistics, the newcomers could hardly supplant and equal the seven battle-experienced American and French divisions.

The Combined Chiefs, Clark thought, were wrong to decide in favor of southern France at the expense of Italy. "It just doesn't make sense," he wrote in his diary. If the Fifth Army with all its units marched overland through northern Italy, Clark could be in southern France before the amphibious forces came ashore from the sea. It was a great shame and pity, he thought, for Anvil, still a tentative operation, to draw resources from the Allied forces in Italy and thus paralyze a great and perhaps total victory north of Rome.

Together with Churchill and Alexander, Clark preferred to overrun northern Italy quickly, then go eastward into the Balkans and meet the Russians as far east as possible. He longed to drive through the Lubljana Gap across Yugoslavia to Vienna, perhaps even to Budapest or Prague in a campaign to rival the exploits of ancient conquerors.

But Roosevelt and Marshall, who wanted to defeat Germany quickly before turning in force against Japan, saw Eisenhower's operations in northwestern Europe as more propitious.

Marshall, accompanied by a small party, came to Italy in June, and Clark met him at an airfield near Rome. While the two rode together for two and a half hours to Clark's command post, Marshall briefed him on the developments in Normandy and in the Pacific. Marshall favored an invasion of southern France because the port of Marseilles would permit sending troops directly from the United States to strengthen Eisenhower's forces.

"I told him," Clark later wrote, "I thought it was all wrong, that they were running for the wrong goal." Losing troops to Anvil "threw a crimp into the victorious advance of this Army." Yet, on the basis that southern France would go, he assured Marshall that he had instructed his staff to comply wholeheartedly with Devers' demands for service units, auxiliary troops, and artillery battalions to be pulled out of Italy for the invasion and subsequent campaign of southern France. Marshall later paid tribute to Clark's loyalty to the chain of command.

Scheduled to lose not only seven divisions and two corps headquarters but also the skilled and veteran Canadian-American Special Service Force, his paratroopers, many artillery battalions, and assorted engineer, signal, and other units, Clark wondered whether it would be possible for the seriously reduced Fifth Army to carry out any significant operations in Italy. Might it be better to transfer what remained of the Fifth Army to southern France?

He was realistic. The British could hardly permit all the Americans to leave Italy. Alexander would never consent to losing them. The Eighth Army, if the truth were known, had, in the battle for Rome, "contributed absolutely nothing but grief."

As long as Clark remained in Italy, Alexander would have to take account of how little the Fifth Army could do. The Eighth Army, Clark noted in his diary, would have to "carry the ball from now on." Alexander had to "give the [diminished] Fifth Army a narrow sector of responsibility commensurate with its means." The Fifth Army would do what it could "until such time as all troops are taken out [of Italy]." Yet in the end, "This will never work, I know, for Eighth Army is incapable of carrying the ball [alone]."

Alexander came to discuss his long-range plans. Having oriented both Allied armies on Bologna, he had given the Eighth Army what Clark considered to be the favorable terrain. Five miles below Bologna, the Fifth Army was to turn over the principal road to the British, who were to take the city. Both armies would then be in the Po valley, and the Fifth Army was to proceed through the Brenner Pass into Austria.

The plan was "lopsided" and "ridiculous," according to Clark. "I told him a little competition between armies would be a good thing." So Alexander redrew the inter-army boundary and ran it through the middle of Bologna, thereby enabling each army to capture half of the city.

Alexander would later change his mind in favor of another plan.

The uncertainty of Anvil weighed heavily on Clark's mind. Becoming convinced that the Allies would in the end invade southern France and that most of the Fifth Army would follow and become part of Eisenhower's forces, Clark wrote to him on June 26. "You can have every single unit I have, and they will leave here the minute the request is made. I have told my staff to give you the best we have, but don't forget the rest of us." He was reminding Eisenhower that his Fifth Army headquarters was also available.

He had perceived the declining importance of the Italian campaign. The bulk of resources in manpower and material would flow to the main Allied effort in France, leaving little for the forces in Italy.

De Gaulle visited Clark toward the end of the month to make him a Grand Officer of the Legion of Honor and to decorate him with the Croix de Guerre with Palm. Intensely interested in Anvil because the invasion would put a substantial number of French troops into metropolitan France to fight for the liberation of their country, De Gaulle saw clearly what Anvil meant for the prospects in Italy. The Fifth Army would lack the strength to cross the northern Apennines.

Clark agreed. In that case, he thought it better for all the American troops to go into southern France and bolster the American and French forces of the Seventh U.S. Army now commanded by Alexander Patch. The French units would probably become a separate field army in the near future. Two armies in southern France, one American, the other French, would require an army group headquarters to coordinate them. He had no idea, he said, who would command the army group.

"General de Gaulle," Clark wrote in his diary, "nodded without replying." De Gaulle saw the logic of moving the Fifth Army headquarters to southern France and upgrading it to army group status. But he was probably aware of another solution being discussed.

The question of Anvil was settled affirmatively on July 2. Three days later, August 15 was designated D-Day. Talk of forming a new army group headquarters with Devers in command removed Clark's uncertainty over his place in the scheme of things. Italy would continue to be Clark's battlefield.

Considering his future in Italy, Clark wrote a lengthy journal entry early in July. He hoped to drive to and across the Arno River without pause, unless he had to stop and let the British catch up. After crossing, he would take Pisa, then rest his troops and accumulate supplies for an attack through the rough mountainous terrain shielding Bologna. Once in the Po valley, both Allied armies should, he thought, move toward the Danube. Or the Fifth Army could march over the Maritime Alps to France.

The major obstacle to success in Italy was the decreasing strength of his Fifth Army. With Devers still Wilson's deputy but now very much involved in preparing the invasion of the Riviera from Mediterranean theater resources, Devers gave the southern France operation priority over the Italian campaign. He constantly drew men, units, equipment, and supplies from Clark's army in order to build up the Anvil forces.

An American division was arriving to bolster Clark's units, but he doubted its capacity for the kind of combat required in the mountains. The 92d Division, made up of black soldiers and mostly white officers, was coming from the United States. Because it required more training before commitment to battle, Clark planned to break in the division gradually, to give it "appropriate" tasks at the outset. "I do not feel it is wise," he wrote, "to count on its offensive ability in a slugging match with the Germans to the same extent as a white division." But he was fair. "I will give it every opportunity to develop its full 100% offensive power if it has the inherent capability of doing so."

Clark needed three more divisions at the very least to make the Fifth Army effective. Alexander was certain to suggest building up the Fifth Army with British troops, and if the Combined Chiefs accepted the proposal, Clark would of course have to go along. But he disliked the idea because of his prior experience with McCreery's British corps.

If, as was likely, the Fifth Army remained in Italy, it should, Clark thought, be an all-American organization. If additional U. S. forces were unavailable, the campaign was hardly worth pursuing. Instead of being asked to cross the Apennines, the Fifth Army should be removed from Italy as fast as it could be assimilated into the Anvil operation. The British Eighth Army had sufficient means to hold the Germans at bay in Italy.

But the Allied strategists, as he already knew, would decide otherwise. Both armies would try, as before, to engage and tie down the maximum number of German divisions in Italy, keeping them away from the more important eastern and western fronts where the Russians and the Anglo-Americans were making the major efforts to win the war.

One possibility offered hope of regaining the spotlight, of changing the course of the war, of attaining a spectacular accomplishment that might end the war quickly. If the two Allied armies could reach the Po valley before the end of 1944, they might compel the Germans in Italy to surrender. If the Germans continued to fight, the Allied leaders at the top political and strategic levels would have to make a decision on objectives. Should the Allied armies sweep across the Po valley toward France or toward the Balkans? Clark preferred the latter, where Vienna and southeastern Europe lay. If the Allied armies in Italy took Bologna, the Balkan vista came within reach. To capture Bologna now became Clark's compelling interest.

Polish units took Ancona and American troops entered Leghorn on July 18. The Germans, before departing, had utterly demolished both ports. The destruction exceeded the magnitude of the wasteland encountered by the Allies in Naples. Sunken ships and mines clogged the harbors, wrecked cranes littered the shorelines. In Leghorn alone, the Germans had planted more than 25,000 deadly booby traps. It would take the Allies over a month to clear the debris and remove the demolitions. And the first Liberty ship would not dock at Leghorn until a month after that. The supply line remained long and fragile.

The Allied pursuit ran its course as exhausted troops approached the Arno River, and a lull in active operations ensued well into August. Before pushing beyond, both Allied armies rested and accumulated supplies. Patrols probed the Arno defenses, and elements prepared for their river crossings.

Lieutenant General Sidney C. Kirkman's British XIII Corps neared Florence, reached the Arno on August 8, and halted. Unwilling to fight in the historic city, the British waited for the Germans to leave.

Having knocked down all the bridges except the fourteenth-century Ponte Vecchio, the Germans started to vacate Florence four days later. Italian partisans tried to hasten their departure, and fighting broke out. Kirkman's troops then crossed the Ponte Vecchio and cleared the streets. Riots and clashes involving partisans and fascists brought two more weeks of violence.

Lemnitzer had meanwhile come to Clark with a new plan from Alexander. Instead of exerting his main effort in the center of the Italian peninsula, in the mountains north of Florence, to capture Bologna, Alexander thought of shifting his strength to the Adriatic sector, where the hills were lower and less defensible. Although he still wished an attack from Florence to Bologna, the limited effectiveness of the Fifth Army would inhibit a real chance of success. Leese and the Eighth Army were to attack toward Rimini on August 25, and Clark, helped by Kirkman's corps, was to head for Bologna around September 1.

With Clark's principal objective, Bologna, in jeopardy, he, Lemnitzer, Gruenther, and Brann flew to the Eighth Army command post to discuss the new operational idea with Alexander, Leese, and Harding. Their major topic was how to coordinate Keyes' corps, which belonged to the Fifth Army, and Kirkman's, which was British, as they attacked together and abreast from Florence to Bologna.

Clark suggested combining the two corps under a single command to facilitate what was essentially a unified effort. But whose command? Alexander was reluctant to put Kirkman under Clark, while Clark was averse to letting Keyes go under Leese, whose main focus would be on the Adriatic sector.

Alexander talked of placing McCreery, his senior British corps commander, over the two corps. Although Clark thought it better to have both corps under the Fifth Army, he accepted Alexander's solution.

Leese then spoke. Clark was right, he said. Kirkman should go under Clark.

Alexander immediately agreed.

As Clark left the conference, he thanked Leese warmly for his unselfish approach to the problem. With Clark pressing the battle, the two corps, he was sure, would get to Bologna and open up exciting possibilities in the Danube region, perhaps bringing the war to an end that year.

A new source of strength for Clark appeared. Brazil had declared war on Germany and was sending combat troops to join the United Nations forces. About 25,000 soldiers, members of the Brazilian Expeditionary Force, poorly clothed and equipped, were arriving in Italy and preparing to go under the Fifth Army. "Handling" them, Clark wrote in his diary, "is a very delicate subject and must be done right." He was reassured when General Mascarenhas de Moraes, the commander, accompanied by several officers, came to his headquarters. Clark received them with an impressive guard of honor, and discussions during and after lunch resulted in mutual respect. Clark promised to speed their entry into battle. They told him how much the people of Brazil admired Clark.

He visited the 92d Division and made a fine welcoming speech. The troops had nothing to fear from the Germans, he said; the Germans were afraid of them.

He gave much the same talk to the Brazilians. Although they displayed high spirits, they had much to learn, particularly the officers who had little understanding of their responsibilities. Clark appointed Vernon Walters, a young captain who was proficient in several languages and who had served as one of his aides, to be liaison officer with the Brazilian force.

In Sicily on August 1, the 6th Army Group headquarters came into being under the command of Devers. Clark recalled Devers' advice to him several months earlier. Devers had counseled Clark to remain in Italy and to have nothing to do with Anvil.

Fifteen days later, Allied units invaded southern France. The landings were a resounding success. Marseilles would soon fall, and the forces would quickly mount a great drive up the Rhone River valley to an eventual meeting with Eisenhower's formations.

After observing the amphibious landings from a warship, Churchill came to Italy. He spent the better part of a day with Clark, who spoke of his friendship with Alexander and of his admiration for British soldiers. Touring the front, Churchill was impressed with Clark's self-confident outlook and leadership.

Buoyed by the Prime Minister's visit, perhaps thinking of Valmontone, Clark was unusually warm when he replied to a message from Alexander. "I...hasten to assure you that I am in complete accord with the way in which you have outlined the forthcoming operations. I assure you that I...have issued orders which carry out your instructions to the letter....Please dismiss from your mind any misgivings you may have as to our desire to push this thing with all our energy. The only thing I do not like is the waiting. We are anxious to get going, and the sooner conditions will permit our attack the better we will like it. I will be ready any time you say the word 'go'."

Leese launched his offensive on August 25, and the Polish Corps advanced swiftly toward Rimini. Everything was going well when heavy rains, as Kesselring had expected, turned the terrain into a bog and mired down the attacking troops.

The Fifth Army crossed the Arno River on September 1 rather easily. On the following day, Allied soldiers entered Pisa, then continued fifteen miles beyond into Pistoia. The 92d Division did well in its initial combat.

Having crossed the Arno and driven the Germans back to the Gothic Line, Clark now had to wait to resume his advance. "The fate of the Fifth Army," he wrote to Marshall, "is tied up with that of the Eighth, which is not progressing any too well." The British were struggling against the weather, the terrain, and the Germans. Clark was ready, even impatient, to thrust over the mountains to Bologna.

Two roads led to Bologna, both through narrow mountain passes. The principal highway went through the Futa Pass and was the obvious opening. A two-lane rural road with many sharp curves through the Gioga Pass, dominated by the 2,000-foot peaks of Monticelli and Monte Altuzzo, was the more difficult approach. Expecting the Germans to mass their defenses in the better avenue, Clark decided to feint toward Futa and to concentrate on getting through Gioga.

The British were sufficiently forward to cover Clark's right flank by September 13, and he unleashed his attack. Small groups of determined and brave men climbed the heights and proceeded from one ledge to another under the eyes of German defenders. The combat was close and fierce.

"We are fighting desperately," Clark wrote to his mother. "I am forward every day looking at these damnable mountains and wonder that any man could ever get through them. We will, but not without the price."

The cost was high. The Fifth Army lost almost 3,000 casualties to break into the Gothic Line, and in those small-unit actions, the Japanese-Americans, the Nisei soldiers, distinguished themselves by their heroism and success. With Monticelli and Monte Altuzzo in American hands, Bologna was less than twenty miles ahead. But still to be conquered were a few miles of extremely broken ground. Only after the Fifth Army penetrated through the highlands would the troops find Bologna uncovered and vulnerable on the Po valley plain.

"We have done a tremendously fine job and are over the mountains now," Clark assured his mother with some exaggeration, for some high ground remained. But the worst seemed to be behind them, and "I would say this is probably one of the biggest accomplishments of the Fifth Army. I hope the press at home has taken some account of it."

The Brazilians had participated in the battle, and Clark congratulated Mascarenhas for the performance of his men in their first combat. They had moved through mines and artillery fire to capture a town and had thereby contributed to the capture of Monte Altuzzo. Crittenberger, in whose corps they were serving, handled them skillfully even though they required a great many interpreters and special liaison officers.

The excellent impressions made by the 92d Division and the Brazilians heartened Clark, but he was sad when he learned that he was about to lose his Japanese-Americans. The Nisei troops were leaving Italy for southern France. Their departure was a great blow to him, for they were among his ablest soldiers.

Devers' 6th Army Group headquarters arrived in France on August 31 and became operational on September 15. Under Eisenhower's overall command, Devers directed the Seventh U. S. Army and the First French Army. Devers, Bradley, and Montgomery were now Eisenhower's army group commanders in northwestern Europe. Yet Devers remained, in addition, the senior American officer in the Mediterranean theater, Wilson's deputy, and responsible for nourishing and regulating the fronts in Italy and in southern France.

When the British captured Rimini toward the end of September, Leese turned his Eighth Army over to McCreery and departed to become the

Commander in Chief of the Allied Land Forces in Southeast Asia.
With both Allied armies having cracked the Gothic Line, they stood
on the threshold of a great victory. But as they took up the offensive
again early in October, they could do little. Torrential rains, fog, low-
hanging clouds, as Kesselring had foreseen, reduced the Allies to painful
fighting and small gains.

The British contended with low, flat, and marshy ground crossed by
thirteen rivers swollen with rain and running in deeply dredged channels
between high flood embankments. They would endeavor to overcome
that maze of obstacles for three months. After crossing seven rivers, the
Eighth Army was exhausted. The units were well under their authorized
strengths. They had to halt their exertions.

The Fifth Army toiled in vain to cross the remaining few heights
interposing before Bologna. And now Clark had the problem of replacing
his combat losses. His lack of individual infantrymen he said, was "crit-
ically serious" and about to "endanger" his operations.

Devers, still the senior American officer at AFHQ looking after both
the 6th Army Group in France and the Fifth Army in Italy, estimated the
replacement problem in the Seventh Army to be worse. If Eisenhower
could replace the wounded and injured in the Seventh Army from European depots, Devers would send the Mediterranean theater infantry
replacements to Clark.

Clark was hardly reassured. Devers was primarily interested in southern
France; the Fifth Army had to be of secondary importance to him.

Clark's impatience and frustration boiled over on October 9, when he
dictated a long and angry entry for his diary in order to recapitulate and
summarize his situation. The conditions were miserable. Heavy rains
inhibited progress. Some roads were under more than four feet of water.
Wounded men had to be evacuated and supplies sent forward on cables
strung over streams. The men were tired, the mountains imposing, the
Germans tough. Bologna, within reach and attainable, eluded Clark's
grasp.

If Alexander had followed his original plan of having the two Allied
Armies crack the Gothic Line together and side by side from Florence,
they would now be in Bologna. Instead, Kirkman's corps, helping to
make the "main wallop" over the mountains, Clark judged, had "been
of little value to me."

If Alexander was at fault for the lack of success toward Bologna, so
was Devers. He was responsible for unduly reducing the Fifth Army.
Guided entirely by his own selfish interests, Devers had diverted troops

badly needed in Italy for his own use in France. Devers had also taken eleven of thirty-three corps artillery battalions from Clark. So few heavy pieces remained that Clark had to group the assault guns of the armored division together to bolster artillery fire.

Now Clark had a shortage of infantrymen. Four American divisions were losing approximately 5,000 soldiers every ten days, and Clark had no way to replace them.

It was inconceivable to Clark how such a disgraceful situation could have developed, and particularly at a time when success was at hand after weeks of great sacrifice. The American officers at AFHQ, Clark was sure, had little concern with the campaign in Italy, failed to support him, and kept the true facts from the War Department.

"In desperation," as he wrote, he radioed directly to Eisenhower. Could Eisenhower sustain the Seventh Army replacement requirements out of European theater resources? There were 5,000 American infantry soldiers in North Africa and Italy, but Devers had earmarked them for himself. If Eisenhower could supply Devers with 5,000 men, Devers could release the 5,000 in the Mediterranean theater to Clark.

Although his Fifth Army had sustained 10,000 casualties in the past month, Clark had no choice except to go on; indeed, "I would not consider any other path." There was little point to stopping and remaining in the mountains for the rest of the winter. He moved his command post into the Apennines even though he thereby created communications difficulties, for he wanted his headquarters staff to appreciate and to share as much as possible the hardships endured by the combat troops. Furthermore, he wished to be as close to Bologna as possible when the final surge, the breakthrough, occurred.

In contrast with his burning desire to get forward to Bologna, he saw the British as nonchalant. Lack of progress seemed to bother them little. They were far behind the Fifth Army and relatively passive. "The Americans have carried the ball every inch of the way in this battle, dragging the British troops on their flank." As an indication of how bad things were, "They have relieved Leese and put in a washout like McCreery. He is a feather duster type."

What was happening, in Clark's opinion, was a repetition of the battle for Rome. The British were always miles behind. Their soldiers were hardly at fault, for individually they were brave and collectively they fought well. What they suffered from was poor leadership. Alexander exercised no influence, was anything but a driver, and was unable to prod the British into serious effort.

Three kilometers (less than two miles) of rugged ground separated him from Bologna, the last of the high ground in front of the city, and Clark lacked the troop strength required for the final push. There was no excuse, Clark thought, for Wilson's AFHQ, Devers' NATOUSA administrative and logistical structure, the Communications Zone supply establishment, and Alexander's army group headquarters to tie up 50,000 people who contributed little to the battle.

Furthermore, his requests for air support were consistently turned down. And, "I could write for hours on the lack of cooperation by the Royal Navy in support of my ground efforts. . . . I have asked for naval gunfire on my west coast. It has been refused repeatedly, yet the Eighth Army has it all the time."

He was discouraged, distressed, and depressed. No one understood the importance of Bologna. His troops were less than fifteen miles from the city and had only a few more heights to conquer to get into the Po valley. They were so close to success that one more effort was bound to do it, one last exertion in the terrible mountains would get them there. They had to keep going.

Yet the replacement problem continued to obstruct his efforts. He desperately needed at least 3,000 more infantrymen.

At a conference with Kirkman, Keyes, and others on October 14, Clark displayed a chart showing the battle casualties during the past month. The Americans had lost more than six times as many men as the British. They had captured fourteen times as many prisoners of war. The figures, he pointed out, made it obvious who was doing the fighting. The Fifth Army had progressed three-quarters of the way, had gained 45 of the 60 miles between Florence and Bologna. There could be no letup. The offensive had to continue day and night.

But the units, now reduced to skeleton proportions, could make no headway.

Clark's frantic struggle to get across the few intervening miles of mountainous ground became obsessive, and he began to ascribe his lack of success to British ineptitude. The Germans were shifting troops from the Eighth Army front to protect Bologna because, Clark felt, the British in the Adriatic sector failed to engage the enemy fully. The British had no will to fight, to tie down and hold the Germans. The situation was "disgraceful."

How could Alexander keep four British infantry divisions and an armored division in reserve behind the Eighth Army when the Fifth Army was fighting with every ounce of strength? He asked Alexander this question on the telephone and received what he termed "evasive" answers.

Actually, the British were close to exhaustion too. But to Clark, Alexander was letting the Germans transfer divisions to the Fifth Army front in order to give the Eighth Army the opportunity to go forward. "If anyone is to advance into the Po valley," he dictated for his diary, "they much prefer that the British Eighth Army gets the credit, rather than the Fifth Army." To him, the reason was clear. "We are caught in the British Empire machine."

As he gradually accepted the possibility of being unable to get into the Po valley in the immediate weeks ahead, he laid the blame on the Eighth Army. Using the excuse of unrelenting rains, the British continued to postpone their efforts.

When Clark expostulated to Alexander that he was driving the Americans hard, Alexander said, "Of course, if you think you had better stop the attack, you do so."

He would not stop, Clark replied, even though he was aware of the limit beyond which men could not be pushed. That point would soon be at hand unless the Eighth Army showed more fight.

Alexander promised to restudy the situation and get in touch with Clark in the morning.

Devers sent a word of advice to Clark on October 20. Clark, it seemed to Devers, was overworking his troops. He was demanding too much of them. Given their reduced numbers and the miserable conditions in the mountains, Clark was asking for the impossible. Devers was reminded, he said, of how Clark had almost pushed his men beyond endurance in February, when he had tried to get into the Liri valley.

Clark dismissed Devers' notion. Devers had made no visit to Clark's front for about two months, and he had no knowledge of the tactical situation, the terrain, the enemy resistance, and what Clark was trying to do. Capturing Bologna in 1944 would bring the war to an end or open up immense new strategic possibilities.

Two days later Devers relinquished his Mediterranean theater responsibilities to Joseph P. McNarney, formerly one of Marshall's principal assistants in the War Department. McNarney became Wilson's American deputy, and Devers turned all his energy to commanding the 6th Army Group in France.

On October 26, Clark very reluctantly concluded that it would be impossible for him to capture Bologna soon. He hated to have his men spend the rest of the winter in the frozen mountains, but there seemed to be no alternative. Four days afterward, he halted his attack. To stop when he was so close to Bologna and the Po valley was, he considered, his toughest decision of the war.

What then could be done? According to Alexander, quite clearly few additional units would be made available to the Italian campaign. An Indian division and a Greek brigade had been sent to Greece and were not likely to return. Two British divisions were about to be disbanded to provide individual replacements for the remaining British units. Only in the spring of 1945, after the troops were rested and good weather prevailed, would they be able to carry out a sustained offensive. Current operations, he suggested, should be suspended in favor of preparing for further effort in the following year.

In the face of all the difficulties, Clark bowed. Three thousand American replacements flew in from France during the last week of October, but they were too late to make possible an immediate resumption of the attack.

So the offensive burned out, and the front became relatively quiet. The men shivered and endured another bleak winter of snow, rain, fog, cold, and general misery.

Clark toured the front and visited his units incessantly, trying to cheer the soldiers and show them his concern for their discomfort. At one place where he wanted to see the men at their gun positions, Henry Gardiner necessarily "walked him through a lot of mud." Clark went willingly. Hiding his disappointment of the failure to get to Bologna, he tried, as best he could, to share his soldiers' existence and to hearten them.

Had the Allies reached Bologna in 1944, moved eastward into the Balkans, and been in eastern Europe before the Russians, Clark would later say, they might have changed "the whole history of relations between the Western world and Soviet Russia." They would have drastically reduced the influence of the Soviet Union, he was sure, in the immediate postwar years.

CHAPTER 19

☆ ☆ ☆ ☆

VICTORY

"darned proud of you—just as is the whole country"

VERY EARLY ON the morning of November 24, 1944, a small British signal office attached to the Fifth Army headquarters received a message addressed personally to Clark. After decoding and typing, the officer in charge delivered the paper. Because awakening the commanding general at 6 A.M. usually signified crisis or trouble, he said, as he handed the sheet to Clark, "This is good news for a change."

"It gives me the greatest pleasure," Churchill had written, "to tell you that the President and his military advisors regard it as a compliment that His Majesty's Government should wish to have you command the 15th Group of Armies."

Sir John Dill, the British Chiefs of Staff representative in Washington, had died, and Wilson was to succeed him. Alexander, to be promoted to field marshal, was to replace Wilson as the Supreme Allied Commander of the Mediterranean theater of operations. Clark was to move up and take Alexander's post as army group commander.

"I am sure," Churchill continued, "we could not be placing our troops, which form the large majority of your command, in better hands, and that your friendship, of which you told me, with General Alexander will at once smooth and propel the course of operations."

After reading the letter, Clark sent for Gruenther. When he appeared, Clark said, "Al, I've been relieved."

He let Gruenther gasp in astonished disbelief before telling him the news.

Replying to Churchill, Clark wrote, "I will be deeply honored to command the 15th Army Group. I fully realize the responsibility this assignment entails and the compliment His Majesty's Government has paid on me in consenting to place your glorious Eighth Army under my command. Please rest assured that its welfare will be carefully guarded.... Please accept my great appreciation for the confidence you have always placed in me."

The appointment was indeed an honor and a compliment to an American in the British arena. Churchill and his military advisers, the Chiefs of Staff in London, set policies, laid out strategy, and allocated resources for the theater. The theater commander, formerly Wilson, now Alexander, was head of the combined ground, sea, and air forces in the area. He carried out instructions, reported on developments, coordinated efforts, and dealt with various political, economic, and administrative matters. Under him, British officers had commanded the Anglo-American ground, sea, and air forces. To have Clark direct the Allied ground forces, to put him so high in the British chain of command was the result of Churchill's esteem, the consequence of association with and admiration for Clark since 1942.

Clark's elevation was recognition of his immense prestige and unique eligibility for the post. He was the logical choice, above all, because of his personal stature and strength. He had dominated the Italian campaign. The British had established the rules, and Alexander had supervised the ground fighting, but Clark had stamped his personality on the events. He, more than any other, was associated with the critical actions at Salerno, Monte Cassino, Anzio, and Rome. To the Allied public, he symbolized the achievements in Italy. Marshall would make the point when he sent his congratulations "just as you are losing the Fifth Army with whose achievements and fame your name will always be associated."

If he had complained in his diary of imagined or real British deficiencies, he had kept his views private. In public, his conduct was irreproachable, fastidiously correct and loyal. Furthermore, he sincerely agreed with the British long-range desire to advance eastward from northern Italy into the Balkans, primarily to block the Russians.

Of unquestioned competence in operations and tactics, with unexcelled ability to manage and direct, a figure of commanding presence and force, steadfast and firm in the face of difficulties, Clark had demonstrated his capacity for higher command.

The changes were to take place in the middle of December. Truscott, who would take command of the Fifth Army, arrived in Florence, and he and Clark had a long talk about the campaign and the coalition.

In a confidential assessment to the War Department, Clark reported the 92d Division to be deficient in combat. Under fire, many junior officers lacked leadership and a sense of responsibility, and much the same was true of the noncommissioned officers. The enlisted men were below average, and many cases of misbehavior before the enemy had been tried by court-martial. Stressing the preliminary nature of his report, Clark hoped to see the division improve.

He spoke often to the troops to hearten them. He decorated and promoted many individual officers and men for bravery and leadership. He sought to give them confidence.

As for the Brazilians, the junior officers were unable to hold their men together, and the poorly trained troops suffered from the extremely cold weather. The division commander was mercurial, a code word for unreliable, made excuses, and saw the presence of the Brazilians in Italy as a means of gaining prestige; they were not there, he told Clark frankly, to be cut to pieces.

Before assuming command of the 15th Army Group, Clark traveled around the Fifth Army area to say goodbye. "I have a real lump in my throat," he wrote to his mother.

As the Germans in northwest Europe quite by coincidence opened their vicious Ardennes counteroffensive on December 16 and started the battle of the Bulge, Clark flew to Siena and took command of the army group. The British had wanted him to have a British chief of staff, but he declined. The relations between a commander and his Chief of Staff were, he said, "almost a family affair" with "mutual respect for each other and understanding" imperative. Gruenther, along with Brann, Saltzman, and several other officers close to Clark, moved with him and continued to exercise the same functions at the higher level.

On the day after Christmas, the Germans struck in the coastal sector where the 92d Division held the left flank and covered Leghorn. Some black soldiers gave way and fled to the rear. Fortunately, Clark had moved a veteran division to back up the Americans, and these troops regained the lost ground.

The top American commanders became convinced of the inability of the 92d Division to achieve a satisfactory level of combat performance. Selecting the best men and organizing them into a single regiment, they sent the others to service units.

Most of the soldiers were poorly motivated, for racial animosity had pursued them from the United States, and subtle discrimination made them feel inferior. But what contributed above all to their poor combat record and to a high incidence of crime was their generally low educational level. There were more men with Army test scores in the two lowest categories, Classes IV and V, than in any other division.

Instead of concentrating so many marginal soldiers in a single organization, the War Department asked, would it be better to disperse them throughout the Army? Like most of his contemporaries, Clark thought not. He was against the indiscriminate mixing of black and white troops. A black battalion of infantry might be grouped with two white battalions to form a regiment, for some black officers were excellent leaders, and the Army had an obligation to give every man his chance. But integrating blacks and whites into the same units would merely pave the way, Clark wrote, "for our biggest defeat." The good of the Army came first, and the fundamental task of the Army was to win wars. Like many others of his generation, he saw no point in diluting the Army's combat capacity by changing the white composition of the fighting forces.

Years later, reflecting on the behavior of the 92d Division, Clark said, "The Negro soldier needed greater incentive and a feeling that he was fighting for his home and country and that he was fighting as an equal." The failure of the division was no reflection on the courage of black soldiers but rather on the society that denied them equality.

The War Department began to move slowly and cautiously toward integrating black and white soldiers. The European theater assembled platoons of black troops and placed them in combat battalions. In the Mediterranean theater, McNarney passed instructions to Clark to permit no organization or unit to establish club, mess, rest center, or recreational facilities exclusively for one race or the other.

The well-known radio news announcer and commentator H. V. Kaltenborn spent several hours with Clark and remarked that his main characteristics were "youth and vigor." He resembled "the faces of those Venetian Doges I've seen in paintings by Titian and Tintoretto." Clark went to the front every day and was "very popular with his troops," who suffered in the mountains and fought the bitter cold and the rough ground as well as the enemy.

McNarney's end of the year rating of Clark was short and to the point. "A cool, exacting combat commander," McNarney wrote. "Has ability to maintain high standards of discipline under most difficult conditions."

On New Year's Day 1945, Clark wrote to Renie. He hoped for complete victory, and looked for the 15th Army Group to play its full part. Reflecting on the hardships and also the blessings of the previous year, he was clear in "my determination that somehow we will carry on . . . there are many problems, the solutions of which are not clear. . . . This is a tremendous job I have, and to do it right, as has always been the case in history, one feels he needs more assistance." He meant more troops. "The trick, of course, is to get the job done with the tools at hand. With God's help, I will do it."

He then flew to Siena, spent two hours in his office on paperwork, and had a reception for the 700 officers of his headquarters. He made a short talk and reminded his staff that their job was to help commanders, not to worry them. That done, he moved the headquarters to Florence, closer to the front. Because he believed it wrong to have military personnel, he said, "holed up and shacked up in a city," where there were "too many dames" to divert them from their work, he established his offices in woods on the outskirts of the city, on the bank of the Arno where the Fifth Army headquarters had formerly been. His men operated out of huts, tents, trucks, where he felt that soldiers in the field belonged.

Clark came to know many civilians in Florence, particularly members of the American colony, most of them women who had married Italian titles and had magnificent villas in the hills. Quite a few asked Clark to occupy their homes in order to protect them from vandalism. Clark accepted one of many offers. He used the property as his personal residence, and there he took baths, entertained important visitors, and played poker and bridge with his friends.

His elevation to army group command did little to allay his private suspicions of the British. When the Canadian corps was pulled out of the Eighth Army and sent to join the Canadian army in Holland, McCreery asked to regain control of two British divisions still in the Fifth Army so that he could make the main effort in the next Allied attack. Clark "heartily" disagreed with the idea. "If there is one thing I am sure of," he wrote in his diary, "the principal 'carrying of the ball' will be done by the American infantry divisions, as they have always done in the past." Transferring the two British divisions to the Eighth Army would weaken the Fifth, expose the port of Leghorn, and make impossible a strong thrust through the mountains to Bologna, the city on the Po River plain.

Explaining some of his difficulties to Renie, he wrote, "I certainly have a hodge-podge outfit—every nationality in the world. It is not like having all Americans like the other commanders in France have. The transportation and all the weapons and ammunition of the British are entirely different from the American. They can't be switched around. The German divisions opposite me are all the same—all German with the same equipment.... I cannot put a British Division or an Indian Division on a snow-capped mountain like I can the Americans." Inflexibility was "inherent in an inter-allied command. There has never been one so complex as my Army Group. I am not complaining."

Members of the House Committee on Military Affairs, among them Representative Clare Booth Luce, toured installations in Italy. She took an immediate liking to Clark, and their friendship would continue into the postwar years. "Clare gave me a great lift—appreciated our hardships—stayed on longer than other Congressmen," Clark wrote in his diary.

In Washington, Mrs. Luce talked about what she called the "forgotten front" in Italy. She told of the abominable weather and terrain, the sufferings of the soldiers. Their morale, she said, was extremely low because the American press gave their activities little attention. Her remarks were widely reported.

To rectify the alleged oversight, Marshall announced his intention to visit Italy on his return from the Yalta Conference. He would show the troops his interest in them and assure them of the affection for them at home. "Do not meet me at the airport," he radioed Clark. "I will come to your headquarters. No honors."

Anxious to demonstrate the diversity of troops serving under him, hoping to have Marshall better understand the variety of problems their presence produced, the differences of language, food, and customs, which required accommodation, Clark, with some trepidation, disregarded Marshall's instructions.

When Marshall saw a guard of honor waiting to greet him, his face hardened into grim lines, then quickly relaxed. Clark had assembled troops from the United States, both colored and white, Brazil, England, Scotland, Ireland, Wales, India, Canada, South Africa, Poland, New Zealand, Italy, both regulars and partisans, as well as nurses and women auxiliaries from several nations. Only the French and the Nisei, who were fighting in western Europe, were missing.

Speaking to the officers of Clark's headquarters, Marshall cited the Italian campaign as the most perfect example of the teamwork among many nations united in a common cause. To newsmen he explained how the 15th Army Group was holding down Germans who might otherwise bolster the fighting fronts elsewhere.

Clark took Marshall to the 92d Division, which now consisted of a black regiment and a provisional regiment made up mainly of antiaircraft units. At Clark's request, in order to provide the customary third regiment, Marshall directed Eisenhower to return the Japanese-American 442d Infantry Regiment. The Nisei would be back in Italy in March.

The communiqué issued by Roosevelt, Churchill, and Stalin after their Yalta Conference endorsed the Curzon Line as the eastern boundary of postwar Poland, and the news created turmoil in the Polish Corps. Many soldiers had lived in territory east of the line, and that part was to be ceded to the Soviet Union. Having been taken prisoners of war by the Russians during the defeat and partition of Poland in 1939, later released to fight in Italy, they were vehemently anti-Russian.

The men were so upset that General Wladyslaw Anders, the Polish Corps commander, doubted whether they would continue to fight. To withdraw 100,000 Polish soldiers from the front line would cripple the Allied forces.

McCreery talked with Anders, then sent him to Clark. They had a private conversation in Clark's van, and Clark sought to soothe and reassure Anders. He talked of Kosciusko and Pulaski, and advised Anders to trust Roosevelt. The United States, Clark sincerely believed, would never let postwar Poland go under Bolshevik control.

Anders then proceeded to London for discussions with the Polish government in exile. Returning from England, he informed Clark of his determination to resume the struggle.

The valor displayed by the Polish soldiers throughout the Italian campaign, it was clear to Clark, earned Poland the right to sovereignty. The failure of the western Allies after the war to support a free and independent Poland was, to Clark, a betrayal. He felt bitterly that the United States government should have stood up to Stalin and the Russians.

"This being a high commander of the armies in Italy," Clark wrote to Renie, "requires much logistical planning not necessarily closely related to fighting." The most important thing he was doing was "careful and detailed planning" during "a hard period of inactivity" to prepare for what all hoped would be the final offensive.

Clark visits the Japanese-American soldiers of the 442nd Regiment. Spurned by other commanders, then given a chance by Clark, his beloved Nisei warriors repaid him with extraordinary bravery.

Clark shows off Indian troops, another element of his multinational command, to his boss, General George C. Marshall.

May 1945: At the end of a long and bloody campaign, Clark receives the surrender of the German forces in Italy from the brilliant German general Fridolin von Senger.

Back in the U.S. for the victory celebrations, Clark visits President Truman.

Clark was greatly responsible, as American High Commissioner in Austria, for saving that country from the Russians. The bouquet given him as he departed symbolized the Austrians' affection and gratitude.

He was delighted to hear about Renie's forthcoming trip to Fort Benning to speak to the Women's Club. "Under no conditions should you accept any fee for speaking there," he advised, then added, "I am glad you came to that decision yourself. Naturally, they should pay your expenses." He was glad about her continuing efforts in the Treasury Department war bond campaign, pleased to know of her visits to military hospitals.

His son Bill at West Point had rejected all branches of the service except the infantry—"more power to that kid!" He respected daughter Ann's religious choice in favor of Christian Science.

The recent death of his Cub pilot, Lieutenant Colonel Jack Walker, had been, he said, a "terrible blow" to him. Walker had flown Clark for seventeen months, and they had been together almost every day, spending hundreds of hours in the air. They had made at least forty hazardous flights in and out of Anzio, traveling over water about five feet above the surface. Once they had struck a barrage balloon, and the plane had almost gone out of control; only Walker's skill had saved them. Because the airfield at Anzio was heavily shelled by the Germans and because the roads were mined, Walker fixed pontoons on the plane so that he could land on water. One day as they bounced into the air on a take-off, the pontoons collapsed. Walker had to come down. After flying for an hour and a half to use up fuel, he brought the plane into a sheltered bay near the beach. As they hit the water, the pontoons broke off. By racing the motor before the plane went under, Walker got them close enough to the shore so that they could swim to safety.

Clark had selected Walker and several others who had been overseas for a long time to go home for a visit with their families. As the plane in which Walker was riding as a passenger left the ground, one motor cut out, and the craft crashed into a railroad embankment and burst into flame. No one lived.

In February, the commander of the German SS forces in Italy made secret contact with Allen Dulles, the American intelligence chief in Switzerland, and began negotiations to surrender. Alexander quickly became involved. The western Allies informed the Russians, who, fearing a separate peace, protested. Although the talks continued intermittently, the end of the fighting would come only after the defeat of the German military forces.

The Italian partisans, numbering somewhere around 50,000 persons, became bolder. Operating behind the German lines, armed with weapons captured from the Germans or dropped by Allied aircraft, sometimes organized and trained by Allied officers parachuted into northern Italy, partisan bands cut telegraph wires, dynamited culverts, bridges, roads, and railways, and ambushed small parties of German troops.

"The German soldier in the infested areas," Kesselring later reported, "could not help seeing in every civilian of either sex a fanatical assassin or expected to be fired at from every house." Although the Germans executed ten civilian hostages for every soldier killed, the partisans waged a murderous warfare. Controlled in the main by the Communist party, the Italians struck down fascists and other political opponents as well as Germans.

President Roosevelt nominated Clark on March 15 for promotion to full four-star general, along with Devers, Bradley, McNarney, and five others. "Renie darling, Hi, small fry!" he wrote on the following day. "So you didn't think your old man would ever amount to anything. Weren't you surprised when I got nominated for the four stars? I know how happy you were, as I was."

The recommendation was, he said, "recognition . . . for the work which has been done in Italy. I feel it is a compliment mainly to the officers and men of my command who gave their lives here in Italy and to those who have carried on with me and made it possible for us to accomplish our mission."

As a four-star general, he would have the same pay but an increased allowance of $2,200 a year. He would put it in bonds or send it back in cash, whichever Renie desired. There was no point to change the allotments; the paperwork took too long. If Renie mailed him stars of rank, he wanted small ones, not the large size.

The Senate approved the President's nominations, and the War Department listed him with rank from March 10. Official word reached him on March 30. Instead of putting on his stars at once, Clark waited one day for his son Bill's birthday. That made the event a family matter. Gruenther pinned on his stars before a few old friends. Clark allowed a photographer to take some pictures but permitted no publicity.

Hitler recalled Kesselring in March 1945 and put him in command of the troops in Germany. Vietinghoff replaced him as the commander in chief in Italy.

By then, to the Allies, the end of the war seemed very close. In western Europe, Anglo-American units were crossing the Rhine River and heading toward junction with the Russians, who were near Berlin. With the German military machine crumbling, what should the Allied forces in northern Italy do?

Because the Germans were losing power and heart, the longer the Allies waited to attack in Italy, the easier their task would be. The British, Clark suspected, wished to defer an offensive until May, when a crushing Allied blow was likely to be mortal to the Germans. To postpone a final drive, Clark thought, would be a great error. In his opinion, the 15th Army Group had to contribute its full share to the work of destroying the Germans. Otherwise the Italian campaign made little sense.

Clark called a conference of his major subordinate commanders. They had all been drawing battle plans, including diversionary measures to deceive the Germans. The general discussion gave Clark a better overview of what was possible.

Having crystallized his thoughts, Clark issued his operational instructions to the army commanders. With improved weather and favorable ground conditions, with satisfactory ammunition stocks and replacements on hand for at least two months of combat, the two Allied armies were to launch an all-out attack to destroy the Germans south of the Po. They were then to cross the river and capture Bologna and Verona. Featured were close ground and air coordination and the element of surprise.

Clark toured the front from the Adriatic to the Tyrrhenian Sea, talking with troops of all nationalities. It was, he said, "quite an experience."

The offensive started on April 5, when the Nisei feinted in the coastal sector and drew German reserves to that area. Four days later, after a skillful artillery and air preparation designed to confuse the Germans, McCreery's men jumped off. In five days the Eighth Army broke through all the major river defenses below the Po. On April 14, Truscott's Fifth Army started toward Bologna and in six days broke through the mountains protecting the city.

"I hope and pray," Clark wrote to his mother. To Renie, he expected "a great victory." According to the newspapers he received from home, the combat consisted of only minor actions. In reality, "it is just as severe, just as bloody, as desperate, and just as important as any in Europe."

Thousands of Germans surrendered as Allied units streamed across the Po valley. Bologna fell to Polish and American units on April 21. "You can imagine," he wrote to Renie, "what that means to me after these long, difficult months. The battle is going well. I hope for a great success."

Linking up beyond Bologna, the Fifth and Eighth Armies drove fleeing

Germans toward the Alps. The Italian partisans rose up openly. When American forces entered Genoa and Turin, they found these cities already under the control of the guerrillas.

"Renie darling," he wrote on April 24, "Here it is . . . a beautiful day— beautiful in many ways for at last I have seen unfolded the great victory which my two armies deserve; the fulfillment of the plans which I and my staff have worked on for so many tiresome months in the Apennine Mountains. I always prayed that the 15th Army Group, with my old Fifth Army and companion British Eighth Army, should have the chance to contribute a mighty last blow to the tottering enemy. . . . I rested my troops, saved the ammunition, built up replacements, trained and planned, and raised the morale so that when proper weather came I might hit a successful blow. It was not easy to delay . . . for it looked as though the war might fold up with me sitting on my royal behind. However, I had to keep on waiting until my resources were at their best.

"Finally we struck. . . . We have shattered the two last great German armies in the field." In comparison with their losses, "my casualties have been extremely low . . .

"I don't see what holds the Germans together. . . . I hope it will be over soon."

As Clark's forces raced to the Austrian and French frontiers to seal the Alpine passes and block German escape routes, with Mussolini captured and killed by Italian partisans, the campaign neared its end. On April 29, at Alexander's AFHQ located in Caserta, two German plenipotentiaries, one representing the Wehrmacht, the other the German SS and Police forces in Italy, signed and made official Vietinghoff's unconditional surrender of all the German land, sea, and air forces in Italy, a million men, effective at noon, May 2.

Clark did his utmost to make the effective date May 1. "What could be more appropriate," he wrote in his diary, "than on my 49th birthday for the Allied 15th Army Group to reach the climax of its twenty-month campaign in Italy? One of the most complete and decisive victories in military history has been recorded by these two armies in a period of approximately three weeks."

When Alexander informed Clark of the day when hostilities were to cease, Clark wrote in his diary, "Just missed my birthday." He would have liked the fighting to have ended on a personal note.

Like the Allied entry into Rome just ahead of the Normandy invasion, the war in Italy ended a few days before the final German surrender.

Problems remained. Allied troops had to prevent Italian partisans from killing Germans after their surrender. The Yugoslav leader Tito had ambitions around Trieste and created tensions.

Vietinghoff's representative, General Fridolin von Senger und Etterlin, a former Rhodes scholar at Oxford, dapper, with an Iron Cross around his neck, who had commanded the XIV Panzer Corps throughout the campaign, made a harrowing trip through partisan-controlled areas and came to Clark's office on May 4. In the presence of Clark, Truscott, McCreery, Gruenther, and Air Force Major General Benjamin W. Chidlaw, Senger stood at attention, saluted, and asked to receive the Allied orders for the surrendered German land forces.

Clark handed him written instructions on how the German units were to turn themselves in to Allied custody. Gruenther and Senger, together with their staffs, were to work out the details.

Senger saluted and was about to leave when Clark noticed that he was wearing a pistol. Understanding his need to be armed during his trip, the American gently asked him to take off the weapon. Senger complied.

"I was rather overwhelmed," Clark wrote to Renie, "that here after almost two years should come this General representing the complete surrender of the hundreds of thousands of men whom we have fought against so desperately."

He now had to round up Germans in the Alps, disarm them, and feed them. He was concerned about the Trieste area. On May 5, when the Fifth and Seventh U. S. Armies met in the Brenner Pass just below Innsbruck, Clark was in Trieste, where the atmosphere was tense. Showing firmness, Clark packed the area with Allied troops and moved Americans in to augment the British. When he learned of the unconditional surrender of Germany, effective May 8, he instructed McCreery to occupy southern Austria before Yugoslavs or Russians arrived.

"I have been exceptionally busy lately," he wrote to his mother. There were "many, many problems." Trieste demanded much of his time. "My last battle worked out precisely as I had hoped and planned. It could not have been more successful, and I am delighted, for these two armies which have fought for so long deserve the break they got. A few months ago it would have been hard to forecast that the first great surrender could come here."

Eisenhower sent Clark a personal letter of congratulations. After recalling their duties together at Fort Lewis, in North Africa, in Italy, he wrote, "Your accomplishments . . . are among the notable ones of the war and I realize more keenly than most how difficult your task has often been. The fact that you have kept up your optimism and drive and your sense of balance is almost remarkable. . . . I am darned proud of you— just as is the whole country." He hoped for an early meeting between them for "a real talk" and a "big evening."

Clark replied warmly, spoke of Eisenhower's great contributions to the war, and hoped to see him soon.

For the Allied forces, the immediate postwar days were euphoric. The guns were still, except for those fired in half-hearted training exercises, and the danger of death and injury receded. The weather was never more beautiful, and everyone relaxed. "Fifth Army," Henry Gardiner noted, "was living like royalty, having moved in on all of the best that Lake Garda has to offer." Clark had a sumptuous villa at Sirmione on the lake where he fished, sailed, swam, and entertained important visitors. He had his own C-47 plane and traveled to visit troops and commanders and to participate in ceremonies.

Taking stock of his personal situation, Clark could be well satisfied. By his accomplishments he had inscribed his name in the annals of history. He could wear the American Distinguished Service Cross, the Distinguished Service Medal, and the Legion of Merit; Britain, France, the Soviet Union, Brazil, Poland, Italy, Malta, and Morocco had bestowed high decorations on him. The War Department would soon award him an Oak Leaf Cluster to the Distinguished Service Medal for his "extraordinary versatility and uniformly superior ability and leadership as organizer, administrator, and combat leader." By his foresight, tactical and administrative ability, leadership and personal courage, he was a continuous inspiration to all" and was "remarkable . . . in producing harmonious teamwork of allies."

Now it was time for the people to celebrate the victory in Europe, and in that display of glad emotion, Clark would be conspicuous. The next two months would be a great personal triumph for him, replete with honors.

In mid-May Clark received an order to return temporarily to the United States. Marshall planned to have six parties of officers and men visit major cities for celebrations: Courtney Hodges to head a group in Atlanta, Bradley in Washington, Patton in Los Angeles, Ira Eaker in San Antonio, Eisenhower in New York, Clark in Chicago. All the junior officers and enlisted men were to be residents of the particular city and eligible for discharge.

Henry Gardiner was in Clark's party, which left in two planes from Florence, stayed in Paris a few days, then flew across the Atlantic.

Approaching Chicago, they picked up a fighter escort of 24 aircraft. After flying directly over the Loop, they landed at Chicago Municipal Airport. The group climbed into open cars and paraded through the city in a triumphant ticker-tape ride down Michigan Avenue, along State Street, through the Loop district, to the stadium on the lake front. Dignitaries spoke briefly, and Clark addressed an enthusiastic crowd. Renie came from Washington, and that evening there was a banquet with entertainment and more speeches.

While Gardiner and the others were separated from the service, Clark and Renie flew to Washington. His mother Beckie met them at the airport. The Clarks went home to the Kennedy-Warren House. Clark talked with Marshall and President Truman. He attended Ann's graduation at the Marjorie Webster Junior College, then left for West Point and Bill's graduation, where Bradley gave the commencement address and Clark handed Bill his diploma. His mother had a cocktail party for old family friends in her home on Kalorama Road, and Lieutenant General DeWitt, head of the Army-Navy Staff College, attended.

Clark was the guest of honor at a luncheon hosted by Congressman Henry Jackson, who then escorted him to a private dining room in the Senate where Clark spoke on the problems of Trieste. Senator Alben Barkley of Kentucky took Clark on the floor of the Senate and presented each senator present to Clark, the first officer of the war to receive this honor.

Accompanied by Bill, Clark returned to Europe in June. In Rome they saw the Pope and Prince Umberto. They stopped in Florence before landing at Verona. He spent a week showing Bill around Italy. Then his son left for the United States and parachute training at Fort Benning. "I am very proud of him," he wrote. "He is very polite and manly, and I hated to see him go."

Clark's trip to the United States had been a whirlwind of acclamation. It confirmed his status as a figure of world importance.

But more was to come. The Italian-American Labor Council selected Clark to receive its Annual Four Freedoms Award in New York City on Columbus Day. Oxford University invited him to accept the honorary degree of Doctor of Civil Law in October. The Masonic Order wished to confer the thirty-third degree on him. The government of Brazil asked him to travel to Rio de Janeiro to welcome home the veterans of the Expeditionary Force.

His earlier dissatisfaction with the Brazilian troops had vanished. The men had learned to be adequate combat soldiers, and Clark had managed to have the organization accept the surrender of a German infantry division. There was good feeling on both sides.

Clark departed for Rio de Janeiro in July with Crittenberger, Brann, and several others. High government officials met them, a huge crowd welcomed them. Renie flew down from Washington.

Everywhere they went, the people, recognizing Clark's tall figure, shouted a diminutive expressing affection, "Markie Clarkie, Markie Clarkie." At the review of the veterans in the downtown area, according to Clark's aide, the spectators "broke loose and formed a solid mass in the street, making it impossible for the cars to move." The Military Academy renamed the sports arena the Mark Clark Stadium. At Bela Horizonta, "the crowds literally picked him up and carried him to the hotel on their shoulders." In São Paulo, supposed to be "emotionally cold," the Opera House had 3,000 seats, but an audience of 8,000 came to hear him speak. At the Jockey Club, he watched the horses run the newly named "Mark Clark Handicap Race."

And so it went, Brazilians chanting "Markie Clarkie" everywhere.

Finally, Clark's party flew to Natal, where they divided. Most traveled to the United States, including Renie. Clark headed for northern Italy.

The Brazilians having worked him "to a frazzle with entertainment and talks," he wrote to his mother, he was about to go to Austria, where problems of power politics and the cold war awaited him.

CHAPTER 20

☆ ☆ ☆ ☆

AUSTRIA

"being firm"

LONG BEFORE THE defeat of the German military forces, the Allies planned to occupy Germany after the war and root out Nazism, foster democratic institutions, and cripple the industrial war-making capacity. They decided to dissolve Hitler's Anschluss of 1938, which had incorporated Austria into Greater Germany, and to restore Austria as a free and independent state. There would thus be two separate occupations, one in Germany, the other in Austria, both with the same forms but with different Allied commanders and military forces.

In Austria, as in Germany, instead of administering the conquered territory jointly in a continuation of the wartime coalition, the victorious powers divided the land into national occupation zones and, in the capital, sectors. To deal with policies of common interest transcending zonal boundaries and to act as the supreme authority in the country, the chiefs of the four military occupation forces in Austria were to sit together periodically in Vienna as the Allied Control Council.

Until the four-power occupation machinery was installed, each Allied nation exercised local control. The military maintained order, guarded prisoners of war, and helped refugees, the displaced persons from all over Europe, the French in the western part, the British in the south, the Americans in upper Austria, and the Russians in a large eastern zone including Vienna.

Having arrived in the capital in the closing days of the war, the Russians controlled the routes of access—roads, railways, and flight paths—to Vienna, as well as telephone and telegraph installations inside the city. The geographical position of Austria itself was on the seam between western and eastern Europe and perilously close to, almost surrounded by, what appeared already to be a Soviet controlled bloc.

On May 14, 1945, hardly a week after the war ended, a Provisional Republic of Austria under Dr. Karl Renner came into being. Hurriedly constituted as a coalition of Socialist, Communist, and People's Parties, and composed of able men free of Nzi taint, the government, established in Vienna, pledged to pay the occupation costs, to develop a sound economy devoted to peaceful pursuits, and to set up freely elected national and local ruling bodies.

Shortly thereafter, Clark learned officially of his selection to command the U. S. Forces in Austria and to be the American High Commissioner. Together with Lieutenant General E. M. Bethouart for the French, McCreery for the British, and Marshal Ivan S. Koniev for the Russians, he was a member of the Allied Control Council. Before the Council could function, the Allies had to ratify the occupation agreements.

This occurred in July at the Potsdam conference, which formally approved the occupation arrangements and, further, authorized the removal of industrial equipment from both occupied states as war reparations. In Austria, determining the ownership of German assets was extremely difficult, for after the Anschluss, Germans had seized, confiscated, and purchased much Austrian property. How to untangle conflicting claims under different Russian and Western interpretations was a source of unending trouble. The Russians began at once to take compensation. They dismantled factories, heavy machinery, and other capital goods and shipped them to the Soviet Union.

During preliminary meetings among representatives of the four occupying powers in Austria, Gruenther, who would continue as Clark's Chief of Staff and Deputy, acted for him. Gruenther set up the American headquarters in Salzburg, traveled to Vienna to consult with the Russians, and generally laid the groundwork. He reported the Russians to be friendly if somewhat guarded.

Clark himself went to Austria on August 12. He motored with Saltzman from Verona to Salzburg. He took possession of the Schloss Klessheim, formerly a guest house for Hitler's Eagle Nest, as his residence and headquarters. He would use a hunting and fishing lodge at Hinterstoder, a village in the Tyrolean Alps, for relaxation.

After a brief inspection of his new quarters, Clark drove with Gruenther to the Festspielhaus, there to open for the first time after the war the Salzburg Music Festival, the great annual tribute to Mozart. Despite devastation and personal dislocation, the trappings of the major event had somehow been assembled.

Inside the theater, Clark was escorted to his seat. Ruffles and flourishes sounded. A detachment of American troops paraded with flags. An official of the province made a short speech. Then Clark spoke.

"I am indeed gratified," he said, "that my first official utterance to the Austrian people, dwelling in the zone occupied by the U. S. Forces, which I have the honor to command, should be on the occasion of a celebration of a rebirth of Austrian cultural freedom. The United Nations are giving Austria an opportunity to work her way back to liberty, to independence, and to an honored place in the community of peace-loving nations."

All connections with Nazi Germany, he continued, had been severed. Final arrangements for quadripartite control were in process. Handling and disposing of prisoners of war and of displaced persons had begun. A relentless search for individual Nazis went on. Local governments had been established in the provinces. Democratic political parties, the rights of assembly and public discussion, the resumption of trade union activities were being encouraged. Austrian courts were already functioning. Plans for publishing Austrian newspapers, magazines, and books were under way.

A short musical program followed his remarks.

Clark was anxious to have the Allied Control Council meet quickly, for numerous problems clamored for attention, among them, arranging for the distribution of food and fuel to the civilian population to prevent them from starving and to keep them from freezing during the winter. The Russians seemed hardly anxious to convene the body. As hosts, for they were in Vienna, they delayed, meanwhile establishing control over their zone and sector and continuing to send capital assets to the Soviet

Union. Under pressure from Clark, they finally agreed to a meeting at the end of the month.

In apparent recognition of the power of the United States, Koniev invited Clark to visit his headquarters in a suburb of Vienna the day before. Clark accepted, and he and Gruenther were treated to an exhausting day of festivities, food, and drink most of the afternoon and evening, a performance of Russian musicians at the opera house, a movie at midnight, a late supper, and vodka into the morning hours. Koniev excused himself early, but his deputy, Colonel-General Alexis Zheltov, a big bull of a man who was a former heavyweight wrestling champion of the Soviet Union, stayed to the last. After several hours of sleep, then a swim in the pool, a set of tennis, Clark and Gruenther departed for Vienna.

Later that day, escorted by six motorcycles through streets lined with American and Russian soldiers, Clark drove to the Imperial Hotel and attended the first meeting of the Allied Control Council. The session was mainly ceremonial, but all four general officers remarked on the gravity of the food and fuel shortages.

On his return to Salzburg, Clark sent Koniev a letter of thanks, praising "your understanding, your cooperation, and your genuine desire to solve our Austrian problems in cooperation with our Allies."

"I feel that our relations have improved considerably," Clark cabled Washington, "with indications that he [Koniev] will make some concessions."

Understanding the profoundly different national interests and outlooks of the United States and the Soviet Union and following the example of Roosevelt, who had attempted to win over Stalin, Clark sought to establish a personal friendship with Koniev in the hope of keeping friction to a minimum.

Eisenhower and his son John arrived, and Clark took them to Venice, where they toured the city, then to Rome, where they saw the sights, had an audience with the Pope, and lunched with Crown Prince Umberto. They flew to Nice, then motored to Eisenhower's villa in Cannes for a vacation.

They were relaxing on the beach when a message from Washington startled them. President Truman was upset over the housing and other facilities of the displaced persons, particularly the Jewish refugees who apprently received less consideration than the others. Eisenhower and Clark returned at once to their headquarters.

The allegations may have been true in Germany, but not in Austria.

Inspecting nine installations housing displaced persons, Clark was, his aide noted, "exceptionally pleased with the conditions of the camps." Whether he felt the tug of his mother's heritage or whether he was simply manifesting a sense of humanity, his treatment of the refugees was exemplary. Agencies and individuals especially concerned with Jewish displaced persons were gratified with what they called the enlightened attitude of Clark's administration. He and his staff had improved housing, diet, and medical care, provided schools, vocational training, social programs, and warm clothing, and made available religious facilities.

"I have never been more busy in my life," he wrote to his mother. His biggest task was to keep the Austrians from freezing or starving to death during the winter.

Early in October, Clark went to Rome to bestow an American decoration on the Italian prime minister. In Vienna he met with McCloy, who had come from Frankfurt, and with Averell Harriman, who had come from Berlin. Flying to Paris, he saw Juin, now a member of De Gaulle's government. In New York at the Biltmore Hotel, he was the honored guest of the Italian-American Labor Council, called the American Garibaldi who had restored liberty to Italy, and given the Four Freedoms Award. Speaking to an audience of 800 and over a national radio network, he said that the Allies were making progress in Austria. Although the problem of food had yet to be solved, postal and telegraph services were functioning, trains were running, motor travel was possible. He envisioned the early formation of a democratic government in Vienna. His relationship with Koniev, he said, was perfect.

In Washington he lunched at his apartment in the Kennedy-Warren, dined with his mother and Aunt Zettie Marshall, then went to Palm Beach, Florida, for a week of vacation.

In England, together with Eisenhower, Freyberg, Montgomery, and other high-ranking commanders, Clark received the honorary Doctor of Civil Law degree from Oxford University. In Paris he met with De Gaulle and Juin. His son Bill, assigned to the 44th Division in Austria, joined him and accompanied him to Salzburg.

Clark had a close relationship with Renner and the Austrian government, which he thought had done a good job. They had maintained a working unity, had a good legislative record, displayed vision and force in reconstructing the country, and enjoyed the confidence of the population. When they proposed national elections on November 25, Clark endorsed the action.

Chancellor Renner lauded Clark's efforts on behalf of Austria. "Ever since his arrival," Renner said, "he has shown himself to be a warm and unselfish friend of our people and of our country. This great American personality, who obviously combines superior diplomatic powers with his military prowess, has clearly demonstrated himself as a warm intercessor for our country. . . . We have every reason to face the future with confidence when men like General Clark . . . so actively sponsor our cause."

At a press conference shortly before the Austrian national elections, Clark announced an improvement in food deliveries and spoke warmly of Austrian progress. Whether his words or simply his presence affected the population or whether the initial brutality of the Russians lingered, the balloting was favorable to the West. The Social Democratic and the People's Parties split the vote, the latter gaining a slight majority, and Dr. Leopold Figl became the new Chancellor. The Communist Party received only five percent of the votes, and the Russians were stunned.

When Figl sent the Allied Control Council a list of the members of his government, Clark expected the Russians, still shocked by the erosion of their prestige, to protest the names of several proposed Cabinet ministers on the excuse of previous Nazi association. Although Clark's, McCreery's, and Bethouart's intelligence officers found all above suspicion, Clark worked out a private understanding in order to keep his relations with Koniev, as he said, "extremely cordial."

A day or so later Figl told Clark of his friendly conference with Koniev, who had objected to three of Figl's nominees. No doubt with a slight smile and perhaps a wink, Figl expressed his willingness to substitute three names. Renner was to be the President of Austria.

On December 19, with the other members of the Council, Clark attended the opening of the Austrian Parliament.

Clark tried personally to brighten Christmas for the Austrian children. He donated $500 to a fund for holiday parties, encouraged his troops to contribute warm clothing, toys, and candy, had girls and boys in for cake and hot chocolate. Citizens spontaneously wrote him nearly seventy-five Christmas letters, some containing poems composed by children, to thank him for food packages and other parcels and for what the Americans were doing for Austria.

The Russians, often irritating and inconsistent in their behavior, began to be intimidating. They occasionally closed the most direct highway from the American zone to Vienna and harassed and held up on one pretext or another the Mozart Express, the American train running twice a day between Vienna and Salzburg. Brawls and thefts became common, and ugly incidents occurred. Clark ordered armed guards on the train and gave them authority to fire their weapons in self-defense. When two Russian officers menaced passengers, an American sergeant shot and killed one, seriously wounding the other.

Koniev immediately demanded the delivery of the sergeant to Soviet custody to stand trial. Clark refused.

Russian fighters buzzed and fired on American transport planes and held target practice dangerously close to the American airfield. A Soviet antiaircraft battery shelled an American plane flying in the designated corridor. Clark instructed crews to respond to threats and warned the Russians of countermeasures.

The American outlook toward the Russians changed to hostility in the spring of 1946, not only because of the annoyances the Russians created but also because the Western world understood their attempts to shape eastern Europe forcibly into the Soviet image.

In Texas, a small group of 36th Division veterans planned to destroy Clark's military reputation by questioning his competence at the Rapido River. They quoted the protests of Walker, the division commander, against what he termed Clark's unjustified orders.

Gruenther, now assistant commandant of the National War College in Washington, D. C., got wind of the action and telephoned Walker, who was at Fort Belvoir, Virginia, awaiting retirement. Admitting his ignorance of the connection between the Rapido crossings and the Anzio landings, Walker demolished the validity of the charge.

Drew Pearson, a Washington journalist who specialized in the sensational—he had publicized Patton's slapping incidents—made a Sunday night broadcast and predicted a congressional inquiry to determine responsibility for the heavy loss of life along the Rapido.

The Senate Military Affairs Committee was about to approve the promotions of Clark and several others to the permanent rank of major general. The members decided to wait.

At the division reunion in Brownwood, Texas, a resolution termed the Rapido crossings "suicidal," one of the war's "colossal blunders," a "blood bath," and placed the blame squarely on Clark, who had ignored Walker's warnings of imminent catastrophe. Although subsequent statements were emotional and factually inaccurate, the military committees of both houses reluctantly scheduled hearings.

Clark declined to comment. The War Department released a history of the operation and considered Clark's instructions to have been proper.

The testimony of the 36th Division Texans was less than convincing.

After a delay of five months, the senate confirmed Clark's Regular Army promotion to major general.

Commenting on the desire of the masonic order to present Clark with the thirty-third degree, Irving W. Lemaux, an old Indianapolis friend, wrote, "it seems to me like you have already had the thirty-sixth."

In Austria, Clark worked to clarify the German assets in order to sustain the economy, to abolish the zonal demarcation lines in order to promote internal trade, to reduce the number of troops in order to relieve the country of excessive occupation costs. "No progress whatsoever has been made on any of these matters," he reported. "The Soviet element uses every means to block progress."

A group of American reporters touring Europe arrived in Austria, and Clark set up conferences with governmental officials and briefed them personally. The Allies, he said, were making progress despite obstacles erected by what he called the "attitude of our Soviet friends." The main source of trouble was reparations. The Western allies had ceased shipping German external assets from their zones because of the ruthless Soviet acquisition of resources. The Russians sometimes imposed annoying difficulties on American movements. At first Clark had tried to be cooperative, and he had made concessions, expecting the Russians to reciprocate. Now he was honest and direct with them. When the Americans were tough, he said, they got better results.

The reporters approved Clark's firmness in dealing with the Russians, called the American presence in Austria "a real first-class and big-time set up," and paid tribute to Clark and his staff. According to Walter Lippmann, "Our interests in Austria are in the best possible hands."

The War Department allowed families of servicemen to join their husbands in Europe, and among the initial group were Renie and Ann. The dependents arrived in Bremen, where Clark had trains waiting for them. His son Bill escorted the party from Salzburg to Vienna. To Clark's great joy, they were there on his fiftieth birthday, May 1.

Clark returned to the United States in the fall of 1946 to receive Masonic honors, and his travels were a triumphant tour. Everywhere he was acclaimed, interviewed, quoted, photographed. He was pictured as a man of action, a tough campaigner, a skilled diplomat.

Speaking to the students at the National War College, Clark told of his initial determination "to get along with our Soviet friends.... At the very beginning we went in for a form of appeasement. We gave in often." They "resisted every step we took to create an independent and democratic

Austria. . . . I have found by being firm we were able to get along better with them." He saw his main mission as preventing Austria from sinking into the Soviet sphere of influence.

When General Joseph Stilwell, commander of the Sixth Army at the Presidio of San Francisco, died in November 1946, Eisenhower offered the post to Clark. He accepted.

But he was soon requested to attend the meetings of the Council of Foreign Ministers in London. The purpose of the conference was to draw the basis of a peace treaty with Austria, this to be concluded later in Moscow. Secretary of State James F. Byrnes wished Clark's expert advice.

He was in London almost all of January and February, 1947, staying at the Hotel Dorchester, taking most of his meals at the Hotel Connaught, before moving into an apartment on Park Street overlooking Hyde Park. "I am at 20 Grosvenor Square," he wrote to Eisenhower, "right where we started out. It brings back many memories. I look out the same windows and into the square where they are erecting a monument to the late FDR. I used to look out these windows almost five years ago and wondered what the future held, and I must say I am still wondering, for we have a long and difficult road to go before we make the peace secure that we fought so hard to win."

Byrnes did not come to London, and Robert Murphy acted for him. The peace talks, held at the Lancaster House, discussed the German assets, Yugoslav reparations, the withdrawal of the occupying armies. The American delegates, searching for compromises in order to gain Soviet agreement to postwar peace treaties and a four-power pact, were inclined to accept Russian proposals to treat Austria, in Clark's opinion, much like Bulgaria, Rumania, and Hungary, states in the Soviet orbit. Clark insisted on bestowing full sovereignty on Austria. The Soviets were intransigent, the meetings fruitless.

Soon after Clark returned to Vienna, Byrnes resigned and Marshall succeeded him as Secretary of State. He asked Clark to accompany him to Moscow, to meet him first in Berlin. Clark flew to Berlin early in March and shared his views with Marshall and his assistants, among them John Foster Dulles, Benjamin Cohen, Murphy, Lucius Clay, and McNarney, on what he thought was fair for Austria.

From Moscow, in a letter to Renie, Clark described the depressing conditions: "up to my neck in work and difficulties," his hotel room cold, "not even 60" degrees, "the futile childlike approach the Soviets take to the matters under discussion." "I feel like I am going to kindergarten every day.... They have not given in on a single point since we started. They delay the conferences, drag them out, hesitate on discussions, and are unable to delegate authority. This is all part of their pattern to confuse and wear down all of us and get us to give in."

A few days later, "This is the toughest assignment I ever had and one I find hard to endure.... Sometimes I am ashamed to be a party to our deliberations when Soviets treat us as if we were a fifth rate country. It worries me sick. I hardly sleep any more, for the whole mess disturbs my very concept of what things should be."

In what he called "endless and hopeless" debates, Clark argued for true Austrian independence. The meetings ended in stalemate.

As the conference broke up, Clark requested and received permission to stop briefly in Warsaw on his way back to Vienna. At the war memorial in Warsaw, Clark, in a thumbed nose gesture and to the consternation of the Communists, placed a wreath to the memory of the Polish soldiers who had fought so valiantly in Italy.

During his preparations to leave for the United States, Austrian officials tendered Clark a farewell party. The Federal Chancellor paid tribute to his efforts, thanked him for quickly re-establishing a civil administration in the American zone, for contributing to the abolition of the zonal borders, for helping overcome food shortages, and for the "hard battles you fought at the Foreign Ministers' Conferences in London and Moscow for...the conversion of Austria from a liberated to a free country." Coming to know Clark the soldier, the statesman, and the man had been one of his few pleasant personal experiences in a time of care and trouble. Thousands of Austrian children, he concluded, would always remember the Clarks for what they had both done for them.

The Chancellor's remarks reflected a widespread and sincere affection for Clark in the country. As his time of departure approached, many warm letters and small gifts came to him from strangers who expressed gratitude for his work. He had projected himself as the protector of the Austrians, concerned for their welfare. He had symbolized not only to the Austrians but also to the Russians, British, and French the great strength, prestige, fairness, and generosity of the United States, its people, and government. He had impressed everyone with his firmness and flexibility. He had in effect waged a successful public relations campaign, not for himself but rather for the American image. But the publicity would have fallen flat without the substance of his skill as a diplomat. He had been the leader of the Western presence and as such had orchestrated a program to keep Austria solvent and independent. He had towered above his colleagues.

His final view of his Austrian experience concerned the Russians and the need for power in dealing with them. As he wrote in 1950, "there is nothing the Soviets would not do to achieve world domination...they respect nothing...except force. And when confronted with strength and determination, they stop, look, and listen....We must build a national military team that will make it unavoidably clear that anybody who endangers our way of life will risk destroying himself."

He left Vienna for Salzburg on May 4, and on the following day set out for home. At the railroad stations, his aide recorded, "Hundreds of people were gathered...and there was a genuine sense of regret expressed at the General's relinquishment of his command and his departure."

He, Renie, and Ann traveled to Trieste, Florence, and Rome, went to the Riviera, then on to Paris. At Boulogne, they boarded the *S. S. America* for their Atlantic crossing. He looked forward to a pleasant tour at San Francisco, then perhaps retiring quietly to Camano Island.

CHAPTER 21

☆ ☆ ☆ ☆

KOREA

"with misgivings"

ABOARD THE *AMERICA*, Clark received a cable asking him to talk on his recent experiences over a radio network in New York and to the National Press Club in Washington. He accepted.

In New York he blasted the Russians for "failing to cooperate" in the postwar world, warned the Americans that the Soviets were on a collision course with the United States, and advised the nation to prepare for a showdown. He said much the same thing in Washington, calling on America to be strong, to make no further concessions to the Reds, and to block them from gaining world domination.

Traveling cross-country, he addressed audiences and called the peace tougher to win than the war and termed the Soviets dangerous. By the time he reached the west coast, he had gained a reputation as an exponent of firmness when dealing with Moscow and an "outspoken foe of Communism."

When he assumed command of the Sixth Army, San Francisco celebrated General Mark Clark Day, and four thousand civic and church leaders, attending a reception for him at the National Guard Armory, praised him as an exemplary soldier–diplomat.

Columnist George E. Sokolsky deplored what he called Clark's exile to California, "where he can twiddle his thumbs in the pursuit of paper routine." Foreshadowing Senator Joseph McCarthy's later charges, Sokolsky mistakenly ascribed Clark's assignment to the "little men who run the State Department" and who wanted him out of the way so that they could hand Austria over to the Russians. His "natural gifts and his vast experience" were being wasted, for he was "beyond doubt one of the most competent statesmen in the service of the American people." He had a "genius for handling the Russians."

There was a quiet boom to nominate Clark for Vice President on the Republican ticket in 1948 or to run with Truman. He promised Renie, who was not altogether well, never to seek political office.

Clark applauded the unification of the armed forces under a Department of Defense. He was instrumental in abolishing duplicate functions and facilities of the military services and instituted on the west coast what was later called the single-manager concept.

Departing with Renie and Ann by ship from New Orleans on a goodwill tour of Brazil early in 1949, Clark spoke to the press of the military weakness of the United States. Reporters characterized him as "a legendary figure," wrote of his "fabulous wartime achievements," and described him as "unassuming and modest, with an unquenchable boyish personality."

Bradley, who was the army Chief of Staff, rated Clark, praised his performance, and added "Very ambitious and somewhat inclined to seek publicity."

When he and Renie voyaged to Italy, a good-natured cartoon appeared in an Italian paper. It showed two prostitutes in a bar. One said, You heard that General Clark is coming to Rome? Yes, said the other, I hope he's bringing the Fifth Army with him.

The Clarks were received warmly everywhere they went. At the American cemetery at Anzio, Clark warned against would-be aggressors.

Bradley moved up to be Chairman of the Joint Chiefs of Staff, J. Lawton Collins, Clark's classmate, became the Army Chief of Staff, Devers retired, and Clark succeeded him as Chief of the Army Field Forces at Fort Monroe, Virginia.

In that post, Clark was primarily responsible for training the combat troops. He was also involved in squabbles arising out of unification, how to balance conflicting claims of the services for manpower, weapons, and missions. He traveled a great deal, chaired conferences, made inspections, observed maneuvers, and gave speeches warning that force was the only virtue understood by the Russians.

Rating Clark again, Bradley listed his self-confidence, ability to make decisions, willingness to accept responsibility. "Even though he has what I consider too much desire for publicity, I still rate him one of the six most capable officers in the Army."

In July 1950, the Communist forces of North Korea overran the 38th parallel and invaded the Republic of Korea. President Truman committed United States military forces to oppose them. The United Nations supported him, and member states sent units to join MacArthur's American and South Korean troops. Clark was all in favor of what he called the government's "courageous action" and strong stand against aggression, which, he said, would deter the Soviet Union from starting World War III.

Training troops for combat had become vital and urgent, and, as the McNair of the Korean War, Clark stressed realism and ruggedness and the use of live ammunition in his exercises. Against what he called "the ruthlessness of the enemy" who "flaunts the accepted rules of land warfare," Clark hardened American soldiers and worked to "eliminate all the frills" in training. Technological progress and the development of push-button weapons, he said, hardly relegated the infantryman to oblivion; he still remained the essential force in war, the indispensable element in battle.

The entry of the Chinese Communists into Korea raised the spector of a monolithic enemy. Outraged, Clark privately advocated bombing "military targets in Manchuria and China in retaliation" for the Communist aggression. "Unhappily," he said, "the Soviets are calling the signals and we are conforming to their movements. They have the initiative and we have been following."

In February 1951, with his old friend Major Generals O'Daniel and Sullivan, Clark, like McNair in World War II, traveled to Korea to observe the battle and the performance of the American troops. His classmate Ridgway commanded the Eighth Army in Korea, and he asked Clark to intensify training for combat at night. Clark agreed and promised also to experiment with illuminating the battlefield by searchlights, flares, and shells.

Clark had a pleasant visit with his son Bill, who commanded an infantry company in the 2d Division. Bill would be wounded three times, the last during the fighting on Heartbreak Ridge. For his gallantry in action, he received two Silver Stars and the Distinguished Service Cross.

Detractors scurrilously ascribed the latter award to Clark's influence and pressure. In truth, had Bill not been his father's son, he might well have received the Medal of Honor.

In Japan, Clark called on MacArthur, who inquired after his mother. He complained of the Chinese sanctuary north of the Yalu River, the boundary between North Korea and China. Like Clark, he believed that military targets in China should be bombed.

As May 1, 1951, his fifty-fifth birthday, approached, Clark thought seriously of retiring from the Army. The University of California at Los Angeles had asked him to become its first Chancellor, and the opportunity enchanted him. But when President Truman asked him to remain on active duty, Clark cancelled further talks with the institution.

The President relieved MacArthur from his command with dramatic suddenness in April and at once moved Ridgway to replace MacArthur in Tokyo. Clark had mixed emotions and said nothing.

Early in 1952, speaking at Watertown, New York, Clark described the "spreading tide of Communist aggression" as an "evil force bent on world domination and the imposition of . . . tyranny and despotism." The Communists had engaged in insidious infiltration as the last shots were fired in World War II. Now they were responsible for the bloodshed in Korea.

At his fifty-sixth birthday in 1952, Clark would complete thirty-five years of active service and have more than five years in the permanent grade of major general. Under Army regulations, he would have to retire unless the Secretary of the Army specifically asked to retain him on active duty until he reached age sixty. At the President's behest, the Secretary did the required paperwork.

When Eisenhower decided to run for the presidency of the United States, Truman appointed Ridgway to take his place in Paris as Supreme Allied Commander in the North Atlantic Treaty Organization. To succeed Ridgway in Tokyo, he named Clark.

As Commander in Chief, United Nations Command, Clark would be at the head of the allied forces engaged in Korea; as Commander in Chief, Far East, he would direct the American ground, naval, and air forces in the region.

Large-scale fighting in Korea had come to a stalemated end a year earlier, with the front stabilized. Armistice talks to bring the hostilities to a close had foundered on the question of repatriating prisoners of war.

Nearly 100,000 Chinese and North Korean soldiers captured by the United Nations preferred release to Taiwan, governed by Chiang Kai-shek, or to South Korea. The United Nations Command was ready to do so, but the Communists insisted on having all the prisoners returned to them, by force if necessary. The situation resembled Europe after World War II, when many prisoners and refugees had refused repatriation to Soviet-controlled countries.

Clark's photograph appeared on the cover of *Time* magazine, which said, "In an age when the line between political and military affairs is blurred or non-existent," Clark perfectly embodied the complementary impulses of policy and strategy.

After consultations with Truman, Bradley, Collins, and others in Washington and with Secretary-General Trygve Lie at the United Nations in New York, about to depart for the Far East, Clark talked with newsmen. His primary task, he said, was to "obtain an honorable armistice." The United States had decided against seeking a military decision in Korea, and Clark had neither the authority nor the resources to gain victory on the battlefield. Although he had no sympathy for terminating the war without a military triumph, he had his instructions and would carry them out faithfully.

Renie, who would join her husband in Tokyo later, remained at Fort Monroe because Ann was about to marry Gordon Oosting, a former aide of Clark. The father of the bride promised to return for the wedding, and Bradley approved the trip in advance.

At Haneda Airport in Tokyo on the afternoon of May 7, 1952, Clark was met by Ridgway and by the newly appointed U. S. Ambassador to Japan, his old friend Robert Murphy. On the following morning, as Clark and Ridgway flew to Korea to acquaint Clark with the conditions and problems and to allow Ridgway to make his farewells, Clark learned of a nasty turn of events.

On the previous evening, on the island of Koje, where the United Nations had a large prisoner of war installation, Chinese and North Korean inmates had captured Brigadier General Francis I. Dodd, the camp commander, and were holding him hostage in the compound. Their purpose was to generate propaganda, and they complained of mistreatment at the hands of their captors and of the "forcible retention" of those who refused return to North Korea and China.

For more than a year, prisoners at Koje-do had demonstrated, rioted, disobeyed orders, held kangaroo courts, and murdered captives who wished repatriation to South Korea or Taiwan. The camp authorities on occasion had to suppress disorder by force, and some deaths and injuries among the inmates had resulted.

Their kidnapping of Dodd created an international sensation in the news media. The Communist press screamed vituperation and tried to discredit Clark, who would now head the United Nations efforts to negotiate an armistice settlement.

Ridgway immediately made some minor but widely publicized concessions at Koje-do, and the Communists released Dodd unharmed on May 10. Two days later Ridgway departed Japan, and Clark assumed command.

The incident made it impossible for Clark to return to Fort Monroe for Ann's wedding.

Although armistice teams continued to meet intermittently, they could make no progress toward a truce. Clark suspended the sessions in October.

Sensitive to the ability of the Communists to turn from the bargaining table to the battlefield, Clark strengthened the United Nations military positions and intensified training the South Korean forces. A planning group he set up in his headquarters studied how to stop a Communist attack and also how to bring the war to a victorious conclusion. The members found no remunerative targets for atomic weapons, but suggested bombing north of the Yalu River in Communist China and moving at least two divisions of Chiang Kai-shek's Army from Taiwan to Korea. Authorization to do so was lacking.

Renie came to Tokyo, and the Clarks lived in the Maeda House, a 32-room mansion. Their social obligations were heavy and included the emperor and empress of Japan. Renie immediately became involved in charity work with orphans and sick children. She visited American hospitals to cheer the wounded.

During the election campaign of 1952, Eisenhower promised to terminate the Korean War if he gained the presidency and, further, to visit the Far East to expedite the end of the fighting. After winning at the polls, he flew directly to Korea. Early in December Clark met him there and tried vainly to persuade him to strike for military victory. Eisenhower was resolved to have an armistice. But he removed some restrictions and allowed Clark to bomb some targets formerly forbidden—the North Korean capital Pyongyang, hydroelectric power plants along the Yalu River, and dikes protecting rice fields.

Shortly thereafter, Red Cross organizations meeting in Geneva proposed that the belligerents in Korea exchange their sick and wounded prisoners of war. With Washington's approval, Clark suggested this course

Clark in Korea with his West Point classmate Matthew B. Ridgway, whom he was about to succeed as Commander in Chief of the UN Command in the Far East.

In August 1953, Clark presents the Korean armistice documents to the man with whom his whole adult life had been involved, and who was now the president of the United States.

A ticker-tape parade up Broadway, in New York City, for Clark, the returning hero, celebrated the end of the Korean conflict.

to his opposite numbers, the commanders of the Korean People's Army and of the Chinese People's Volunteers. Could they discuss repatriating the seriously sick and wounded?

The death of Stalin in March 1953, the bombings authorized by Eisenhower, talk in Washington of using atomic weapons, and perhaps the visit of the Clarks to Taipei, Taiwan, which looked like a veiled threat to bring Chinese Nationalists into the Korean conflict, led the Communists to temper their demands. Late that month the two Communist military leaders replied to Clark and indicated their willingness to take up the question.

Resuming the talks suspended for nearly six months, both sides quickly agreed not only on the sick and wounded exchange but also on the larger issue of prisoner repatriation. A commission of representatives from neutral nations was to meet in the demilitarized zone between the opposing front lines to screen the captives and determine their disposition.

All seemed to be moving toward a swift conclusion when the President of the Republic of Korea, Syngman Rhee, threatened to disrupt the endeavors. A national patriot who had opposed the Japanese in Korea before the war and who had lived in exile most of his adult life, Rhee wished above all to re-unify North and South Korea, split since the end of World War II. If an armistic came into being, the United Nations forces would no doubt leave South Korea while the Chinese troops would probably remain in the North. The Republic would again be vulnerable to Communist attack.

To prevent a truce agreement, Rhee made known his options. He could withdraw the South Korean representative from the armistice delegation. He could refuse to permit the neutral nations representatives on South Korean soil. He could unilaterally release from their camps those Korean prisoners who wished to remain in the south. He could attack to the north himself. In short, he could repudiate, violate, and nullify an armistice.

The truce talks became deadlocked again.

Clark conferred periodically with Rhee. He admired the spunky Korean leader, but he had his instructions too. He attempted vainly to win Rhee over to an armistice.

In May, Clark sought to resolve the impasse. He authorized Major General William A. Harrison, Jr., a West Point classmate who had succeeded Admiral Turner C. Joy as chief of the United Nations armistice delegation, to recess the meetings for several days. During that time the United Nations Command would formulate a final position paper on the major issue. The United Nations was unwilling to accept forced repatriation of prisoners but willing to let a commission of neutral nations determine where each captive was to go. If the Communists balked, Clark was ready to terminate the negotiations and resume military operations to force an agreement.

On May 25, Harrison traveled to Panmunjom and presented the terms to the Communists. They were receptive and agreed to study the proposal.

In Seoul, Clark and the U. S. Ambassador to Korea, Ellis O. Briggs, met with Rhee and informed him of their intention to conclude an armistice. The Americans were firm but also apprehensive. Rhee could offer a separate proposal to the Communists. He could withdraw his military forces from the United Nations Command. He could refuse to pull his troops out of a demilitarized zone. He could block the meetings of neutral nations representatives. He could stage-manage riots and demonstrations against a cease-fire. He could finally attack to the north with South Korean troops.

Rhee was adamant. An armistice was unacceptable to him.

The Communists were inclined to accept the United Nations plan, and agreement on a truce appeared settled on June 8, when Harrison and his opposite numbers signed a document called the Terms of Reference. They now set about to determine whether the Neutral Nations Commission, representatives of Switzerland, Sweden, India, Czechoslovakia, and Poland, would actually serve. If so, what remained for the belligerents to do was to draw the demarcation line to conform with the contact along the front and to iron out several very small issues.

Clark was certain of signing in about ten days. The sessions continued smoothly, and both sides accepted all the articles. The only details remaining were decisions on when and how to sign, when to make the armistice effective, and when to exchange the prisoners of war.

At this time in Tokyo Renie had a slight heart attack. Hospitalized and instructed to rest, she had to lessen her charitable work and to withdraw from her strenuous social obligations. To her husband, the prospect of bringing the negotiations to a quick end promised to give him more time to be with Renie.

Rhee then upset the deliberations. On June 18, on his own authority, he released all the Korean prisoners of war who refused repatriation to North Korea, some 27,000 soldiers who melted into the civilian population.

The Communists recessed further meetings at Panmunjom.

Clark tried to make Rhee understand and accept two basic premises: having renounced attempts to eject Chinese Communist troops from Korea by force, the United States was determined to secure an armistice; the only way for Rhee to unify Korea was by political means, by a series of political conferences, for the South Korean Army alone had no chance of success against the Communists. An armistice, Clark emphasized, would gain time and American help for Rhee to build up his military forces.

The Repulic of Korea, Rhee said, would have nothing to do with an armistice.

Collins, the Army Chief of Staff, and Assistant Secretary of State Walter Robertson flew to Tokyo and conferred with Clark, Briggs, and Murphy. Although Clark had authority to conclude the cease-fire over Rhee's objections, it was better, they decided, to gain Rhee's acquiescence.

Robertson went to Korea and met with Rhee daily for two weeks, like Clark before him, cajoling, threatening, and promising American aid in order to obtain Rhee's approval.

Meanwhile, Clark informed his opposite numbers of his willingness to honor the Terms of Reference and requested sessions to be reconvened on July 10.

Instead, the Communist forces launched an attack in the center of the Korean peninsula and inaugurated a week of fighting.

The Communists then returned to the negotiating table. The two delegations worked out the final details—how to move prisoners to the demilitarized zone and into the custody of the neutral nations representatives, how to revise the demarcation line and the demilitarized zone to conform to the changes created by the last battle, and how to sign the armistice.

After what Robertson termed "the battle of Syngman Rhee," he won Rhee over. Rhee agreed to do nothing to obstruct the terms of a truce. In return, the United States pledged a mutual security pact, long-term economic aid, and assistance to expand and improve the South Korean military forces.

Returned to Washington, Robertson wrote to thank Clark for "your wise counsel" and "your unfailing courtesy and consideration." He said, "To you, more than any other single individual, should go the credit for this great achievement. I think I have some idea of the difficulties you have had to surmount on all sides."

On July 26, a telephone call from Harrison apprised Clark of the latest developments. The senior delegates would sign the armistice on the following day. Early on the morning of July 27, 1953, as though to serve notice of their ability to resume hostilities if the United Nations violated the armistice, Communist forces struck again. The United Nations fought back, and Air Force and Navy planes pounded the enemy front and supply lines.

At 10 A.M. in Panmunjom, Harrison and his North Korean counterpart signed a military armistice between the United Nations Command and the armed forces of North Korea and Communist China. The documents were brought to the Advance Headquarters of the United Nations Command at Mansan-ni.

Clark had flown to Korea that morning and, accompanied by Ambassador Briggs, called on Rhee. Then Clark proceeded to Mansan-ni. In the apple orchard, at 1 P.M. on a beautiful and hot afternoon, Clark entered the theater. Under the lights of still and newsreel cameras and under the view of several selected observers, he signed the documents.

An hour later he broadcast a short message to the world. "I cannot find it in me to exult in this hour," he said. "Rather, it is a time for prayer, that we may succeed in our difficult endeavor to turn this armistice to the advantage of mankind. If we extract hope from this occasion, it must be diluted with recognition that our salvation requires unrelaxing vigilance and effort."

He had felt profoundly his duty to sign. But according to his conviction, victory had been possible and was preferable in the long run.

At 10 P.M., in accordance with the truce, all military hostilities in Korea and its surrounding waters came to a halt.

Clark made his feelings explicit in his book, *From the Danube to the Yalu*, published in 1954. Signing the armistice, he wrote, "capped my career, but it was a cap without a feather." He regretted "being the first United States Army commander in history to sign an armistice without victory." His greatest emotion was a "sense of frustration." Thankful for stopping the bloodshed, he regarded the truce as a lull in "unfinished business." The United Nations could have won the war by being "tougher faster," by increasing the resources committed, and by dropping the atomic bomb. Everywhere in dealing with the Communists, he had found them "to be the same breed of bandits. They are ruthless in their exploitation of weakness."

Seeing himself as the victim of a lack of an American will to win, he had carried out his orders "with misgivings."

He departed immediately for the United States.

CHAPTER 22

☆ ☆ ☆ ☆

THE CITADEL

"you have achieved so much for the college"

WHILE FLYING FROM Japan to the United States, Clark decided to retire from the Army. Renie was not entirely well and required a quieter existence. He was bitter over signing the armistice instead of going for victory. His seniority made it difficult to find an appropriate assignment. Because he had served continuously as a four-star general since his temporary promotion in March 1944, he was entitled to that permanent rank without Senate confirmation. And finally, he wished to be free to speak out, in a way impossible in uniform, on the dangers facing the United States from the Red menace.

After stopping in New Orleans to be Bill's best man at his wedding, Clark went on to Washington, where he presented a copy of the truce documents to Eisenhower and told him of his wish to retire. As always, Clark called him "Ike." To Clark's mild amusement, Eisenhower seemed uncomfortable. He wanted to be addressed as "Mr. President," and Clark obliged.

Returning to Japan, he prepared to depart. Letters paid tribute to his performance. Harrison wrote, "I am proud to have served under you and to have had the opportunity to witness the steadfast and sure way in which you upheld the interest of our country in these difficult days." Vice Admiral J. J. "Jocko" Clark, commander of the Seventh Fleet, said, "I know that if your policies had been followed, we would have won more than an armistice; we would have won the kind of victory to which our country is entitled—unconditional surrender."

Parades in San Francisco and New York welcomed and cheered the Clarks.

By prearrangement, they met with Governor James F. Byrnes of South Carolina, former Secretary of State, to discuss a subject broached several months earlier. Would Clark assume the presidency of The Citadel, the Military College of South Carolina?

As a state-supported institution of higher learning for young men, The Citadel was much like the Virginia Military Institute. The college had been in existence since 1842. The corps of cadets had fired the guns along the Charleston waterfront in April 1861 against Fort Sumter to open the Civil War. Originally occupying the Arsenal buildings near Francis Marion Square, the school had moved uptown to a new campus on the bank of the Ashley River.

General Charles P. Summerall had been President for twenty-two years. Early in 1953, at age 86, he made known his intention to retire.

Governor Byrnes and the Board of Visitors inquired whether General Lucius Clay, who had been the American High Commissioner in Germany and was then President of the Continental Can Corporation, might be available. His business obligations led him to decline.

Learning that Clark was eligible to retire from the Army, Byrnes cabled him in Korea. Clark replied that he was "definitely interested."

In New York, Byrnes persuaded the Clarks to accompany him to Charleston. He showed them around the campus. Clark commented favorably on the cadet retreat parade. He remarked on the excellent record made in the armed forces by Citadel graduates.

"How should we announce your acceptance?" Byrnes asked.

Clark had yet to make up his mind. He had many offers of employment from prominent business concerns.

Continuing their tour of the school, they stopped at the President's house. Renie was quiet, and Byrnes, understanding, said, "We'll tear it down and build one to your specifications."

Clark promised to let Byrnes know his decision shortly after his Army retirement.

That occurred on October 31, 1953, at Fort McNair. Ridgway and many others lauded his forty years of active duty, his courage, integrity, and high professional competence. He received the third Oak Leaf Cluster to the Distinguished Service Medal for his achievements in Korea.

Shortly afterward, Clark received a formal offer from The Citadel. He advised Byrnes of his acceptance.

At age 57, too young to withdraw into seclusion, he wanted to speak out on the questions of passionate concern to him: preparedness, patriotism, and the Communist threat. He needed a home base, a forum. Camano Island was remote, and the rainy weather was bad for Renie. Charleston had sunshine and an airport and was reasonably close to Washington, D.C. and other important centers.

That Byrnes, a national figure, had asked him was a prominent factor in his decision. Byrnes' selection and friendship promised Clark widespread acceptance by the people who counted in South Carolina.

Although the national movement for civil rights was gaining momentum and the process of integrating blacks into the armed forces was well under way, the state in particular and the South in general provided a comfortable environment for Clark. Conservative politics reigned, and traditional values thrived.

The city also represented his convictions. As he later said, "Charleston is all-American. Charleston believes in the military, believes in being strong, believes in national defense. Their sons have volunteered more readily. They respect the uniform. They respect the flag."

Interested in training young leaders, Clark additionally regarded The Citadel as a challenge. The College seemed to be marking time. The physical plant had deteriorated. The officials were elderly, too old to pursue new programs vigorously. The Regular Army officers assigned to the Reserve Officers Training Corps were mediocre. Few faculty members had doctors' degrees. The library was in cramped and crowded quarters, laboratories were small and old-fashioned. The campus appeared to be an enclave separate from and out of touch with the mainstream of American life and the real world.

Clark resolved to turn the college around, restore its vitality, give it a renewed sense of purpose, improve and shine its image. By his energy, managerial skills, standing in the nation, flair for public relations, acquaintance with almost everyone of consequence in the country, he would transform a provincial school into a national institution. The tasks were designed precisely for his strengths.

He officially became President on March 1, 1954. At his inauguration, he spoke briefly and promised the students a sound education reinforced by the best features of military training. He would enhance character building among the cadets, improve their appearance, insist on the highest standards, and enlarge the awareness and the understanding throughout the country of the school's ideals.

The United States, he concluded, could never match the manpower resources of the Communist areas. America's real strength lay in technology and leadership. The development of leaders, both civilian and military, was all-important for what he called "the eventual showdown with Communism."

The media coverage was extensive.

Clark brought to the college his enormous personal prestige. Everywhere he spoke—to civic, business, and church organizations, to the press, on television, he linked The Citadel to him, and the school shared in and benefited from his high public visibility.

He ran the college the only way he knew how, as a military commander. With Sullivan as his principal assistant to supervise the daily operations, with a few other old friends on whom he could depend to look after routine matters, Clark made the decisions, issued directives, and expected his staff to carry out his policies.

He had little conception of the traditional functions and prerogatives of the faculty, their concerns with academic freedom, their desire to participate in professional appointments and curricular changes. To him they were teachers, and their instruction, no matter in what subject, was supposed to enhance Americanism, which he equated with anti-Communism. To some professors, Clark appeared to have an intuitive aversion to scholars who continued to debate questions that he had long ago resolved and settled in his mind. Others characterized his political philosophy as simplistic in its anti-Communist thrust.

Yet Clark raised faculty salaries, improved professors' living quarters on campus, provided them with better facilities—more classroom space and laboratories, gave them sabbatical years off to pursue their doctoral degrees. All he asked in return was for them to do their duty in the classroom, to observe the customs and courtesies of the military services, and to keep their hair cut short, their belt buckles and shoes shined and polished, their carriages erect, their salutes crisp.

Never altogether comfortable with the faculty, he appointed Dr. William Duckett, Head of the Chemistry Department, to be the Dean. Clark dealt directly with Duckett, who kept him abreast of academic problems and handled the professors.

Clark cultivated wealthy benefactors and the alumni for funds. He wooed and charmed legislators and other state officials in quest of appropriations and support. He upgraded the athletic and military training programs. He increased the enrollment to 2,000 cadets, the maximum number that could be housed. Most of all, he stirred a strong sense of excitement and pride. When he presided over the Friday afternoon parades, his tall figure personified and projected confidence in the changes he had put into motion on that well-ordered campus.

The college demolished Summerall's residence and constructed a one-story rambler for the Clarks. Renie had requested no steps because of her heart attack, and she was frequently—some good-natured observers said constantly—at the site to consult with the builders.

When he greeted the freshmen in the fall, he invariably said, "Mrs. Clark and I will soon schedule a visit to our home." The youngsters thrilled to them.

He restored an honor system, then worked very hard, harder, he said, than on anything else, to make certain of its proper functioning. Establishing an Educational Fund for student scholarships, he donated the honorariums he received for speaking. He formed The Citadel Development Foundation to raise money from private sources to supplement state budgets. He appointed a retired military chaplain to the staff to have a spiritual leader permanently on campus for worship and counseling. He eliminated older staff members who were past their prime, and gradually obtained a younger and more efficient group of administrators, engineers, and financial experts.

Traveling to Washington and talking with the Secretary of the Army, Clark secured the promise of getting outstanding colonels to serve as the Commandant of Cadets, responsible for military training and student deportment. The first officer who came was Reuben Tucker, a superior paratroop commander in World War II. He was soon promoted to brigadier general. The pattern continued. Among other able officers who served tours of duty at The Citadel was William McCaffery, who later retired as a lieutenant general. The corps of cadets benefited.

Unwilling, Clark said, to "be satisfied with mediocrity in any department of the college," he had alumni committees composed of professionals—chemists, physicians, lawyers—visit the campus to report on facilities, courses, faculty, and to suggest improvements. They recommended more classroom space, more course electives, and higher salaries for senior faculty members.

He established the Great Issue Lecture Series and many prominent leaders, most of them his friends, came to the campus and inspired the students while they saw at close hand what The Citadel was all about. When the White House announced President Eisenhower's intention to speak at the school, the publicity was extensive. "It's difficult to realize," an alumnus wrote to Clark, "that you have achieved so much for the college within the period of only a year. You continue to astound me, and this has not been my first exposure to a natural leader... deeply grateful for your brilliant and devoted service to 'the West Point of the South.'"

Reviewing the cadet corps, Eisenhower leaned over and whispered, "You know, Wayne, that sure looks like West Point to me." It was the ultimate compliment.

On the go almost constantly, followed by journalists and photographers, Clark met with MacArthur at the Waldorf-Astoria in New York, accepted the national chairmanship of the Heart Fund, was the Grand Marshal of the Cherry Blossom Parade in Washington, D.C., where the Summerall Guards paraded and attracted favorable comment.

Clark's remarks on television in 1954 echoed Senator Joseph McCarthy's claim of Communist penetration into American councils of state. "Gradually," Clark said, "an uneasy frightening suspicion entered my mind.... There were indications that Communists had been planted in our Army to try to sap the power of the United States.... When the Alger Hiss case broke, the nagging fear was that perhaps the Communists had wormed their way so deeply into our own government on both the working and planning levels that they were able to exercise an inordinate degree of power in shaping the course of America in the dangerous postwar era. I could not help wondering and worrying whether we were faced with open enemies across the conference table and hidden enemies who sat with us in our most secret councils."

He described the United Nations as a place that gave the Soviet Union and its satellites a sounding board for propaganda and a haven for spies and saboteurs. "We have confronted the Soviets with one concession after another," Clark said. What the Foreign Service of the State Department needed badly were "honest-to-God, red-blooded Americans" who could stand up under pressure.

The Hoover Commission on Organization of the Executive Branch of the Government was deliberating when Herbert Hoover, the former President, asked Clark to chair a Task Force on Intelligence Activities. He agreed. They were warm friends. Hoover had visited Clark in Austria, Clark had dined with Hoover at his home in New York; at Hoover's invitation, Clark had attended several meetings of prominent and conservative businessmen at the Bohemian Grove near San Francisco.

Clark's report recommended measures to correct weaknesses, improve quality, and increase efficiency in the rapidly shrinking world of electronics, nuclear weapons, and supersonic planes. With Senator McCarthy discredited, the paper found no valid ground for suspecting any organized subversive or Communist clique to have contaminated any agency of the intelligence family.

Most of the suggested reforms, as Hoover later informed him, "I am unhappy to report," were rejected.

On the west coast where Renie and Clark were visiting their son Bill and his family—he had retired from the Army because of his wounds in Korea—and their daughter Ann Oosting and her husband, they received an invitation from Darryl F. Zanuck to a television studio to see an advance showing of a film. There, to their great astonishment, they found themselves appearing on the popular program "This Is Your Life," which featured a celebrity who was confronted unexpectedly by figures out of his past, school teachers and other old friends who had contributed to his career.

If the public thought of Clark as the proverbial military officer, stern and unbending, rather distant and cold, the television viewers saw a man who struggled to control his emotions as acquaintances of his childhood and early Army years appeared. He was obviously surprised and pleased. He and Renie were an extremely likeable couple. She remarked that she had met him on a blind date for a picnic. "He was a complete bust," she said. He told how she had sat on a bee. "We got to know each other better."

The most obvious changes at The Citadel came from Clark's building program. In addition to renovating and air-conditioning the mess hall and the chapel, rehabilitating the barracks, making on-campus housing available to faculty and staff members at extremely low rentals, he was responsible for several handsome new structures—a student union named Mark Clark Hall, with a large auditorium-banquet facility, offices for student activities, a canteen, and a few suites for important visitors; an impressive library and museum dedicated to R. Hugh Daniel and Charles

As president of The Citadel, the military college in Charleston, South Carolina, Clark salutes the colors.

A four-star family: Clark's wife, Renie; his daughter, Ann Oosting; and his son, William.

The old soldier, last of his breed, in September 1983.

E. Daniel, businessmen and benefactors; plus a splendid Military Science edifice.

He started a summer camp at the college for boys 12 to 15 years of age. Housed in the barracks, fed in the mess hall, they utilized facilities otherwise idle and participated in a large sports program. Staff officers, faculty members, and students provided counseling and individual tutoring. For Clark, the successful business venture was also a way to get, he said, "an early look at youngsters who may develop into the sort of men The Citadel desires to enroll as cadets." What pleased him most of all was that the boys became better acquainted with the Constitution and the Bill of Rights; they stood at attention as they watched the flag go up in the morning and come down at night.

He was disappointed in Eisenhower as President. Eisenhower should have been, he thought, more forthright in warning Americans about Communism. He should have told "the sordid story of our efforts to get along with the Communists." The United States "usually negotiated from weakness . . . made too many concessions." He wrote less frequently to his old friend.

What The Citadel stood for, he reiterated, was what had made America great. He inaugurated an annual Cold War Seminar to alert community leaders to the menace of Communism and had cadets majoring in political science, history, and education attend the sessions. He made J. Edgar Hoover's book, *Masters of Deceit: The Story of Communism in America and How to Fight It*, required reading for all cadets. "I know from intimate personal experience," he said, "that evil forces are loose in the world, and that their sinister aim is to destroy our free way of life—by subversion if possible, by overt hostility if necessary."

Rebecca Clark, his mother, almost 95 years of age, died in Walter Reed Hospital in April 1962. A vital and charming person, she was a grande dame known to her friends as The Colonel's Lady and The Dowager Queen. At age 70 in 1939, she turned the acreage around her home in Arlington into a colony of small houses set in gardens. She had personally supervised the construction in order to be sure of roomy closets and adequate kitchens and baths. A photograph in a Washington newspaper showed her beautifully dressed, wearing a fur jacket and a chic hat, gloves and necklace. Her hair was light, her smile self-assured. She was striking. When her grandson Bill came from West Point to visit her, he took her out to dinner. Very lively, very good company, she seemed to know every maitre d'hotel and headwaiter in town.

Renie fell ill and was unable to accompany her husband to Hawaii, where he delivered a major address and met again with his wonderful Nisei soldiers, who gave him a warm and affectionate welcome and reception.

On a Sunday night, Clark received a telephone call from his son-in-law. Ann was sick, but as a devout Christian Scientist she believed her illness to be hardly serious. Clark reached her bedside on the following day just before she died of meningitis at the age of 36. A portrait painter, she had also worked with disadvantaged children and elderly shut-ins.

In November 1963, Clark dedicated a unique monument on campus. A concrete shell with an opening for visitors encased the forward hatch of the *Seraph*, the submarine that had taken him to North Africa. The boat had come to the end of its useful life in the Royal Navy, and Mountbatten, Clark's old friend, had helped transfer that part of the vessel to Charleston.

Parents Weekend followed, and 7,000 visitors came to the campus, among them former King Umberto of Italy and his entourage.

In the spring of 1964, Clark announced his intention to retire. Renie required care and attention. Ten years as President were enough. He had given the college a modern and impressive physical plant. He had expanded the prestige and influence of the institution. He had increased the number of professors with doctoral degrees to ensure academic respectability. It was time for him to go. Younger leaders were better attuned to the newer problems of dealing with the admission of women and black cadets.

The Board of Visitors persuaded him to stay another year until they found a successor. He and Renie moved into a spacious penthouse apartment atop the Francis Marion Hotel, which gave them a marvelous view of the city.

The Board of Visitors praised Clark for advancing the quality of every aspect of life at The Citadel. His lofty prestige in military and diplomatic circles around the world had brought eminence to the school. Named President Emeritus, he left active office on July 1, 1965.

Renie continued in poor health until she died on her seventy-fourth birthday in October 1966. Devoted to her husband during forty-two years of marriage, she built his confidence and contributed to his image and legend. By her natural warmth and grace, she had captured the affection of the cadets, who called her the First Lady of The Citadel. They sponsored her for the Palmetto Award for service to the state. She placed her prize in the case containing her husband's decorations, and to visitors spoke of the display as "our medals."

Lonely after her death, referring to Renie constantly in his conversation, Clark tried to keep busy. He reviewed books, wrote inspirational messages, delivered speeches, served on corporate boards, advocated military victory in Vietnam. He advised and assisted the college administration, made appearances before the cadets, became a member of The Citadel Development Foundation, was a source of wisdom for the Board of Visitors. He gave generously of his funds to the school, capping his donations with half a million dollars in 1981.

Occasionally, he was hospitalized for a digestive, respiratory, or cardiac ailment. He had a heart pacemaker installed. At Walter Reed Hospital for a hernia operation, he saw Eisenhower, who was there after a heart attack. The two old friends who had drifted apart were both happy to reminisce and forget their differences.

In October 1967, Clark married a family friend, Mary Applegate of Muncie, Indiana, and Leland, Michigan, whose husband had died four days after Renie. Military life, the bride told reporters, was entirely new to her.

Clark campaigned for Richard Nixon and Spiro Agnew, and he and Mary were in Washington for the inauguration. They were guests of the government of South Africa, lunched in Rhodesia with Prime Minister Ian Smith, and met with veterans of both countries who had served in Italy.

He was gratified in December 1969 when President Nixon appointed him to succeed Devers, who had resigned, as a member of the American Battle Monuments Commission, made up of distinguished citizens and retired military officers. Several months later his colleagues elected him their chairman. With a small headquarters in Washington, D.C., the Commission administered about thirty cemeteries for American war dead and other memorials in foreign countries. Clark made periodic trips overseas to inspect the facilities and services.

In 1974, he and Mary went to Austria, where Clark stirred a welcome remarkable for its sincerity and warmth. Enthusiastic crowds greeted him, extensive news coverage kept him in the public eye. Reporters and television cameras followed him everywhere: to Hinterstoder, where the entire population turned out with American flags to meet him; during his appearances in Salzburg; while he laid wreaths to Austria's military and civilian dead at the Heldenplatz in Vienna. He addressed the cadets at

Wiener Neustadt, spent an evening in the Imperial Box at the opera, attended a performance of the Lippizaner horses at the Spanish Riding School, and was present at a mass sung by the Vienna Boys Choir. At a dinner in his honor hosted by Chancellor Bruno Kreisky, Austrian leaders paid tribute to his contributions to Austria's peaceful and democratic reconstruction, acclaimed him as Austria's savior who had led the country to independence, who had rescued the inhabitants from starvation, and who had laid the foundations of the new state.

After living in Charleston's Francis Marion Hotel for ten years, a time when Clark's morning and evening strolls were a famous tourist attraction, he and Mary decided to move. The downtown city had deteriorated and become congested. They temporarily occupied an apartment in Mark Clark Hall. Mary adored the bugle calls on campus.

About a year later they moved into a large suburban house with a swimming pool and a lovely garden of tall trees and Southern flowers on the fringe of Charleston. Their home was filled with gifts from the Japanese and Austrian governments, paintings by his daughter Ann, mementos and memorabilia, including the blue and white Roma sign. In his study was the massive desk he had used in World War II, as well as photographs of his friends Churchill, Roosevelt, Truman, Eisenhower.

He lived quietly, spoke occasionally in public, attended meetings, answered his correspondence, and thought of his full life.

CHAPTER 23

☆ ☆ ☆ ☆

IN RETROSPECT

"a constant inspiration . . . as long as I shall live"

LOOKING BACK, CLARK could well be satisfied with his accomplishments. As the recipient of many tributes, accolades, decorations, and honors, he had reached extraordinary heights. He had shaped the history of his time and had hobnobbed with the famous figures of his world.

"The people who knew him at the time we did," an old friend, Ruth Liebe, said, referring to Fort Lewis before World War II, "never dreamed that he would ever go so far." Like her, Clark himself found it difficult to believe the reality of his eminence. Constantly astonished, he pinched himself occasionally to be certain of the actuality—being promoted to general officer rank, dining with leaders of the British Empire, commanding the Fifth Army, capturing Rome, bringing about the German surrender in Italy. As he wrote to his mother, it was hard for him to imagine that he was running the show.

Michael A. Musmanno, in a brief biography of Clark published in Italy, revered him as the leader of a great Crusade in the Middle Ages,

281

a tall figure in plaited mail, kneeling before the cross, with a long sword trailing at his side, receiving God's blessing. When the British monarch visited Clark in North Africa, a soldier said, "I thought that the real tall man with the three stars was the king." Because of his imperious bearing, the troops in Italy sometimes called him Marcus Aurelius Clarkus.

These were mistaken impressions. For Clark was unlike, say, Patton and MacArthur, who saw themselves in the aristocratic mold, throwbacks to the heroic medieval knight and other Romantic personages. They regarded success and triumph as natural attributes of their inherently brilliant status and station, and they were comfortable with the rightness of their fame and fortune. They took for granted their eligibility for honors.

Clark in contrast had no flights of fancy. Solidly American, businesslike and workmanlike, he was a manager and executive in the Horatio Alger mold, modest in his hopes. Uncomplaining attention to duty led to achievement and advancement, and although the rewards were expected, they were never wholly certain, and it was always at least a little surprising when they arrived. Much like Eisenhower, Ridgway, and Collins, Clark was solidly planted in twentieth-century, middle-class America. Markie Clarkie, as the Brazilians affectionately called him, was down to earth, real, no mysterious, other-worldly type or figment of the imagination.

Mrs. Liebe remembered her husband's remark, "Mark Clark must have had something that none of us recognized." What they overlooked, although surely it was evident, was his intensity. He was dedicated to the service, devoted to his duty. He practiced an outstanding proficiency in all aspects of the military profession.

His motivation to excel probably stemmed from his desire first to emulate, then to redeem his father. Colonel Charles Carr Clark had an ordinary career. Yet his solid soldierly qualities were his son's model, and Mark Clark sought to prove the validity of integrity and hard work, his father's virtues, as the basic features of an honorable life. His father had missed greatness because the accident of historical circumstance had prevented him from reaching prominence and high rank. To Mark Clark, the only difference between them was that he had been more fortunate in his opportunities.

Having built on his father's foundation, he was unusually aware of family continuity. In an address on the 100th anniversary of MacArthur's birth, he said that MacArthur's "sense of purpose came to him naturally from a soldier father and a Scottish immigrant grandfather." Clark was no doubt reminding himself of his own soldier father and immigrant grandfather.

Frequently, when he received promotion or tribute, he wrote to his mother, "Dad would be happy to know," or "Dad would be satisfied." Beckie gloried in her son's progress, and she rejoiced at every step of his way. For Mark fulfilled her husband. In the same way, Clark was enormously pleased with his son Bill's attendance at West Point, his choice of the infantry as his branch of service, his combat record in Korea. The Clarks were part of a military tradition going back to grandfather Clark's service in the Civil War.

The Liebes were both "very pleased for him," and the reason they ascribed to Clark's prominence was, to a certain extent, correct. "It sometimes pays," Mrs. Liebe said, "to be at the right place at the right time—and know the right people." Marshall was Clark's significant contact, McNair his essential mentor, and Eisenhower his indispensable friend. But those relationships were no more than half the story. All three of Clark's superiors insisted on the highest standards of performance. Unless Clark had met their expectations, he would have lost their interest and support. At every stage in his career, he rose to the requirements and mastered the demands of his post.

Four main ingredients explained his success. He was highly intelligent and quick. He had an awesome capacity for work. He prompted the best from his subordinates. He was a master of human relations.

On the last point: Frank S. Russell hitched a ride in Clark's plane shortly after the war in Europe, and he saw Clark, after the landing, step into the pilot's cabin and thank him for the good flight. When Joe Gray, one of his political advisers in Austria, left for home, he thanked Clark for "innumerable courtesies and kindnesses." Major General John E. Leonard wrote to him, "How do you find time to be so thoughtful and considerate?"

Obedience to the chain of command and fidelity to superiors and subordinates are among the most cherished military values. Whatever reservations clouded Clark's judgment of decisions reached and announced, whatever resentments, whether real or imagined, boiled beneath Clark's exterior, he was fastidiously loyal in public to the military system. No one suspected his private thoughts when he differed with the accepted course of action. No one but his aides knew the comments he recorded in the privacy of his journal to vent his sense of frustration. Much like Patton, who wrote scathing remarks in his diary to rid himself of personal outrage, Clark, anguished and tormented, controlled his impulses and followed faithfully the necessities of teamwork in war.

Although Clark wished to continue the Italian campaign into the Balkans, he refrained from criticizing the strategists who decided otherwise. Marshall understood Clark's conviction and appreciated his restraint. Many years later, Marshall, referring to Clark's behavior, remarked, "He never said a word at the time. He was a very good soldier and very loyal."

Before the Salerno invasion, when Eisenhower questioned Dawley's competence, Clark defended his subordinate. When he relieved Lucas at Anzio, he showed consideration and tried to avoid humiliating him. When McMahon, his roommate at Braden's and West Point, was removed from command of the 8th Division in Normandy and reduced from major general to colonel, Clark asked for him, obtained his transfer, and appointed him his G-1, personnel officer, at the Fifth Army headquarters; at the end of the war, Clark promoted him to brigadier general.

O'Daniel, to whom Clark had turned over his infantry company in 1918, was Clark's favorite trouble-shooter, and he eventually rose to the grade of lieutenant general. Clark called specifically for Edwin Howard, his G-2 assistant at Fort Lewis, to be his intelligence officer at the Fifth Army. He kept his classmate Sullivan close to him as a trusted friend and associate. He pushed Gruenther and Lemnitzer, both of whom became Supreme Allied Commanders in Europe during the postwar years.

To some detractors, "the personal factor," as one has said, "was always in the front of Clark's mind." But Clark would hardly have kept his friends in important positions unless their abilities and performance warranted his confidence.

Clark's concern with publicity stemmed from his desire to make good in the normally fierce military rivalry. The profession of arms is the most competitive of all occupations. There are just so many positions fixed by law, just so many jobs stipulated by regulations, just so many promotions possible. A military man lacking ambition has no chance to advance. All those who rose to eminence were not only superb leaders but also ruthless in the pursuit of their goal. Some concealed their lust for power better than others.

The arduous road they traveled to preferment was littered with obstacles and obstructed by ordeals, and those who followed the path were determined as well as good. Those who reach the objective and become mighty attract invidious remarks, pernicious slander, malevolent gossip. "The more stars you have," Clark once said, "the higher you climb the flagpole, the more of your ass is exposed. People are always watching for opportunities to misconstrue your actions and to jump all over you."

In the case of Clark, the disapproval was excessive. Clark's rise in rank was quick, but so was Eisenhower's. Clark skipped the rank of colonel, but so did Bradley. Clark was frequently in the news, but so was Patton. They all wanted public applause. What was the difference among them? Was Clark's ability to dissemble his craving for rank and responsibility less than theirs? Did Renie Clark do him an injustice by seeming to be, in her appearances on the speaker's platform, a deliberate extension of himself? Did some observers regard her talks as a conscious program on his part to benefit himself? Was a latent anti-Semitism making itself felt? Or was it simply that Clark, unlike the others, was involved in Italy, a subsidiary campaign? Ironically, Clark was a magnificent practitioner of the art of public relations, but in the end he failed to obtain a consistently good press.

The drumbeat of his rhetoric when he returned from Austria and again when he came back from Korea coupled with his pronouncements on and warnings against Communism alienated some of those who admired his wartime record, for they judged his activities to be a continuing search for attention and glory and felt it unseemly for him to enter the political arena. His remarks in the style of Senator Joseph McCarthy's unfounded charges of Communists in government separated Clark from some who had earlier respected him.

His postwar comments stemmed from his simplistic view of a more innocent world. To a large extent Clark was the prisoner of his early notions. He was the captive of the cherished convictions of his formative years. Theodore Roosevelt had imbued Clark with his outlook of a strong and righteous America, the Military Academy had reinforced his uncomplicated patriotic belief in his country, and his vision consistently turned back to the early years of the twentieth century when he had grown to manhood.

In many respects, World War II was the culmination of that kind of thought. The conflict was a crusade against tyranny, a struggle for decency, and the moral questions were simple and clear. To crush evil totally, total war in quest of total victory made sense.

After all the effort and exertion to make the world perfect, another tyranny arose, this one stronger, more malevolent and infinitely more dangerous. To Clark, it was mandatory to extinguish the peril again. Instead, according to his view, America hesitated, drew back from the contest, and, in his eyes, allowed Communism to flourish.

Like MacArthur, he was unable to understand the necessity of limited war in a nuclear age, the need for political restraint in a world dominated by two superpowers and teetering on the edge of complete destruction. He paid the risks little heed as he called relentlessly to extirpate the false doctrine even if the struggle required World War III.

For what Clark saw as a Kremlin plot to take over the United States, he blamed the Communists for fostering: "intermarriages of the races, all the things that are bad for our country," subverting American youth by drugs, destroying respect for the military. He railed against juvenile delinquents, draft-dodgers, peaceniks, troublemakers, flag burners, rioters, looters, influence peddlers, and hippies, who, he thought, were being led by sinister forces. "I am concerned about the turn my country is taking," he said. "We've got this disgraceful lawlessness...which I believe is being encouraged." He had no need to add who he thought was responsible for the corruption, the racial conflict, the pornography in literature, the filth on movie screens, the crookedness in high places, the crime on the streets. America was in decline, the victim of a gigantic conspiracy, "our expiring country." If only Americans could shake off the "dust of disgrace and recover from what appears to be a terminal illness," all the complex problems could be solved by the ancient and simple virtues.

If his postwar preaching tarnished the brilliance of his wartime achievements, his primary claim to fame rests on his military accomplishments. The centrality of his position in the affairs of Europe during World War II made him undeniably a shaper of history, a dominant force in London, where he prepared the invasion of North Africa, in Algiers, where he brought the French to the Allied side, and in Italy, where he drove the campaign. His strong support of an independent Austria during the occupation influenced his times significantly. Concluding the armistice negotiations in Korea, despite his personal reservations, further formed his age.

He had an extraordinary strength of character and will, a personal power of direction that forced results and also bred resentment. Many British historians and writers disliked Clark precisely because of his drive. As late as 1978, one called him a "self-opinionated and self-centered personality," an observation related to Clark's effect on the Italian campaign.

The British supervised the Mediterranean theater after 1943, and Italy was supposed to be their arena. Instead, the weight of American resources and Clark's tenacity overwhelmed them. Earlier heroic deeds by the

British—the evacuation from Dunkirk, the battle of Britain, the victory at El Alamein (which Montgomery added to his title, calling himself Lord Montgomery of Alamein), the entry into Tunis (Alexander of Tunis)— dimmed and faded in the light of later Allied triumphs, which were, in large part, produced by the American partner.

As Eric Sevareid noted shortly after the war, the British in Italy suffered from the neurosis of a growing sense of inferiority with respect to the Americans. Montgomery's British Eighth Army in Italy, Sevareid wrote, "felt its desert glory slipping." Clark, who "thought and spoke exclusively in terms of his own Fifth Army," made the campaign his own. He grew larger in stature than his immediate superior, Alexander, a soldier dearly loved by the British people.

The growing strength of the United States and the Soviet Union at the end of 1943 and the accompanying decline of British influence in the Allied coalition dismayed Churchill. He sought to turn around the waning British prestige by making possible a British victory in Italy. He had to do so before the Normandy and southern France invasions reduced the Italian battlefield to a relatively minor sideshow. With his eyes fixed on Rome, the only place where the British could gain a significant triumph, Churchill, against the advice and over the objections of the experts, put on Anzio, undoubtedly the most dramatic ordeal of the Italian campaign.

According to Nigel Nicolson, who wrote a sympathetic biography of Alexander, "The operation was mounted in insufficient strength and with unjustifiable optimism; the objective was not feasible nor the method clear. Nobody... specified in writing before hand exactly what was to happen once the troops were ashore." The failure, in short, was Alexander's.

"Our disagreements served to strengthen rather than lessen my friendship for General Alexander and most of his British colleagues," Clark said. "Our differences were very real and very important."

What is telling is that in the critical moments Clark usually had his way. But they were all gentlemen, and whatever animosities they buried during the coalition experience dissolved in the glow of ultimate victory, only to return during the postwar dissection and analysis of the events.

Was the Italian campaign worth pursuing in the dreadful conditions of terrain and weather? Hitler, by changing his mind, by deciding first to abandon Italy, then to battle for it, unknowingly lured and trapped the Allies, who had formulated and enunciated no clear rationale before invading the Italian mainland. The fighting became a vast holding action, each side, with approximately equal numbers, pinning down the other's forces and preventing their employment elsewhere. For both opponents, the strategic connection between the combat in Italy and the operations in northwestern Europe and on the eastern front was slim, even debatable. If the Allied armies in Italy ground down and wore out a part of the German military machine that might have more profitably fought on the eastern or western fronts, the Germans tied down Allied troops who might have reinforced the great thrust from the west across France into Germany. Yet perhaps without the heartbreaking fighting in Italy, the decisive effort under Eisenhower might well have suffered similar anguish and frustration and the Russian tide to the west might have slowed.

In contrast to the large landscapes on the two main fronts in Europe, where maneuver was possible, the terrain in Italy inhibited the exercise of generalship in the grand manner, particularly where mechanized units, tied more or less to the road system, were involved. The allied routes of advance were all too obvious to the German defenders who occupied ground perfectly suited to their blocking efforts. The true war in Italy took place on the level of platoons, companies, and battalions that battled from one hill to the next.

Clark exercised his leadership in a personal way. To the extent that any army commander can do so, he shared the dangers of his men. His appearances on the Salerno and Anzio beachheads, his presence near the front throughout the campaign, heartened, comforted, and inspired his soldiers. By quiet, almost casual, valor, Clark welded the Fifth Army into a superb fighting force. He similarly molded his polyglot elements of the 15th Army Group, a conglomerate of ethnically diverse types, all with varying customs and habits, into a powerful, synchronized organization.

De Gaulle called Clark "simple and direct," Juin termed him "clairvoyant and energetic," and McNarney rated him immediately after World War II as a model commander who displayed the traditional strengths cited in military textbooks and manuals: highly intelligent, of unquestioned physical and moral courage, loyal to both subordinates and superiors, mentally stable, able to work under high pressure, capable of quick and decisive action, caring for the welfare of his men. If Clark was "extremely ambitious," if his "drive to reach the top sometimes causes him to seek personal publicity, this trait has become less noticeable in recent months." McNarney concluded that Clark's success as a field commander was "attested by the final breakthrough, vigorous pursuit, and capitulation of enemy forces in Italy."

With the American public, Clark struck a responsive chord. Hundreds of letters from strangers sympathized with and encouraged him. Mrs. Joseph Bunton of Tucson, Arizona, for example, wrote in August 1944, "You seemed closer than the usual news story personality.... You were like someone we knew, whose daily doings we watched with friendly interest."

Embodying the American virtues, Mark Clark touched and warmed the American people. Whatever his failings, he towered above his generation and helped to shape the events of his time. He is an authentic historical figure and an American hero.

Mark Wayne Clark died on April 17, 1984, two weeks before his eighty-eighth birthday, in Charleston, South Carolina.

AUTHOR'S NOTE

THIS BOOK IS based on the literature of World War II and the Korean War; on sources at the National Archives, the Library of Congress, the U. S. Army Military History Institute, the U. S. Army Military Personnel Center, and the Archives of The Citadel; on interviews with a host of individuals; and on extensive discussions and correspondence with General Clark.

Readers who wish specific references to certain points should write to the author in care of the publisher, whose address is 298 Fifth Avenue, New York, N.Y. 10001.

I met General Clark in the early 1960s when he was President of The Citadel and I was working on a book about the Italian campaign. He graciously permitted me to consult his wartime diary, and I spent several days on the campus in Charleston. Several years later, at a convention of the American Historical Association in New Orleans, General Clark and I renewed our acquaintance when we were part of a panel discussing the invasion of North Africa. Many years afterward, when I asked whether he would be receptive to the idea of my studying his life, he assured me of his cooperation.

He gave me access to his Army personal and medical files in the custody of The Adjutant General's Office. He arranged with The Citadel Development Foundation to have me at the college for a year as the Mark W. Clark Visiting Professor of History. With a very light teaching load and an office in the Library, I studied General Clark's papers, never before, so far as I know, opened in their entirety. He and I spent many hours together talking.

At The Citadel, archivist Malachy Collet facilitated my research; George M. Seignious, II, Charles Anger, and members of the History Department, William Duckett, D. D. Nicholson, James Wood, and many others of the faculty and staff were more than helpful.

Those whose contributions to my knowledge and understanding are greater than they suspect include Theodore Antonelli, Marie Capps, William D. Clark, J. Lawton Collins, James L. Collins, Roma Danysh, Harold Deutsch, William C. Faught, William S. Fiske, Joseph R. Friedman, Stanley L. Falk, Arthur L. Funk, Henry Gardiner, James Gavin, Dominick Graham, Teddy Greenberg, Blanche Gregory, Thomas E. Griess, Alfred M. Gruenther, E. B. Haslam, Lyman L. Lemnitzer, Claire M. Marche, William McCaffery, Timothy Nenninger, Forrest C. Pogue, Buddy Rogers, Charles E. Saltzman, DeWitt Smith, Richard C. Sommers, Mrs. Joseph Sullivan, Vernon Walters, William C. Westmoreland, and Hannah Zeiklik.

My wife is always a partner in my work.

To all those named above, and to others I may have unintentionally omitted, I wish to record my gratitude and thanks.

I alone am responsible for whatever deficiencies are in the narrative.

M. B.

CHRONOLOGY

1896	MAY 1	born Watertown, New York
1913	JUNE 14	entered U. S. Military Academy, West Point, New York
1917	APRIL 20	graduated from West Point and commissioned Second Lieutenant, Infantry
	MAY 15	promoted temporarily to First Lieutenant
	JUNE 12	assigned 11th Infantry, Chickamauga Park, Georgia, and appointed Platoon Leader, Company E
	JUNE 24	on sick leave, Chicago, Illinois, and Walter Reed Hospital
	AUGUST 23	promoted temporarily to Captain
	DECEMBER 1	appointed Commanding Officer, Company K, 11th Infantry
1918	MAY 1	arrived in France
	JUNE 12	appointed Commanding Officer, 3d Battalion, 11th Infantry
	JUNE 14	wounded, Anould Sector of the Western Front
	JULY 30	discharged from hospital

	AUGUST 1	assigned as staff officer, Supply Section, First Army
1919	APRIL	appointed Post Commandant, port of Antwerp
	JUNE 5	sailed for the United States
	AUGUST	assigned 49th Infantry, Fort Snelling, Minnesota, and appointed Commanding Officer, Headquarters Company
	NOVEMBER	promoted to Captain, Regular Army
1920	MARCH	appointed Commanding Officer, Company H, 49th Infantry, Fort Crook, Nebraska
1921	JANUARY	appointed Detachment Commander on Chautauqua tour
	NOVEMBER	assigned as Assistant to the Chief, Sales Promotion Section, Office of the Assistant Secretary of War, Washington, D. C.
1924	MAY 17	married Maurine Doran
	JULY	student, Advanced Officers Course, Fort Benning, Georgia
1925	MARCH 31	birth of son, William D. Clark
	JULY 1	assigned 30th Infantry, The Presidio, San Francisco, California, and appointed Commanding Officer, Company I
1926	JANUARY	hospitalized Letterman General Hospital, San Francisco
	SPRING	birth of daughter, Ann Clark
		appointed Post Exchange Officer, The Presidio
1928	SPRING	appointed Executive Officer, 4th Brigade, Fort Russell, Wyoming
	AUGUST	hospitalized Fitzsimmons General Hospital, Denver, Colorado
929	SPRING	assigned as Instructor in Infantry and Adviser to the 38th Division, Indiana National Guard, Indianapolis, Indiana
1933	JANUARY 14	promoted to Major
	AUGUST	student, Command and General Staff College, Fort Leavenworth, Kansas
1935	SEPTEMBER	assigned 2d Division, Fort Sam Houson, San Antonio, Texas, and appointed Assistant Chief of Staff, G-3
	OCTOBER	assigned 7th Corps Area headquarters, Fort Crook, Nebraska, and appointed Assistant Chief of Staff, G-2 and G-3, and Deputy Chief of Staff for the Civilian Conservation Corps
1936	AUGUST	student, Army War College, Washington, D. C.
1937	JULY 27	assigned 3d Division, Fort Lewis, Washington, and appointed Assistant Chief of Staff, G-2 and G-3
1940	JULY 1	promoted to Lieutenant Colonel
	AUGUST 17	assigned as staff officer, GHQ, Washington, D. C.

1941   JUNE 18   appointed Assistant Chief of Staff, G-3, GHQ
         AUGUST 4   promoted to Brigadier General
         DECEMBER 9   appointed Deputy Chief of Staff for Training, GHQ
1942   MARCH   appointed Acting Chief of Staff, Army Ground Forces
         APRIL 17   promoted to Major General and appointed Chief of Staff, Army Ground forces
         JUNE 13   appointed Commanding General, II Corps
         JUNE 23   traveled to England
         AUGUST 12   appointed Deputy Supreme Allied Commander, Allied Force Headquarters, London
         SEPTEMBER 23–30   visited Washington, D. C., in connection with plans for Torch
1942   OCTOBER 18–25   proceeded on secret submarine voyage to Algeria
         NOVEMBER 5   traveled to Gibraltar with Eisenhower and opened AFHQ
         NOVEMBER 8   Torch landings in French Northwest Africa
         NOVEMBER 9   traveled to Algiers to negotiate with the French
         NOVEMBER 10   opened negotiations with Admiral Darlan and arranged armistice in Algeria and French Morocco
         NOVEMBER 11   promoted to Lieutenant General
         NOVEMBER 22   signed Clark–Darlan agreement
1943   JANUARY 4   appointed Commanding General, Fifth U. S. Army, North Africa
         SEPTEMBER 1   promoted Brigadier General, Regular Army
         SEPTEMBER 9   invaded Salerno, Italy
         OCTOBER 1   captured Naples, Italy
1944   JANUARY 22   invaded Anzio, Italy
         JANUARY 22–23   failure at the Rapido River
         FEBRUARY 15   bombing and destruction of the Benedictine abbey of Monte Cassino
         MARCH 15   bombing and destruction of the town of Cassino
         APRIL 9–23   returned to the United States for rest
         MAY 11   spring offensive started
         MAY 25   linked up with the Anzio beachhead
         JUNE 5   captured Rome
         OCTOBER 30   halted Fifth Army attack to Bologna
         DECEMBER 16   appointed Commanding General, 15th Army Group
1945   MARCH 10   promoted to General
         APRIL 2   German surrender in Italy
         APRIL 8   unconditional German surrender
         MAY 25–JUNE 20   victory celebration in the United States
         JULY 5   15th Army Group disbanded
1945   JULY 6   appointed Commander, U. S. Forces, Austria
         JULY 14–30   celebration in Brazil
         AUGUST 12   traveled to Salzburg

AUGUST 23 attended first meeting, Allied Control Council, Vienna

OCTOBER 29 nominated to be Major General, Regular Army

1946   JUNE 20 confirmed as Major General, Regular Army with date of rank from October 1, 1944

1947   JANUARY–FEBRUARY Foreign Ministers Meeting, London

MARCH–APRIL Foreign Ministers Meeting, Moscow

MAY 5 departed Austria

JUNE 19 assumed command of Sixth Army, The Presidio of San Francisco

1949   OCTOBER 1 became Chief, Army Field Forces, Fort Monroe, Virginia

1952   MAY 12 became Commander in Chief, United Nations Command and Commander in Chief, Far East, Tokyo, Japan

1953   JULY 27 signed Korean armistice

OCTOBER 31 retired from the Army

NOVEMBER 1 advanced to the grade of General on the U. S. Army Retired List

1954   MARCH 1 became President, The Citadel, Charleston, South Carolina

1965   JULY 1 became President Emeritus, The Citadel

1966   OCTOBER 5 death of Renie Clark

1967   OCTOBER 17 married Mary Applegate

1969   DECEMBER 11 appointed to American Battle Monuments Commission and elected Chairman

1984   APRIL 17 died Charleston, South Carolina

DECORATIONS AND AWARDS

Distinguished Service Cross

Distinguished Service Medal with three Oak Leaf Clusters

Distinguished Service Medal (Navy)

Legion of Merit

Bronze Star Medal with V device

Purple Heart

Mexican Border Service Medal

World War I Victory Medal with battle clasps for St. Mihiel, Meuse-Argonne, and Anould Defensive Sector

Army of Occupation of Germany Medal, World War I

American Defense Service Medal

Europe-Africa-Mediterranean Campaign Medal with one silver service star (in lieu of five bronze stars) and Arrowhead

Army of Occupation Medal with German and Japanese clasps for World War II

Korean Service Medal with three bronze service stars

National Defense Service Medal

United Nations Service Medal

Victory Ribbon, World War II

FOREIGN

Belgium: Order of the Crown with Palm, rank of Grand Officer; Croix de Guerre, 1940, with Palm

Brazil: Order of the Southern Cross, Rank of Grand Officer; Order of Military Merit; Medal of War with Campaign Cross

Czechoslovakia: Order of the White Lion for Victory, First Class; Military Cross of 1939

France: Legion of Honor, Rank of Commander; Legion of Honor, Rank of Grand Officer; Croix de Guerre with Palm

Great Britain: Honorary Knight Commander of the Order of the British Empire

Italy: Order of Saints Maurice and Lazarus, Rank of Knight Officer; Military Order of Italy, degree of Grand Officer; Silver Medal for Military Valor

Malta: Order of Malta

Morocco: Grand Cross of the Order of Oussam Alouite Cherifa, First Class

Poland: Virtuti Militari, Fifth Class

Soviet Union: Military Order of Suvorov, First Class

Greece: Grand Cross of George I with Swords

Philippines: Legion of Honor, degree of Commander

Japan: Japanese Grand Cordon of the Imperial Order of the Rising Sun

Republic of Korea: Order of Taeguk with Gold Star

INDEX

299